TAKE ME HOME, UNITED ROAD

THIS IS A CARLTON BOOK

This edition published in 2005
Copyright © 2002, 2005 Manchester United plc
Text and Design copyright © 2002, 2005
Carlton Books Limited

First published in 2002 as *United We Stand*

A CIP catalogue record for this book is
available from the British Library.

ISBN: 0 233 00156 5

Managing Editor: Nigel Matheson
Editor: Vanessa Daubney
Project Art Director: Luke Griffin
Picture Research: Tom Wright
Production: Lisa French

Printed and bound in Great Britain

TAKE ME HOME, UNITED ROAD

General Editor **Graham McColl**

CARLTON
BOOKS

Contents

Foreword
by Sir Alex Ferguson

Some time ago I remember reading a book by a supporter of Manchester United and being impressed with the way he remembered events, which, although I'd been involved with them, seemed very fresh and distinctive when told in his words. And that's what makes this book different. Just about everyone who has contributed to the book is – by the very fact that they have had something to do with the club, whether as a player, staff member or supporter – woven into the fabric of the place and you'll find that each person has their own story to tell.

I know that, just as I like to think I'm committed to Manchester United, everyone else who works at the club is too. Many have been working here for forty or fifty years, such as Nesta Burgess, who contributes to this book. Others, like a number of the stewards, have taken over their positions from their fathers and even their grandfathers. For them, their whole life is this club, and to be able to get their views about it, how it has evolved and what it has achieved is very important.

There's no doubt that Manchester United has had plenty of drama in its history and these are the people who have witnessed it first hand. My own memories are still very vivid, right from the Friday morning that I flew down from Aberdeen and met the team in order to prepare for my first match in charge. And as you will see in some of the later chapters, like me, the majority of supporters care not just about winning, but about how we play. When I first saw Manchester United play – in Glasgow in the Coronation Cup in 1953, I remember being impressed not just by the fact that they beat Rangers(!), but also by the players, such as Roger Byrne, who just seemed to fly, he was so quick. The need to win is always there, but how we win is just as important.

Indeed, much of the drama associated with the team comes because of what has happened in the last 20 minutes or so of a match.

If we're losing, then we'll throw everything, including the kitchen sink, into the penalty box. Sometimes it doesn't work, but a lot of the time it does and when it does, it's a fantastic feeling. I remember one time when we were down 1–0 to Sheffield United with ten minutes to go at Old Trafford and we scored two in a minute. The excitement that generates is unbelievable and fans go away thinking, 'That's Manchester United'.

Some people in this book may make comparisons between players or between managers, like Sir Matt Busby and myself, but I never think about that. My agenda is simply to maintain what has been achieved in the past. In the case of every manager, it's a different job, with different players, in a different era.

As for comparing players, to my mind great players will always find a way, no matter what era they may play in. Sir Bobby Charlton always maintains that Duncan Edwards was the greatest player he has ever seen, but people often question whether he could have played in this day and age. I say, yes, he could. While many players today may get by because of their athleticism, or commitment, or because of a certain talent they've got, in general the footballers of previous times were probably more rounded.

And, if they played today, they too would have the benefits of science that players have now.

The memories that have been collected here reflect not just these debates and the talents of the players, or the great moments of the club, but the depth of feeling that surrounds Manchester United. It is a testament to the dedication of people to the club to the extent that it becomes their life and shows how many ways there are of interpreting what has happened on and off the pitch.

Sir Alex Ferguson
July 2002

Introduction

There is a raw immediacy about this oral history which does justice to the passions that have made Manchester United one of the most inspiring and unpredictable football clubs on the planet. Those passions are reflected by the voices which clamour to recall every aspect of the club's history, from the days when the club captain kept the club mascot – a goat – in his backyard, through the 20th century, when star players would cycle or take the bus to Old Trafford, to the modern multimedia stardom of United's most glamorous football players.

The voices range across the spectrum, from stalwart Stretford Enders to the boardroom. Individual supporters separate themselves from the crowd briefly to get across their own individual points of view. Those from the cloth cap era mingle in these pages with followers of United from Europe and Asia who keep in contact with the club through the Internet. Players, both retired and current stars, jostle to take possession of a few paragraphs. A rich variety of characters who have played an active role behind the scenes at Old Trafford lay down the tools of their trades briefly to provide their special insights into what they have seen and heard while helping to build the club.

The book is divided into three sections. The first sets the scene, with an overall appraisal of the special nature of the club. This outlines why Manchester United plays such a special, central role in so many lives. Detailed descriptions of the ground include Sir Bobby Charlton reminiscing about the days when he would come to Old Trafford just to enjoy a bath. On a more sombre note, the tragic but momentous Munich disaster is described by some who were closest to the impact, including Sandy Busby, who recalls the days when his father hovered between life and death. The final chapter in this section puts United in perspective by showing how the club has thrived on friendships and rivalries with various others down the years. Liverpool and Manchester City battle it out here to win the title of United's fiercest rivals and Sammy McIlroy and Lou Macari are among those with unusual, intriguing stories to tell.

The second section profiles the people who have breathed life into the club: managers, players, supporters and staff. It begins with the men who have laid down the rules – the managers – and includes a powerful description by Sir Alex Ferguson of how he set about imposing his personality on the club. Nesta Burgess, Old Trafford's tea lady extraordinaire, contributes illuminating insights from her own unique niche at the club to that chapter, as she does to the succeeding one which focuses on United's players, from the Billy Meredith era to the present day. Dennis Giggs, Ryan's grandfather, is among those who add illumination here. The supporters then take centre stage, from Jimmy Billington, who recalls the pre-war era, through *United Review* editorial consultant Cliff Butler's vivid descriptions of the sights and sounds of 1960s Old Trafford, to Angus Deayton's insights into following United passionately from all corners of the globe. The Manchester United staff complete the contributions to this section. Club President Martin Edwards is one of the many who explain how the club's triumphs on the field have been subtly supported by the back-up the players have received from behind the scenes.

The third section shows how all these ingredients have blended together to bring numerous trophies from home and abroad to Old Trafford. Bill Foulkes is among those who recall some of United's exciting, championship-winning seasons. Wilf McGuinness contributes some concise, precise memories of the most momentous FA Cup Finals to that chapter, which focuses on United's Wembley outings. Phil and Gary Neville provide some marvellously detailed descriptions of the club's recent adventures in Europe, which sit well with others' tales of the earliest days in European competition. This section reaches its climax with a rich variety of descriptions from a wide range of angles of three of the greatest days in the club's history: the days when Manchester United triumphed in European finals.

The structure of the book is designed to build a composite picture of the club. It is not, though, absolutely necessary to follow the structure to extract full enjoyment from this book. The beauty of this oral history is that it is possible to dip into any page to find people discussing Manchester United with passion and commitment. Their words, and the stirring way in which they relate their stories, encapsulate the qualities which have made Manchester United such an engaging institution throughout its history.

Part One:
The Club

1

The Wonder of U-ni-ted

Every follower of Manchester United knows that the club has a special appeal but this appeal transmits itself to everyone in a different way. Some have deep, profound reasons for their support of the club and look to the past for the roots of their respect for it as a great institution. Others revel in the things they see all around them on matchdays: the colourfulness, size and variety of United's support and its appeal to followers far and wide. Some enjoy the cosmopolitan feel of the club; others like the way it has retained strong local roots whilst claiming a place at the centre of world football's attention. All are agreed that the mystique of Manchester United makes the club a unique, unrivalled attraction. No two individuals have the same opinion as to why United are so special, and that is one of the key elements in the Reds' mystique.

Chris Yeamans: Following United has always been an adventure. More than any other club we've had an impact on people's lives that sometimes transcends football: the Munich disaster, George Best superstar, the Cantona kung-fu kick, Beckham the most famous man on the planet, Fergie being such an immense man. And the thing is, whatever we've done, we've always done it with style and panache and with none of the cynical professionalism of the successful Leeds and Liverpool teams.

Nesta Burgess: I did retire at 70 but Mr Olive said, 'Keep coming in and look after the lads.' I know their families, you see; they come to me. Roy Keane's mum and dad know me and I look after them when they come in. If you keep the family right, your players are right. We were taught that by Matt – he always used to say, 'Make everybody feel welcome.' That was his thing. The club was noted for it. That made a lot of difference.

Voni von Arx: I'm one of these old-fashioned-type United fans who likes singing, likes going to Europe to meet other United fans and who likes talking to different United fans, wherever they come from. I think that's the really cool thing about United – it's not only Manchester itself, it's Wales, it's Ireland, it's Scotland and it's Europe as well.

Anna Deakin: Manchester United are a special club for so many reasons. The dedication and demands of the fans mean that players arriving at Manchester United have to play with passion to fit in. Players like Eric Cantona, Mark Hughes and Roy Keane all play with such passion that you are either going to appreciate their charisma or see it as arrogance – for United fans it is always going to be the first. The Reds' youth system is also an important factor. As a fan, it is brilliant to see players come up through the ranks and remain loyal to the club. The Neville brothers, Giggs and Scholes are all loved by the fans for being United through and through.

Dennis Giggs: The youth policy at United has always been fantastic. I can't speak too highly of Mr Ferguson. His son was there at the time Ryan went to the club and Ryan palled up with Darren and Mr Ferguson treated Ryan exactly like Darren. They have got this family attitude to players and Ryan was fortunate to grow up with the five or six that made it through to the first team from the youth system, like the Neville brothers, Scholes, Butt, Beckham. Alex Ferguson knows every relative and will go out of his way to speak to them. If he's walking down the tunnel at half-time and he sees me there he'll say hello. I was at a youth match one time and I couldn't get over the fact that a manager of his high profile came down to Southampton in his car and not on the coach

– he would travel all over the country to watch players. The facilities are fantastic at the club. They genuinely do look after the players.

Swallay Bandhoo: Manchester United has always been in the hearts of many Mauritians as Mauritius was a British colony until 12 March 1968 when we got our independence. Hence support for Manchester United has been transmitted from generation to generation. My grandfather was a great United fan, so too my extended family. That's the reason why I still support this team and my five-year-old son does the same now.

Ron Snellen: To me, United is indeed the number one club in the world. But then again, that's what the Scousers think about their teams and the Geordies about Newcastle. The thing that would put United above even other big clubs such as Real Madrid and AC Milan is, first of all, the supporters. United is the only club in Europe – and perhaps in the world – that has a full stadium every game. The Reds also follow their team in thousands across Europe. Just look at Bayern Munich when they played their first Champions League match in front of 10,000 spectators or Juve playing a cup tie before 872 paying spectators!

Ole Pedersen: English is spoken in a lot of countries, there has always been a lot of world-wide interest in what's happening in Britain, and then you have the special attraction that Manchester United has always held. They have always played entertaining football; the Munich air disaster and the club's history, notably the tradition of bringing through United players, from the Busby Babes to Fergie's Fledglings. For me, it was partly the name, the shirt and Steve Coppell, not to mention a rosette from the 1977 FA Cup Final that my uncle brought back to me!

Angus Deayton: I certainly get the feeling that it has much more of a family atmosphere than certain clubs. It doesn't have that sort of dictatorial stamp that a lot of clubs have, where there is basically one person, one sugar-daddy, in charge. I think one of the reasons why a lot of the players stay there is that they do create that kind of a familial set-up and care about the players and attempt to integrate the players into the community. It seems to pay off. That's why I was so relieved in some respects when the takeover didn't happen, whether that's something that will happen eventually... I think the owners have to be football people, whoever it is. Martin Edwards is part of a very, very long tradition and I think that shows. How long it will last I don't know.

Chris Yeamans: When I think of my childhood, my memories of it are inextricably linked with the club. I didn't consciously choose United; they've just always been there. The past ten years of our domination have been beyond the wildest dreams I had as a kid and it makes all those lean years worth the effort. Even if we never won anything again, I would die a happy fan.

Martin C.Y. Lai: You hear all this nonsense about supporters not being from Manchester. It makes no difference whatsoever. United should be proud of the wide fan base that they have – Manchester is not big enough for all the United fans to live in!

Cameron Erskine: When they sing the song 'Do You Come From Manchester?', I say, 'I wish I did... It would be a lot cheaper!'

Gary Neville: It's a great experience to be here. Some days are better than others but I enjoy every single day here; it's never like work. To actually go into that changing room is the best experience I could have every morning, to be around 25 lads who are all having a decent time, are all good mates, all having a laugh together, all taking the mickey out of each other and going out and playing football. That's the way I see it, but it is pretty serious stuff because it affects hundreds of thousands of people's lives. If we don't do well it affects their lives and it affects our lives as well. There are 67,000 people watching us and if we don't win they're going home upset or disappointed. They're not happy and we're not happy. We go home disappointed as well.

2

Old Trafford – The Dream Home

Matt Busby described Old Trafford as his 'haven'. Every morning, on arriving at the ground, he would walk round its entire circumference, drinking in deep draughts of satisfaction at the sight of the stadium, the solid, standing embodiment of the magnificent club that he had reconstructed in his own inimitable fashion during the post-war years. Busby had first arrived at the club in 1945, taking over as manager even after seeing the devastated north terracing and the main stand, both of which had been destroyed by German bombers one night in March 1941. It would take eight years for the ground to be restored to a condition suitable for spectators. Old Trafford would then grow in stature in tandem with the ongoing successes of Busby's teams of the 1940s, 1950s and 1960s.

The club's first ground, in its days as Newton Heath, had been to the north of the city centre, in North Road, now Northampton Road, on a site currently occupied by Moston Brook High School. After 15 years of struggling with that ground's quagmire of a playing surface, Newton Heath moved to Bank Street, Clayton, in 1893. It, too, was far from ideal, but it was still their home when they changed their name to Manchester United in 1902 and they remained there until 1910 when they moved to Old Trafford. The club's new home, five miles south-east of Bank Street, was an impressive edifice, holding 80,000 and being described in the first matchday programme for Old Trafford as having 'no superior'. The *Umpire* magazine described it thus: 'The grandstand, with its 60 rows of seats, is considerably larger than any stand on any football ground in the kingdom and yet the ground is so compact that, unlike the Crystal Palace and other grounds, you always seem near the playing pitch.'

United's subsequent dearth of successes in the 1920s and 1930s meant few changes were made to the ground in those pre-war years.

In modern times, United have been trendsetters in stadium design, pioneering the use of executive boxes after opening their first set in the new two-tier stand on the United Road side of Old Trafford in 1965. The club had also embraced increased seating capacity long before the 1989 Hillsborough disaster prompted the Taylor Report and the consequent instruction from the government that all Premier League grounds should be all-seater. As with Matt Busby in the past, so too in the modern era, winning sides – this time created by Alex Ferguson – have fuelled the expansion of Old Trafford into the best club ground in the country for the all-seater era. Its capacity was increased to 67,700 in January 2000, making it the biggest club ground in Britain. Old Trafford is now very much a stadium for the 21st century but in its scope it remains close to the original idea of the expansive United chairman John Henry Davies, a century ago, for his club to have the swankiest, most stylish stadium in the land.

Nesta Burgess: I wasn't with the club during the war when we had a bomb here and, of course, they couldn't play here. They used to bring Italian prisoners of war to the stadium to clean it up. They had been looking for Trafford Park and they bombed the ground.

Sir Bobby Charlton: My first memory is of coming down from the North-East and seeing how stark it was in Manchester. With the Industrial Revolution all the buildings were black but I'd committed myself. I wanted to be a footballer so here I was, and there was passion here for the club. It wasn't a holiday here, it was a real working place; and, of course, Old Trafford was where everybody came for their pleasure, and they did enjoy it. I came maybe at the right time... in 1953 and it was just a period where after the end of the war every ground was full almost every week, especially here. They used to just squeeze as many people into the grounds as they possibly could and it was no different here. This ground, when I first came here, had an old stand where the modern South Stand is and there was a tiny little cover on the other side and the rest of it was just open to the elements and, of course, the pitches in those days, they didn't treat them like they do now. By the beginning of October it was brown. All the grass had gone, apart from just a little in the corners, but the ground was the place of pleasure for the working-class people. Matt Busby always felt that the public had to enjoy their football and for them to enjoy it you had to play a bit of adventurous football.

Wilf McGuinness: In those days the stadium wasn't repaired properly: on what they call the South Stand now, the roof wasn't on properly. At the Manchester end they had a wooden scoreboard with A, B, C up to Z, where they gave you the half-time scores. It was a bit primitive.

Nesta Burgess: I've lived just up the street from the ground for most of my life so I've lived with the club. When my children were smaller and City played they used to come on bikes and my kids used to take bikes into the yard for threepence. So they made quite a bit of money!

Sir Bobby Charlton: I couldn't get down here to Old Trafford enough; I used to come down here on a Sunday morning. There was nothing to do but I used to come down and have a bath and if Jimmy Murphy was there he would tell me to get changed and take me out there on the pitch and he would hit a few balls to me and give me a little bit of extra stuff about how to do things professionally. I only lived a couple of hundred yards from the stadium here; I used to walk down. It was a magical time. It was just after the Busby Babes started and Matt threw in 16-year-olds, which nobody had ever considered. In those days you almost had to be in your twenties before you got a chance in the first-team. Yet he dropped three or four international players because he said that he wasn't satisfied with them – some of them had probably just gone over the hill. He just threw in 16- and 17-year-olds. I remember the headlines, 'What's going on? Kids playing football!' But they were coached properly and professionally and obviously they were good players because they were the lads that were actually winning the Youth Cup as well. In the 1950s it was just brilliant here: European matches starting, Youth Cups, FA Cup runs. Everything was happening and the fans flocked to it.

The ground itself wasn't anything special architecturally but it created a fantastic atmosphere. Even then, when you went on, you felt like you were on a stage. When you are on that pitch and you look around, it is like a theatre, especially at a night match, when you have all those people looking down on you. It has always had this, even without the stands that you have got now. Everybody used to love playing at United – it has always created a special atmosphere I haven't seen anywhere else. I watch the other team when they are warming up, because you can pick little things up that give you an idea of how their minds are working and some of them will look round and you can see there's a bit of trepidation there. Of course, it has become bigger and bigger, but it retains the same feeling for players and fans. .

Cliff Butler: I loved the Old Trafford crowd. It did something to me; the passion and the noise and the smoke – a lot more people smoked cigarettes in those days. Then you had the railway and the steam engines; the engines would be getting ready to take people back into the city after the match and the steam used to come over the roof and that helped add to the atmosphere as well. So matches in the build-up to Christmas and around New Year had something special about them. There was a fantasy atmosphere in a way. The smoke used to swirl round the lights and I'd be watching the crowd sway on the popular side or the Scoreboard End – someone once said it looked like a field of wheat blowing in the wind, and that's a great description.

Ken Merrett: I remember one game – it must have been in the 1960s – that was postponed because of poor visibility. Fifteen minutes after everyone had gone home, you could see everything clearly – the lack of visibility had been caused by smoke from a train in the station!

Roy Williamson: There is no comparison between the current situation and times gone by. My first game at Old Trafford was versus Sheffield United in 1962 and I was taken by my older brother. I can never forget walking down Warwick Road, now Sir Matt Busby Way, milling amongst thousands of others, mostly wearing the old 'bar' red and white scarf. There was a bloke on the corner near the ground selling star-shaped pin badges with the players' pictures on them. I think they were sixpence each. Apart from that and the match programme, with a colour photo of the team on the front cover, there was little for sale. Certainly nobody wore replica shirts. The atmosphere and the build-up was something else. Climbing the steps behind the Stretford End, once inside the ground, was the greatest thrill, reaching the top and coming out on the terrace with the field laid out before you. This feeling lasted for years. I remember my second game, versus Liverpool, standing by the fence at the front of the Stretford End Paddock. And I distinctly remember them playing Susan Maughan's 'Bobby's Girl' over the tannoy.

Ken Merrett: They used to have a turnstile control in my office so I would be in my office until after the game had started. If the Stretford End, for example, was full, the control would ring a bell in all the turnstiles and then the turnstile supervisor for that area closed those turnstiles down because if it wasn't an all-ticket match people used to pay at the turnstiles. At the majority of games here, people just queued. Once one section was full they went to the next section, if they could. In the end they all used to close and then there used to be 20,000 maybe, at big games, who would walk slowly away. Some people used to just stand in the forecourt and listen to the noise and some would just drift away. They would try and get in at three-quarter time, when the gates opened, but if it was a full house you couldn't do that.

Cliff Butler: It had to be a packed crowd for me. I didn't like seeing gaps in the crowd. When it was a big game you knew that when you got to Old Trafford it was going to be jam-packed so you waited for the moment when it started swaying and that was lovely, seeing all those people swaying backwards and forwards, and then when a goal was scored they all tumbled down the terraces. It's really dramatic, isn't it?

Ken Merrett: The original North Stand was completed in '66. When I joined in January '66 it wasn't complete but it had started to be used and, while I was here during the course of that season, it all came on stream. It had the first private boxes in this country – at the back of the North Stand. I understand it was the architects who suggested them. They'd been abroad and had seen them. Louis Edwards was the chairman in those days and they sold the idea to him. They were just five-seater boxes with a waiter service to serve drinks. There were 30 of them and we sold them for the season. In those days quite a lot of companies had them but individuals also had them, which tends not to be the case these days. They were a success because when we then built the next development, which was in '72, when we took the line of seats round to the Scoreboard End – or K Stand – we carried on with the line of boxes right along behind the goal. Then, in '75, we had our next development. That's when we got the restaurant – the Trafford Suite was the first one – and we introduced exec seats, where you had a padded seat in the stand with the use of a lounge behind it. Then every development after that included either boxes or corporate hospitality.

Chris Yeamans: To tell the truth, I can't remember who we played first time I went to Old Trafford. I can remember it being a glorious sunny day, though. I went with my dad and stood at the Scoreboard End in the days when it had that huge scoreboard and no roof. I was perched on one of the safety barriers while my dad stood behind and held me there, because I was too small to see anything otherwise. I do remember reading the match programme and the name Carlo Sartori sticking in my head because it was such an unusual name. The smell of cigar smoke, meat pies and hot Bovril combined with the atmosphere of 50-odd thousand other people chanting and screaming was like nothing else I'd ever experienced. I remember noticing the weird echo that clapping made as it reverberated round the ground. At that age – seven or eight – the sheer number of people and the volume of noise they made was exhilarating and yet scary at the same time. It was like I'd stumbled into the secret world of older boys and men and feeling really grown up to be part of it. The deep red colour of the shirts and socks – it seemed just the best colour you could imagine for a team to wear.

Cameron Erskine: Our first game was in September 1972, against Derby. Ken Ramsden was the ticket manager and said he would organize tickets for us. There were no places for handicapped people at Old Trafford at the time so I'd carry Nigel up into the stand over where the North Stand is now. Then we got him into B Stand. Eventually, we got a ticket right down where the manager used to sit and Ken Ramsden made sure that those became season tickets for us. There was just one other handicapped person who had a place down there. Phillip Downs, who is now the secretary of the Manchester United Disabled Supporters' Association, later arranged for wheelchairs to be allowed down on to the running track but because of the camber on the pitch you couldn't see very well from there.

Chris Yeamans: One strong memory of Old Trafford in the Seventies is all the bomb scares that used to happen every week, around the time when the IRA was bombing the mainland. For a while they used to announce it over the tannoy – at which point, the Stretford End would sing, 'We're Gonna Get Our ****in' Balls Blown Off.' The bomb scares became so regular that they actually stopped announcing them after a while. Instead, they had a police-style blue flashing light that was situated just above the dugout, and they switched that on if a bomb scare was received.

Angus Deayton: It is not something that people who live close to the team they support would be able to identify with, but having supported someone for over 10 years, and read about them, and read about Old Trafford, and seen photographs and all the rest of it, to actually go there after that length of time was a very spiritual experience. I remember getting into the cab and saying, 'Old Trafford, please,' and the cab driver saying, 'Ah, the temple.' And I thought, 'Yes, that's exactly how

I'm viewing it at the moment.' It is virtually like a religious experience. It was fantastic to see the Munich clock and to walk down Matt Busby Way. It still is a thrill to go there. It was more cosy at that time, more manageable as a stadium. Now, I think stadia are like foreign stadia used to be. You used to read about San Siro being three-tier and it was sort of out of your sphere of reference. You had to imagine what it was like, whereas now that's sort of what Old Trafford is like. It is kind of less cosy, less sort of intimate. That first time I went it felt like being home because of being with people who all shared the same passion as you.

Martin C.Y. Lai: When we had the terraces a fantastic atmosphere was created by thousands of guys singing their hearts out at 1.30 p.m. on the afternoon of a match. You stood in the same place, saw the same faces, and the swaying and the support was the best buzz there was in life. Then came the all-seaters – with a reserved seat you don't have to turn up early to get a good view.

Jonathan Deakin: My real interest started in 1989–90 when I used to pay on the door and sit at the back of the Stretford End with my Dad in E Stand. There were around 2,000 bench seats. I sat on the back row with my Dad, enabling us to sit, or stand if we preferred, watching the mass of the Stretford End below us.

Cameron Erskine: We had our season tickets beside the manager for 18 years until they built the handicapped platform in the corner of the ground. You've got a seat for the helper and a place for the handicapped person. There's a blind section and a section for the 'walking wounded' as we call them – people who are handicapped and not in wheelchairs. We've got St John's Ambulance people on hand: they supply you with capes if it gets wet because although it is sheltered, when the wind gets up it can blow the rain in there. It's very good – we've been all over and the facilities for handicapped people at Old Trafford are first-class, the best there are anywhere. The view is also first-class. You are situated underneath the away supporters and there's no one in front of you at all.

Roy Williamson: As a youngster in the Sixties and Seventies you would stand on the Stretford End. There was a choice to make: you were either a 'right-sider', a 'left-sider' or you stood on the tunnel. During quiet spells in the match your allegiance to one area or another led to competitive chanting, 'We are the left side', 'We are the right side' – all part of the match-day culture. In your twenties and thirties, a move to the Stretford End Paddock was acceptable – to give the new breed of youngsters a chance to re-shape the Stretford End in their own style. Those of us close to reaching, or even past, the half-century mark still have to 'do the business' in the Stretford End or K Stand at the Scoreboard End because there aren't enough youngsters getting in to replace us. So I have to stand up, shout and sing like a 16-year-old! I think a return to safe standing areas would allow young and excluded fans to come to the games, at affordable prices, stand with their mates and recreate the bygone match-day experiences.

Anna Deakin: The main change at Old Trafford since I started going has been the size of the ground. Apart from South Stand, where I sit, all the other areas have been dramatically increased. The increased capacity has affected the atmosphere – in both positive and negative ways. At big games and in times of exciting play there are near on 60,000 Reds all willing the team on, making for an unbeatable atmosphere. Likewise, on more low-key occasions the hardcore Reds are more spread out and the atmosphere can seem a little subdued.

Ole Pedersen: The crowd became a bit muted in the last few years, before the singing section was introduced. I always sit in Stretford End Tier 1, and the singing section above has certainly helped. Otherwise, we United supporters moan a lot. We do not appreciate the good times we are experiencing, and we should recognize that these days will probably never be matched again!

James Marshall: The fans in the upper Stretford want United to be the old way it was, with the fans singing; the old Stretford End, the scarves, the shouting and the banter between the fans. I think that's what everyone wants and it is slowly getting back to that. You can see a lot more fans singing in the Stretford End and in parts of the East Stand.

Anna Deakin: Facilities for female supporters have always been good at Old Trafford, but in recent years the number of women visiting the ground has increased – so it may not always seem that way!

Paul Hardman: I am quite happy in the executive boxes with the prawn sandwich brigade but it wouldn't be my first choice. I think Roy Keane's comments about the prawn sandwich types was very true. When you have experienced the camaraderie and the freezing cold and watching a game against Bury in an early round of the Cup when you get wet through, you don't have a lot of time for sitting there during a match and eating food. It would be nice, if you had the opportunity, to do it once a season but anything after that it is not really that interesting. Watching a match from behind a perspex screen is a killer. On the other hand, the Premier Lounge, which is where the directors' entrance is, serves food, and then you come up from there and get seats virtually on the halfway line. Apart from the fact that it can be a bit sleepy in comparison to the noise and atmosphere of K Stand, it is not too bad but... in some of the boxes in North Stand they must have magnifying glasses in the windows – I can't understand how anybody can see anything from up there.

Angus Deayton: I have a friend who is a director so I very often get to sit in the directors' box, which is fantastic. It's obviously slightly less raucous. There are slightly fewer swear words being bandied around and you have to learn not to leap into the air every time there's a controversial decision or a free-kick near the box or whatever. So it's a slightly more controlled and measured response to the game but if it's tense the reaction is still basically the same. It's great – I can't pretend it's not a schoolboy dream – and it's great to meet ex-players. That's fantastic because a lot of them still come up to see the games; people like Bill Foulkes, Bobby Charlton and Martin Buchan. In fact, I actually got to play on Old Trafford against Martin Buchan so I didn't actually get to touch the ball.

It is passionate. People very often say to me, 'How do you feel about Roy Keane's denouncement of the prawn sandwich brigade?' and I say that I feel absolutely fine about it because I don't think he was really talking about people in the directors' box. I think he was talking about people who don't really know anything about football and who go there with Amalgamated Durables and are just there because Amalgamated Durables happen to have a box and don't really have any affiliation to the game or interest in football. I travel with the directors and football is what you talk about with them 90 per cent of the time.

Keith Kent: When I came here the pitch had been redone in the summer of '87 and we had a lot of problems settling it in. The reserves were playing here, the first-team, the youth-team games were here and the pitch didn't have time to settle. So the first year was a battle royal. At that time we didn't have a tunnel so to get on and off the pitch with tractors was a nightmare. If you think back to the centre tunnel it was 5 feet 6 inches wide. You couldn't get anything down it.

It all came to a head at the end of the season '91–92. We had lost the League to Leeds and the pitch was one of the problems. Two things happened that summer that changed it. One, we knocked the old Stretford End down and for the first time we had wind howling down the pitch and it made it quite bright. Also, while they were doing that, they put translucent sheets into the South Stand; the sun comes through that and it just lights up the pitch more. Our ground had always been covered in thick, black shade. The second thing was that the manager decided to move the reserves. We only played about 40 games here that season and we won the League.

From '93 until about '98 we had about five reasonably good years with the pitch but with the advent of the all-seater stadium everything conspired against us. We had 54,000 seats but that wasn't big enough so we put two new ends on, the east and west. The sun rises in the east, goes round the back of the South Stand and sets in the west so that has lost no end of hours of sunshine. Grass needs light to produce the energy to grow the roots and that is sadly lacking.

In 1998, I decided to put a new pitch in – the idea with any turfing job is that you water it in until it's established and then you withdraw the water so that in theory the roots go down looking for the water. We had five dry days between August and Christmas, honestly; the wettest autumn on record, '98. So we had to returf during the season and we were the first club ever to do that. In November '98 we played Blackburn on the Saturday and won and the pitch was dreadful. We came in on the Sunday and we took the turf off and it took us 12 days to relay the pitch. It was a nightmare. We played after a fortnight and beat Leeds 3–2 on the Sunday, which was a relief.

We had a survey done from May 2000 to April 2001 and the general conclusion is that the combined effects of the prevailing, adverse environmental conditions and the wear associated with the playing schedule make it highly unlikely that a single pitch could be sustained in top condition throughout that entire playing season, irrespective of the management of the pitch.

At the start of 2002 our pitch deteriorated rapidly. We played Blackburn in mid-January and we had a little meeting, the manager and I and I agreed with him that the pitch had run out of legs. He said, 'We'll go for it: when's the next window?' So I said we would relay the pitch in February. It was almost hassle-free. We started laying at half past seven on the Tuesday and by Friday at quarter past three it was in, done.

Voni von Arx: The biggest change for me is from standing to sitting. When I go to Europe to see United we always stand and it's cool to stand and to sing. Now at Old Trafford if you stand and sing and scream, suddenly there's a steward next to you, 'Sit down, blah, blah, blah': for me as a fan this is something they could bring back again somehow.

Paddy Harverson: We rebuilt the stadium at a cost of something like £120–140 million without borrowing a penny, which is a fantastic achievement. When you look at our main rivals, Newcastle had to borrow to do their stadium; Chelsea have gone even more in debt to build their stadium; and our other rivals, Arsenal and Liverpool, are all facing the prospect of building new stadiums and fund them, mostly through debt. So we are here with the best stadium in the country, the biggest stadium in the country and it's all paid for, which is a tribute to the people who have run this company for the past 10 years. We have a wonderful training centre and a new academy, all of it funded essentially through working capital, which is amazing for a business of our size. The fans, to be honest, don't really recognize that because they're not that interested in cash-flows and debt-equity ratios, but it would be nice if people perhaps understood it a bit more. It's crucially important because it means that 67,500 people are in here every week, and it's good, reliable income. People talk about TV being the biggest source of income for clubs. Well, it is at most clubs, but not here.

Phil Neville: To me, any time you step out on that turf it is like a dream. On the big European nights, when the atmosphere is electric, that's when it's at its best; but for me, any time I drive up to the stadium and see it I have to pinch myself that I'm playing for Man United.

Ken Ramsden: The most positive things over the past three years have happened off the pitch, with a much stronger team really working hard to drive the business and a greater desire to provide more and better fan facilities and the confidence to commit to a £40 million spend on making Old Trafford even bigger.

Sir Alex Ferguson: I can also see the day when we've got a 100,000-seater stadium. Now, some people even within the club thought we wouldn't fill a 67,000-capacity stadium, but I think we could fill 100,000 seats and when you create a stadium of that size, it increases the ambition at the club and puts the foot on the accelerator.

3

The Flowers of Manchester

Manchester United plummeted to an all-time low on 6 February 1958 – a day on which no ball was kicked and no points or trophies were lost. That day the United squad had been en route from Belgrade, where a 3–3 draw with Red Star had given them a place in the 1958 European Cup semi-finals, when their British European Airways flight had stopped at Munich for a scheduled refuelling stop. Mid-afternoon, the co-pilot, Captain Kenneth Rayment, twice attempted take-off from Munich but abandoned his efforts after hearing unusual noises from his engines. Snow was falling heavily as Rayment made his third attempt at lifting the BEA Elizabethan into the sky. Again he failed, but this time the plane had picked up such speed in the attempt that Rayment's efforts at braking the plane were in vain. The aircraft ran out of runway and screeched across a road and into a house, a tree and a hut. Its fuselage, wings and tail were wrenched apart on impact. The collision with the hut, which was stocked with aircraft fuel, ignited a huge explosion. Snow and slush on the runway was the official reason given for the unsuccessful take-off.

Twenty-three people lost their lives as a consequence of the crash. Eight of them were journalists and three were members of the Manchester United backroom staff: coach Bert Whalley, first-team trainer Tom Curry and the club secretary Walter Crickmer. A travel agent, a United supporter who had been along for the match, a member of the aircrew and Captain Rayment, co-pilot of Captain James Thain, also died. Eight United players died as a result of the crash: Geoff Bent, Roger Byrne, Eddie Colman, Duncan

Edwards, Mark Jones, David Pegg, Tommy Taylor and Liam 'Billy' Whelan. Half-back Colman, aged 21, was the youngest of the eight; captain and full-back Byrne, at 28, was the oldest. Edwards did not die immediately: he struggled for his life for 15 days before he finally passed away. Two United players survived unscathed: Harry Gregg and Bill Foulkes – Foulkes had come within an inch of his life as the plane had been sliced apart right beside where he was sitting.

Matt Busby, the manager, suffered severe injuries and in the days following the accident, medical staff at Munich's Rechts der Isar hospital feared that he would join the dead. Instead, Busby, then close to 50 years of age, showed remarkable strength to recover from his life-threatening condition. As he fought back to life, so United began to gather strength once again. Busby would return to Manchester from Munich after ten weeks but the club would not recover fully from the disaster for ten years.

The Munich disaster was to earn Manchester United sympathy world-wide for losing so many great young players – the Busby Babes – in the hour of one of their greatest triumphs. This sympathy was sustained long term by the forbearance with which the club bore its suffering and the dignity and resolve it showed in making its recovery. A plaque and a clock on the external façade at Old Trafford remind all visitors of the victims of the Munich disaster of 6 February 1958. Time ticks on, but the flowers of Manchester will not be forgotten.

Bill Foulkes: It was traumatic. I loved flying. A lot of the lads didn't like flying but I did. I used to laugh at them because they were so nervous at times. I would never do that now. I've flown all over the world to coach for around 20 years and, of course, I had to fly. I hated it – it nearly killed me. Losing all your pals is something that never leaves you. It is with you all the time. I think about it every day. The fear of flying is still with, as are lots of other things that I really don't like to talk about.

Wilf McGuinness: When I was only 20 years of age the Munich crash happened. I was fortunate enough not to go on that trip. I had been on every trip and I was down to go on this one. They told us on Fridays so there wouldn't be too much messing about, because not everybody had a phone in those days, and the first team were playing at Arsenal that Saturday. So the ones who were going were told on the Friday to report on the Monday. I twisted my knee – it was diagnosed cartilage – and I couldn't go. So that was the big piece of good fortune in my life. A lad who actually went in my place, Geoff Bent, died. So it was very sad.

Sandy Busby: At the time of the crash, I was playing for Blackburn Rovers and I was coming back through Victoria Station when a pal of mine said, 'Have you seen the placards?' They said, 'United in air crash.' I ran to the telephone and phoned home and an auntie from Scotland who was staying with us answered it and screamed, 'Get back home, son!' When I got back home it was mayhem. My auntie was there and a few people had come round, wanting to know what had happened, because nothing had come through because of the bad weather.

A great writer called Henry Rose had been on the plane and his girlfriend was at our house. Frank Swift, a great goalkeeper who had become a journalist, was on the plane and his wife and daughter were at our house. As the news started to come through, it became clear there had been deaths and all of a sudden my mother went into a semi-coma. She just stared into the fire and no one could get anything out of her at all. People kept coming on the phone and then we got one person on the phone saying, 'Henry Rose has died.' His girlfriend went into a fit. Then the news came that Frank Swift was dead and someone broke it to his wife and took her back home. She only lived round the corner from us. All this time I was up in my bedroom, sitting on my bed, head between my hands, praying. Then, all of a sudden, I heard this shouting from downstairs and it was this friend of ours – I called him Uncle Johnny, shouting – 'He's alive! He's alive!' My dad was alive – and my mother came round in an instant. She said to my sister and I that we'd better get round to the trainer Tom Curry's house, because he had died. She also told us to go to Mr Crickmer the secretary's house, because he had died.

Ken Ramsden: I was at home that Thursday afternoon, home from school, and a pal of mine came round. He had heard something on the radio so he knocked on the door and told my mum about it. She told him he was a wicked child for telling her such terrible things because she couldn't believe it.

It is interesting to think back to how slowly the news spread. Nowadays, with anything, a war or whatever, they are on the spot within minutes, aren't they? I remember on the Friday afternoon at school someone saying, 'Tommy Taylor's alive.' The truth was that Frank Taylor the journalist had survived and the name Taylor came back.

Nesta Burgess: I had Alex Dawson and Mark Pearson staying with me and they came home and said that the plane had crashed. The secretary, Alma George, had initially taken the message. When she told Jimmy Murphy she said to her: 'What are you talking about?' He couldn't take it in.

You were numb because you couldn't believe it. Bert Whalley went to Munich instead of Jimmy, who was manager of Wales and had a game at the same time. I had said to Bert Whalley: 'You lucky thing, I wish I was going.' 'I don't want to go, Nesta,' he said. 'I don't want to go.' I don't know whether he had a fear of flying or what. He was killed. He didn't come back.

Sir Alex Ferguson: I was in the library that day. I was swotting for my exams and I went from the library to training. I used to train with the local junior team, Benburb. When I got in, a lot of the senior players were sitting crying. It was really emotional. I said, 'What's happened?' I never knew anything about it because I had walked from the library right up to Tinto Park. They cancelled training that night.

Sandy Busby: The morning after the crash we flew off to Munich, stopping at Paris, and when they came to pick us up in the taxis they wanted to take us to the hotel but my mother said, 'No! Take us straight to the hospital.' There, a doctor told us to follow him. We went up to the intensive care unit and were walking along the corridor past these wards and I saw this old chap in an oxygen tent and felt sorry for him, the state he was in. Then it struck me that it was my dad. My mother was five yards behind me so I ran back and grabbed hold of her because

I knew she would have fainted there and then. My father was very grey and very ill and unconscious, of course. We came out and the great Professor Maurer came along with all his assistants, five or six of them. A few of the other families were there and he was going through each patient on his list one by one. When he came to my dad, he said, 'Not good at all, very touch-and-go.' So that was another blow. So we went back to the hotel and Harry Gregg and Bill Foulkes were in their room. They just wanted us to get together with them – nothing was really said about what had happened.

For the next few days we got the same report on our dad. Then, on about the fourth or fifth day, Professor Maurer said to us, 'Strong! Very strong! Very strong man.' He was a lot happier, this Professor Maurer. Oh, he was a brilliant fellow.

You worry about your own first and I was only 22 at the time; I'd received a telegram from my dad on 4 February, wishing me a happy birthday. Then, after that report from Professor Maurer, I went to see the other lads. I went to see Big Dunc. His fiancée Molly and a pal of his were at the side of the bed. She said, 'Sandy's here, Duncan.' But he was gone; he was unconscious.

You've no idea how strong Duncan was; he was an incredibly strong boy, and even though his body had been smashed to bits he was trying to lift himself up in the bed. There was nothing that you could do. People were asking why they couldn't send for different pieces of medical equipment from different countries or get kidney volunteers, but there was nothing that could be done. His body had just been smashed. From there, I went to see Johnny Berry. He was probably a bit older than the younger lads because my dad had signed him from Birmingham. He was just unrecognizable. He lived through it but he was never mentally the same – he never played again, of course. Then I went round to a ward that held Bobby Charlton, Kenny Morgans, Dennis Viollet, Jackie Blanchflower and Albert Scanlon. Jackie was probably the worst – he had smashed his arm completely. Bobby had just a few scratches on him – I think he has said himself that he didn't know what was happening when the crash took place. He was on a plane chair and got thrown out.

Mark Wylie: One thing that's very poignant is a telegram from Duncan Edwards sent from Munich to his landlady, saying, 'All flights cancelled. Flying tomorrow.' And, of course, they tried again and crashed. She got the telegram and soon after she would have heard there had been this crash and that he was lying there injured. So that's a very poignant item we have in the museum.

David Meek: I think, looking back, it must have been an enormous strain for Jimmy Murphy, who took over, because he was dealing with going to funerals and supervising the arrival back home of the bodies from Munich. He recognized that he had to get away and the players had to get away so he took everybody off to Blackpool and they based themselves at the Norbreck Hydro two or three days after Munich and for a couple of weeks they did all their training there. So really it was an unreal atmosphere and situation but by removing themselves from Old Trafford, they were able to focus on keeping the show going.

Nesta Burgess: When Munich happened, the '48 boys were first in to the club to see if there was anything they could help out with. It was such a shock – 6 February.

Ken Ramsden: I came down to Old Trafford and was just hanging around to see what was going on. The atmosphere was just silent; there was total depression and misery. People were simply waiting around because that was the only thing you could do. There was no 24-hour TV news or local radio back then. So you just came down and looked around and talked to people. People came in and out of the stadium but you didn't know what was happening inside.

You simply had to go somewhere, though. It was a process of sharing the sorrow, and people do gather even now – I don't think that's changed, even though there are all the news media that did not exist back then. You wanted to share your feelings with people and feel as if you were a part of it because it was your local club and the boys on that flight were nearly all either local boys or boys who had grown up with the club. Them all being so young also had an impact. The fact that they were boys and that they had grown up here added to the distress.

The coffins came back here and I often think about my mum and my aunt at that time – one week they were washing the strips for the players to go away in and the next week they were polishing the coffins. There was no counselling then for staff; people just took it on the chin and had to face up to it as best they could.

Sandy Busby: My dad gradually got stronger so my mother told me I had to get back home to attend the funerals of the lads who had died. Then I went back to Munich. My dad was in a room of his own by now – he had previously been in a room with Frank Taylor, a writer, and Thain, the pilot. It was a beautiful day. When I had been back home I had been phoning my mother every night and she had been saying to me, 'He's going through terrible pain, Sandy.' His lung had been crushed and the lower part of one of his legs had been smashed as well. So they were giving him lung punctures.

Anyway, this day, when I came back, some of the hospital staff said to my dad, 'It wouldn't do you any harm if you went out because it's a lovely day.' You could see my dad hesitate. He didn't want to go out but we persuaded him and we got the bed and turned it full round and started moving it towards the balcony but he started shouting, 'No! No!' It was too reminiscent for him of the plane situation because we were three or four storeys high. So we took him back in.

It was during that time that my mother had to tell my dad what had happened to the other young lads. She had to tell him who had died – he asked her because she hadn't mentioned it. He just said to her, 'I know it's going to be difficult. I'll name the players and you nod your head: sideways for "No" and straight up and down for "Yes".' When he had gone through all the names he went into a depression, which was only natural, of course. He said to her, 'I'm finished with football. That's me.' I think he was blaming himself for the deaths. My mother said, 'Don't be stupid. Also, don't forget that these young lads who died would want you to carry on and the young lads that are left will, I'm sure, want you to carry on.' He realized that what my mother had said was right.

Nesta Burgess: After Munich, I think the whole of Manchester came in to help and I remember the first match, when we hadn't got a team, and the reserves came out, and you just looked and you could see the first team. It was an awful feeling – an awful feeling.

Ken Ramsden: I came down to those first games after Munich with my dad because we had tickets through my mum working at Old Trafford. At the Sheffield Wednesday game, the first game after Munich, the atmosphere was just incredible. People weren't shouting before the game that night. There was a passion in the air before that game but it wasn't expressed. It was a silent passion – the silence was so heavy. Once the game started, everybody roared; it was as if they were getting everything out of their systems. Looking back, in a mature way, the great thing about that game was that at last you had something to shout about ,because you hadn't been able to shout or get excited since the crash had happened weeks earlier. I got to all the games that season, including the final with Bolton.

That was an amazing time – Doctor Maurer came from Munich with his nurses and Matt Busby's taped message from his hospital bed in Munich was played at one game. Things like that never leave your memory. Hearing Matt Busby's words in that way was eerie because although the tannoy was crackly his voice was very clear because the ground was so silent. It was like a minute's silence because of the respect people had for him and because people were aware they were listening to a man who had nearly died, a man who had been the architect of all United's success and the man who had taken us into Europe. To hear him speaking so clearly and with such a cheerful message must also have been of great encouragement to the players. It would have helped them feel that the club was on the way back.

Sandy Busby: I went back to Manchester and saw the Sheffield Wednesday game and the West Brom game, and then went back to Munich again. It was then that I knew he had got the bug again, because he said to me, 'Can you believe it? They're in the semi-finals of the Cup!' Jimmy had put together a patched-up side and I think it was the fever of the crowds that was getting them through. I had a couple of pals playing for Sheffield Wednesday and I had pals playing for West Brom. I asked them what it was like playing in those cup ties against Manchester United. They said, 'We didn't know what we were doing. The crowds were baying.' They were class sides, West Brom and Sheffield Wednesday, and I'm not being rude but our lads were just ordinary players – it was just a patch-up job – but the lads themselves were on such adrenalin and were so pumped up that it was unbelievable what they achieved.

My dad came back. Manchester United had been very underinsured; they were struggling for money. So he couldn't go out and buy Tom, Dick or Harry. So he started again and through his managerial skills and knowledge of players he started picking up players. He also went to the great Mr Bernabeu in Madrid and said, 'Would you come over and play a game for us because we've got to try and raise some money?' And Bernabeu, a bit sarcastically, turned round and said to my dad, 'You come and ask me that? You, the man that I asked to come to Madrid as my coach – and you refused?' My dad said, 'Yes, Mr Bernabeu, but Manchester is my haven. Manchester United is my haven. That's why I didn't come to Madrid.' Mr Bernabeu turned to his secretary. He said, 'Arrange a date. We go to Manchester – expenses only.' In those days the great Real Madrid could have asked for the full gate money from any game in which they played. So that friendly with Real raised a few bob for United.

Bill Foulkes: You see photographs of that time after the crash and I look like a skeleton. I must have lost two stone. They said in the programmes I was 12 stone 10 pounds. I wasn't: I was about 13 and a half stone. When I was working in the pit, at about 17, I used to push trucks of coal with one arm. I was pretty strong. There is a photograph of that game against Milan at Old Trafford, the first European match after Munich, and I am walking out with Nils Liedholm, the captain of Sweden and Milan. Now I had played against him before and he was just about my height but beside him I look like a skeleton. I should never have been playing football. I played all that season and never missed a game. I played in the Cup Final as well and played all the following season. He made me captain and I remained as captain the following season and I went in to see Matt and said I wanted to be relieved of the captaincy. It was playing on my mind and affecting my form. I also said that I would like a rest from playing. He said, 'No, you'll play, but it's your decision if you want to let go of the captaincy.' I did, and it was a relief. If it hadn't been for the crash, if he had offered me the captaincy I would have snatched it with both hands but I couldn't do it; I didn't want to be captain. That season following Munich we came second – when you think of that, with that depleted team, not many teams in the world could do that.

Ken Merrett: The crash happened at the old airfield in Munich and there is nothing there now, just fields. There is a plaque in the field where the crash happened and when we've played Bayern in recent years English supporters have gone and knocked on the local villagers' doors to find it. We have heard some lovely stories that once the United people have gone, the people who live round there take in the scarves and other things that they have left and keep them, and on 6 February they bring them out and put them all round the plaque. I think the City of Munich are going to make it a bit more prominent so that people can find it more easily but I'm not sure it didn't have something more in being understated. It is very nice of the people of Munich to think about us.

Chris Yeamans: I think the Munich air crash helped create the myth. In the same way that the deaths of people like James Dean and Marilyn Monroe froze them in time, so too, with the unfulfilled potential with the Busby Babes, were they mythologized. United became about more than football.

Cliff Butler: Everybody remembers Munich. It's one of those moments like Kennedy and the New York tragedy. For Manchester, the Munich air disaster is a really major thing.

David Meek: I think Munich made an emotional impact; not just the crash but the question: 'Will this club be able to carry on? Will they recover?' It became a very dramatic, emotional story, so it appealed not just to United fans but to people all over the world. If Munich had not happened, I'm sure United would have been successful, but there wouldn't have been such wide appeal.

Voni von Arx: I think the Munich disaster is the most special reflection of United because it was such a tragedy. My father was 10 years old at the time, living in Switzerland. He had heard about the Busby Babes being such a good team. He was so deeply shocked and it touched him so much that he started to support United. He was at the European Cup final against Benfica 10 years later. It is in a way surprising that such a sad event can bring such feelings even to a person who doesn't live in the country where that team plays. Had the air crash happened to Liverpool, for example, he could have started supporting them, but it happened to Man United. It is thanks to him I support United.

I remember in the Nineties Mr [Alan] Hansen said that you can't win the League with kids in the side. I think in '58 it was no different. They were also young players; 20, 21 years old. It's amazing – you would expect such young, inexperienced players to lose every game and to be unable to do well either in the League or in Europe. That's why I have a feeling for '58 in a way, because the circumstances were the same at the beginning of the Nineties as for the players in '58.

Sir Alex Ferguson: Sympathy for the club after Munich brought people to support the club because of that but that only takes you in there. The content is more important. So those people that were drawn to the club because of the Munich air disaster stayed with them because of the way the club played and right through the history they've always played to win. So therefore the fanbase has got bigger and bigger. It's like a website. You go on the opening page and then you click on it to see the content and if it holds your interest you will stay on that website and keep returning to it. A lot of people have clicked on to Manchester United and I don't think anybody will leave once they get in here. It's an exciting club to support.

4

Friends and Rivals

Manchester United have never been short of friends or rivals. The longest running rivalry has been based on the healthy competition for footballing supremacy inside the city of Manchester. Prior to the Second World War, Manchester City were usually top dogs. At that time United were often bobbing up and down between the First and Second Divisions and, as well as playing second fiddle to City, they could hardly be considered a major threat to the clubs outside the environs of Manchester. The post-war years proved decidedly different. As United became a consistently strong force in the game, powerful rivalries began to build with the other major clubs in the English game. Now, thanks to United's dominance of English football over the past decade, almost every club in the country sees United as the one team that deserves to be knocked off its pedestal.

The modern era has also brought regular competition with major European clubs such as Bayern Munich and Real Madrid and a chance for United to foster friendships with some of the biggest names in Europe. These rivalries are quite different to domestic ones. Familiarity, across greater distances, appears to have led to contentment rather than contempt.

Anna Deakin: United's main rivals are Liverpool, Leeds and, obviously, Manchester City. United, however, are in the unique position of having practically every other team in the Premiership class them as their rivals! No matter where you are in the country, there's always someone who wants to have a go at you. It seems quite bizarre but many people seem to give more respect to a City supporter who has never been to a game than to a United supporter who goes to all the games home and away. Critics can say that it is easy to support United when they're always winning but the fact is that it's harder to get respect for supporting United when everyone hates them and wants to have a pop at you for supporting them.

Voni von Arx: I think United's main rivals are still Liverpool, and it goes back to when they built the canal in Manchester. That's the basis of it – I've read the history of it – it has nothing to do with football. It also has a lot to do with Liverpool being a big club in Europe. They have won the League more than United and they've won the European Cup more. For United fans, it's not jealousy, because United have won a lot as well; it's just that this rivalry has grown over the years. If you had to name our rivals, then Liverpool would always be first; then it would be Leeds, after that Arsenal, and then maybe Man City because these days you just laugh at Man City.

Ole Pedersen: Without question, Liverpool are our main rivals. The reason: they still lead, 18–15 [League titles]. No one else could seriously call themselves our rivals.

Chris Yeamans: For me, Liverpool have always been our main rivals, partly because of the old Manc–Scouse rivalry. My dad's brother and my cousin lived just down the road from us and they were both huge Liverpool fans who used to go every week. The Seventies and Eighties was the time when Liverpool used to win everything in sight, so it was really hard for me and my dad to bear, and this led to many a family feud. After certain games – though funnily enough we usually didn't do too badly against them – we wouldn't speak to each other for weeks. We wouldn't have had to wait 26 years for a League title if it wasn't for them.

Jonathan Deakin: In terms of order, our main rivals are Liverpool, Leeds, City. Liverpool is everything: history, geography, football, culture, music. I work in Chester now, and if anything I get more wound up by them than ever. My girlfriend is Scouse too, which is odd. But United v Liverpool is the biggest game in England: no question. Although I hate Liverpool there's a healthy disrespect if you like – we know they've had good sides. Their fans are clued-up, their city is a good night out and they don't buy into the 'England' scene. We deserve each other's rivalry, if you like.

Roy Williamson: Whilst I don't like Leeds one bit, especially now that I'm exiled in West Yorkshire, nothing can match my hatred of Liverpool Football Club. This doesn't make me anti-Scouse – I'm a huge Beatles fan and I've stood on many a picket line with Scouse trade unionists in my time – but when it comes to Liverpool FC, I just go cold. Someone said that they should produce a series of videos of 'Famous Liverpool 1–0 victories', and that sums it up.

Ron Snellen: Although I'm aware that being a United fan these days is quite easy with all the winning, I did go through the Eighties when those Scousers won everything and put us nowhere. Now it's our turn!

Ken Ramsden: In 1992 we were playing Liverpool late in the season at a time when we were challenging Leeds for the League title. Leeds were playing Sheffield United in an early kick-off and we were playing at Anfield later in the day. I had gone down to Anfield with the kit man early that morning and, getting off the coach, a Liverpool steward approached me and said, 'I hope Leeds win today.' I said, 'Why?' He said, 'So you lot don't win the League.' I said, 'Oh, come on, we've not won it for 25 years. You've won it 18 times. What harm will it do you if we win the League?' He said, 'If you lot win the League once you'll never stop winning it.' And I laughed at him. I think about him now! How prophetic his words were! I've not seen him since – I wish I had. He was only a young lad but, goodness me, how prophetic that was. At the time, I thought, 'Let's just win it once. I won't be greedy. I'll settle for winning it once', but it's just gone on from there. That day we lost to Liverpool and Leeds won at Sheffield and went on to take the title.

Lou Macari: The chance to go to United had never occurred to me – on the Tuesday before the West Ham game in which I made my debut I was at Anfield with Bill Shankly, who had a pen in his hand. I had been picked up in a car that morning by Sean Fallon, the assistant manager at Celtic, and Sean wouldn't tell me where we were going. He just told me I was going to England to talk to a football club. I just remember four or five hours later ending up in Southport and that threw me a little bit because I didn't think there was any club in Southport that I would be signing for – I certainly hoped that wasn't the case! – and, having rarely been out of Scotland previously, I didn't actually have much of an idea where Southport was. Anyway, it turned out we were just stopping for a bite to eat and we then moved on to Liverpool.

Jock Stein must have told Bill Shankly to make sure I signed when I got there – in those days things were different when a player wanted a move from one club to another, and I think big Jock had promised Bill Shankly that if I was ever going to move from Celtic he would arrange for me to sign for Liverpool. By chance, Liverpool happened to be playing that night. I had not yet signed when their game began and through fate they gave me a seat in the stand next to Pat Crerand, who was at that time United's assistant manager. When I got talking to him it became clear that he had been unaware that I was on the verge of signing for Liverpool. At half-time he got on the phone and told Tommy Docherty that I was in Liverpool. The Doc told Pat to tell me not to sign and, although the deal was there on the table from Liverpool, I wanted to go to Old Trafford.

Twenty-four hours later I had agreed to join United, so signing for United all happened so quickly for me. I had a gut feeling that United was a better club for me, even though they weren't as successful as Liverpool. Also, when you're playing for Celtic you tend to lean towards Manchester United. I went to United at a time when Liverpool were winning and Manchester United were losing. I just take the view that my 11 years at Old Trafford couldn't have been bettered even if I had won everything at Liverpool, and I don't mean that to be in any way disrespectful to Liverpool. I think everybody who has been at Old Trafford would have to agree that there is some magic about the place even when they are struggling. That stems from the days of Charlton, Law and Best, who really put the club on the map world-wide. So when you join the club you too get put on the map world-wide, and that's a pretty special feeling.

Voni von Arx: I like Bayern Munich – I think there's something in common with Man United there. They're both big in their countries and they are both hated as much as they are loved in their own countries. Then you have '58, which happened in Munich, and so on. For me, it's always great to go to Munich because the fans are nice. There is never, ever any trouble with them and it's a good city.

Ken Ramsden: I think we play the European clubs too infrequently for any particularly sharp rivalries to build up. In fact, there's a great deal of respect between United and our European rivals. We have a fantastic relationship with Bayern Munich, for example. When we played in Munich late in 2001 the club had got word from a lot of local residents that United fans were turning up and looking for the plaque at the airport to commemorate the Munich disaster. So Bayern put something on their website to tell our fans where it was. They worked with us to make sure that as many people as possible would know where it was – that kind of thing is fantastic. It really builds up relationships between fans. It's a completely different kind of passion and rivalry with European clubs – it's just for the night of the game and then it's all over.

Cliff Butler: We play teams in Europe so regularly now that I know some of Bayern Munich's players better than Manchester City's!

Jimmy Billington: The best team I ever saw was Real Madrid, with Di Stefano, Santamaria – the best centre-half you've ever seen – Puskas and Gento, the outside left. Bill Foulkes had Gento in his pocket every time they played, and Bill Foulkes wasn't a classical player. In one friendly they beat United 5–0. That belied United, because they had played their part in making that one of the best games you ever saw there.

Jonathan Deakin: Leeds are the classic 'one-club city': no balance in their views, no one to counter them, and all the knobs supporting the same side. Leeds fans have consistently been the most disgusting in terms of behaviour at Old Trafford since 1990. Walking across the forecourt, protected by police, singing about 'taking' Old Trafford and about Munich is the epitome of small-time Englanders.

Ken Ramsden: The feeling between our fans and Leeds is as bad as it is anywhere and yet on the pitch the match is almost always played in good spirit, the players are very friendly towards each other and the clubs are very friendly towards each other.

Jimmy Billington: City were definitely our biggest rivals in the Thirties, Forties and Fifties. It was just like Glasgow with Rangers and Celtic. Everybody was waiting for that game, and when it got closer and closer you looked forward to it more and more. My friend was a City supporter and, although you didn't battle, it was ding-dong all the time you were talking in the pub. They hammered us three times in one season – '55, the year they won the Cup.

Tony Whelan: I was a City fan as a young boy. In fact, when I got invited to go on the first-team tour to Bermuda in 1970, they came looking for me at one of the night games. Wilf McGuinness was looking for me to tell me but I wasn't at the match and I should have been, because I was a young player. City were playing Schalke in the Cup-Winners' Cup at Maine Road and I was there with my pals. Wilf McGuinness came round to my house the next morning to find out where I had been and I had to tell him, sheepishly. He was very good about it.

I think the rivalry's intense. It's probably less intense now but certainly I remember, as a younger player at Manchester United, that the derby was a massive game and as a City supporter as a kid it was a massive game. When I came to play here, the first-team game was a massive game, as were the reserve team and 'A' team and 'B' team games. You didn't want to get beaten against City – absolutely no question.

Where I lived, in Wythenshawe, they were all City fans and I had always been a staunch Blue. I had always worn a blue scarf, used to go to away matches. So for me to join United – it was traitorous.

Ken Merrett: I carried on being a City supporter for four years after I had joined the club. I used to go and watch City midweek although I was working here but I decided in 1970, when I was made assistant secretary, that it was a good time to change. I still get stick about it. People say, 'How could you change?' I know people say you can never change but I think that's not strictly true. I think maybe it's harder to change as a supporter but you've got to bear in mind that for the first two or three years I was here, the players were United players so they weren't special to me and I was a City supporter, but after about four years – and don't forget I did the wages, so I came into contact with all the players – players who were youngsters, my age, got into the team. So then I knew them as people and I think it was easier then to support them.

My office in those days overlooked the pitch. It was the only one that did and it had previously been the manager's office, after the war, then the secretary's office. It had bars on the window because it was in the Paddock, the standing area. The players used to train here quite a bit as well and I can remember they used to come up to the window and say, 'This is where we keep City supporters – behind bars.' That would have been in the Bobby Charlton era. In those days a lot of people went to watch City one week and United the next.

Roy Williamson: Many younger fans do not regard City as a serious rival but if you talk to the old stagers the feeling is different. We have had many good days against them but also some memorably bad ones: 1974 and relegation, for instance. There's a myth surrounding this, because we would have gone down anyway, so they did not send us down. Nevertheless, it still sticks in the throat when I remember seeing that Mike Doyle celebrating Denis's goal. In true Red style, though, the King made a dignified exit and let it be known by his lack of enthusiasm that he hated what he had done. Long live the King!

I was away for the 5–1 defeat, years later, but I know Reds who were there and who would put the 5–0 hammering we gave them at Old Trafford in the Nineties near the top of their best results.

Sammy McIlroy: I made my debut against City at Maine Road and the true story is that in those days they had the mini-derby on the Friday night before the first-team derby and Bill Foulkes, the youth team coach, told me I wouldn't be playing in the mini-derby because I would have to report for the first-team on the Saturday. I was annoyed because I thought I would just be helping out with the hampers and the boots and I was very disappointed not to be playing in the mini-derby. So I was very disgruntled when I went to bed that night. At 11 o'clock on the Saturday morning I found out I was playing and the sudden shock of that took away all the nerves. Before the match George actually said to me that he'd give me a bottle of champagne if I scored. He was as good as his word, and I kept the bottle for eight years until I opened it for a special occasion.

In the match itself, it was 0–0 and City were attacking. Alex Stepney threw the ball wide to me and I hit it inside to George and George played a lovely ball out to Brian Kidd and when Kiddo played the ball in, George was having his shirt tugged by Tony Book, so I just put it inside Corrigan. I can remember every detail vividly to this day. It was an unbelievable feeling – it was so joyous I could easily have run right out of the ground. The noise was electrifying – it was deafening. They were two great sides at the time – each with a fantastic forward line. We had Willie Morgan, Bobby Charlton, George Best and they had Colin Bell, Francis Lee and Mike Summerbee – and the place was buzzing.

When I played for City a decade after my debut it was strange. City were then in a transitional period. They had just come up from the old Second Division and were aiming to consolidate, while United had a superb side. It was strange coming out in the blue to play against the red but it was your job and you just had to get on with it. On the day, memories came flooding back to me of my debut back in 1971. We had had an international in midweek in Turkey and I had a horrendous blister on my foot and it got infected. Because it was City–United I didn't want to miss it, but I was in so much discomfort it was unreal. I felt like being sick. At half-time I got the doctor to try to do something about it – no one knows anything about that – and the doctor gave me a tablet to calm me down. I wanted to play because I had just signed for City.

The City–United derby is fierce; it's in the same bracket as Celtic–Rangers and Liverpool–Everton.

Paul Hardman: My father was a City fan – it's a family tradition that everybody in the family is a City fan. I actually went and watched City a few times, but there's a definite romance about United. City fans will say that United are supported by people from London, which isn't the case. What's that song they sing about United being the best-supported team in Singapore or something like that? There is a massive groundswell of support for United in Manchester but you get people thinking they are proper Mancunians because they support City.

I supported City at Wembley in the 1981 Cup Final when they played Tottenham, but I think that might actually have been the turning point because something clicked that meant I wanted to follow United. After that I never watched a game at Maine Road and never really supported them. I actually worked in the ticket office at Maine Road but I was using the money I earned there to buy tickets at United and around about '82–83 we got the opportunity to start going regularly to Old Trafford. When I talk to Sir Alex he shares the feeling that there is a romance about the place, even now. So, fortunately, I am a convert from City.

Dennis Giggs: Ryan was playing with Deans youth club and there was a chap there called Dennis Schofield and he had connections with Manchester City. He saw the potential in Ryan and so he went to their School of Excellence. Then the United scouts saw him and asked my daughter about his availability. She said she'd have to speak to Manchester City first but they weren't interested in keeping him. They said he could do as he wished. They just didn't seem to want to fight to keep him. He was always a Manchester United supporter as a youngster and when asked to join he jumped at it.

Simon Davies: I think that in Manchester the rivalry with City is probably twice what it is with Liverpool. It's just geography – they're our closest rivals. We've been called Stretford Rangers by them because they say we are closer to Salford or Stretford than the city centre. So they claim that all City's fans come from Manchester, that they are the one true Manchester club and that United fans come from Devon and Dorset whereas, in reality, most of City's fans come from Stockport. It's just daft little things like that that keep it going.

Jonathan Deakin: Losing 5–1 to City in 1989 was a defining moment, despite our successes that followed, which is why beating them 5–0 in the 1994–95 season was so important.

Ken Ramsden: As a United fan, I don't tend to think too much about either Chelsea or Arsenal, but the Premier League was seen, for a long time, as a two-horse race and Chelsea have now made it into a three-horse race, which is good for football and good competition for us. We have to raise our own bar. There has, I would say, been nothing memorable about our matches against Chelsea; there's nothing special about playing Chelsea, but the behaviour of Arsenal players following Ruud's penalty miss was disgraceful and certainly sticks in the mind. [*Six Arsenal players were charged by the Football Association with varying offences after the 0–0 draw in a League match at Old Trafford on 21 September 2003 and Arsenal were accused of failing to control their players. Arsenal admitted misconduct charges and were fined £175,000. Five of the players charged were fined five-figure sums and four of them were banned for between one and four matches.*]

Our greatest rivals at the moment are certainly Chelsea. You really can't look beyond them or Arsenal.

Eric Halsall: As far as Chelsea and Arsenal are concerned, they're only a couple of southern – even worse, London – clubs who are having a good spell that will, I suspect, prove to be no more than a blip in the grand scheme of things. After all, in well over a century of championships, clubs from south of the Midlands have yet to manage top spot as many as 20 times. London clubs have yet to show real staying power, never mind the kind of loyal, even fanatical, support that United has enjoyed through thick and thin for a century and more – and it has to be admitted that the thin's been damn near anorexic on occasion.

Adam Bostock: Chelsea's challenge to United may just be another flash in the plan, à la Blackburn in 1995. Whether they can enjoy sustained success and achieve what only United have achieved in the last 20 years – winning successive league titles – will depend on how long Mourinho and Abramovich stay at Stamford Bridge. It's also not clear what the future holds for United – following Malcolm's takeover.

Roy Williamson: As far as Chelsea goes, what right have I to criticize? I am proud of our club's supporters fighting against Murdoch and the rest; we are a club that's not going to be anybody's plaything. The fact that Chelsea have taken the Russian money is up to them. It's not for United to criticize; if other fans want to, then let them get on with it. When at our best over the last decade or more, we have always had a nucleus of home-grown talent and we should be proud of that. I don't hear anyone giving us credit for this, though.

Adam Bostock: I do admire the way Chelsea – i.e. Mourinho – have spent the money and built a championship team without buying the biggest names in world football, such as Ronaldinho, Zidane, Ronaldo et cetera. How many trophies have Real Madrid won since they assembled their so-called 'galacticos'? And how much were the successful FC Porto and Greece teams collectively worth in 2004?

Buying the best, most expensive, most highly-paid individuals doesn't guarantee success. It certainly helps – would United have won the league in 2003 if they hadn't broken the British transfer record for Van Nistelrooy, £19 million, and again for Ferdinand, £30 million? Would United have won the treble if they hadn't spent record amounts on Jaap Stam, £10.75 million, and Dwight Yorke, £12.6 million, in 1998?

Chelsea stand accused [by] some of buying the title with Abramovich's money. But some of their key players in the title campaign were on Chelsea's books long before Abramovich arrived: Frank Lampard, summer 2001, John Terry, trainee, debut 1998, Eidur Gudjohnsen, summer 2000.

Eric Halsall: The quality of football that Mourinho and the players bought by Abramovich have developed at the Bridge, together with the similar quality built up at Highbury by Wenger, has introduced a new dimension of genuine, top-drawer competition in the Premiership. Factor in the ongoing phenomenon that is United and you have something entirely worthwhile – a level of excellence for other teams to aspire to – and to judge by the ridiculous number of points we haemorrhaged to struggling clubs in the 2004–05 season, they're learning the lessons all too well. The second rank of clubs, like Newcastle and Liverpool, and the up-and-comers like Everton and Middlesbrough, are all going to work their socks off to try to prevent the top three from having things all their own way.

So you'd have to be a pretty unimaginative supporter not to enjoy the whole business. It would have taken a great deal of pleasure out of supporting United were we to have dominated the Premiership unchallenged. After all, when questioned in his early days at United about what really drove him, the Wizard [Sir Alex Ferguson] was typically concise – it was, he said, the desire to 'knock Liverpool of their ****** perch'. We've now been on the same perch for an unprecedented spell, so Arsenal and now Chelsea are enjoying the same sort of motivation as we did in the 1980s.

After all, it's entirely legitimate in the world of modern football to try to buy success if you can and United is hardly in a position to whinge about other clubs enjoying the benefits of multi-million-pound revenues. Having said that, I do believe that on purely ethical grounds a rich club should put something back into the wider game – and that's something in which Sir Alex has been an incomparable leader.

Simon Davies: In recent years, Chelsea and Arsenal have become United's major rivals for the championship. The matches with Arsenal seem to have overtaken the derby matches with Manchester City as the clashes with most passion – on the pitch at least.

And in the tunnel... It's probably because the matches are so hyped up by the likes of Sky and the tabloid newspapers but the derby seems to have lost some of its edge. There was the match with City at Old Trafford a couple of years ago that ended 1–1 and I don't think there was a single booking. Compare that with the Arsenal match at Old Trafford in 2004 which is alleged to have ended with the Gunners lobbing food around [*after the League match with Arsenal at Old Trafford on 24 September 2004, which United won 2–0, Arsenal players were reported to have thrown pizza, sandwiches and soup in the direction of Sir Alex Ferguson near the dressing rooms*] and it's pretty easy to see where the passion lies. United and Arsenal just seem to wind each other up, while matches against Chelsea aren't quite that fiery – yet.

Sir Alex Ferguson: They [the Arsenal players] were out of control and out of order when that happened. We've still had no apology yet and that tells you the quality of people you are dealing with. Arsenal won't apologize and that's down to their manager.

Eric Halsall: The Arsenal fixtures have thrown up a bucketful of enjoyment. Probably the game at Old Trafford in September 2004 was the most magical for a whole host of reasons. The day began with a packed Shareholders United/Independent Manchester United Supporters' Association meeting at O'Brien's to discuss the takeover bid by the Glazer family. Then thousands of banner-waving fans gathered in front of Sir Matt Busby's statue. To round off the day, Arsenal's impressive unbeaten run of 49 games in the Premiership without loss was brought to an abrupt halt in a game that was more of a battle than a contest of silky skills.

Simon Davies: The images of Martin Keown towering over Ruud after the penalty miss at Old Trafford were pretty memorable [*Van Nistelrooy struck the crossbar with a penalty in time added on for stoppages at the end of the 0–0 draw at Old Trafford on 21 September 2003 and was immediately surrounded by gloating, goading Arsenal players who had earlier been incensed when their captain, Patrick Vieira, had become the 52nd Arsenal footballer to be dismissed in a seven-year period following an incident involving Van Nistelrooy*], as were the reports that filtered through following the Battle of the Buffet, as the witty tabloids chose to call it. The 6–1 win at the end of the 2000–01 season was absolutely stunning, but the most heartbreaking one was having to report on the scenes as Arsenal won the title at Old Trafford in 2001–02. Lots of United fans stayed on to applaud them, which was impressive – I'm not sure what would happen if we won the League at Highbury. We'd probably end up covered in soup. As for Chelsea matches, nothing really stands out. They don't concede many goals, they don't score that many and we haven't had any major fallings-out yet.

Eric Halsall: Arsenal are operating on a much tighter budget than their more fashionable neighbours and it has to be admitted that they've been doing exceptionally well in the Premiership; in their case largely thanks to a manager who, despite his obvious qualities, seems to have a distinct aversion to British players – as well as serious myopia. Arsenal, like Chelsea, have had their moments in the past, as have Spurs and West Ham, but there's no real reason to think that the current blip is any less of a flash in the pan than those of previous years.

Lately, Arsenal have provided us with some entertainment, but Liverpool, naturally, must always be regarded as our greatest rivals because that's one of the immutable natural laws of the universe. Anyway, unless they, or we, go broke, I would say that Liverpool have the deep-seated traditions, the strong and loyal, if misguided, fan base and, above all, the northern strength and resilience to build back up to a position where they can once again be our strongest competition as well as our favourite enemy.

Simon Davies: For the Premiership title, obviously Chelsea are currently United's greatest rivals, but in terms of being closely matched, I'd say Arsenal. We're both just coming off our peaks, I think, while Chelsea are on the crest of a wave, so it's a great battle of pride with Arsenal. We're like two old boxers who refuse to accept they're past their prime and who will go toe to toe with each other and just slug it out; literally, sometimes.

Eric Halsall: On the footballing side, United have been able, thanks to a successful financial operation grafted on to a peerless footballing tradition, to enjoy a wonderful run of success. But to achieve such success you need a combination of board, executive arm, playing and non-playing staff and, in Chelsea's case, owner, which will work together to generate not just efficiency but teamwork and a winning mentality. It appears – albeit on limited evidence to date – that Abramovich, Kenyon and Mourinho are making a pretty good fist of that. I can't really say I admire this – it just is – and it's up to everyone at United to make sure that in the long run neither Chelsea nor any other pretender to the crown manages better than second-best.

Adam Bostock: Speaking as a Macclesfield Town fan and as a journalist who loves a good story, the rise of Arsenal and Chelsea has ultimately made Premiership football interesting again. Pre-Abramovich, the top flight was in danger of becoming very predictable and logical: the country's biggest football club (United) wins the biggest prize. Even Arsenal were, in financial terms, the underdogs to United – Arsène Wenger deserves respect for making sure the money gap wasn't mirrored on the field. Some of the games played between United and Chelsea, or United and Arsenal in particular, have been very exciting, dramatic, controversial – all that you might expect or want of the biggest stars commanding the biggest salaries.

Eric Halsall: I could also cite the 2004 FA Cup semi-final, with the team playing out of their skins with the kind of passion Reds always expect of their teams but don't always get these days and a phenomenal atmosphere inside Villa Park, with the team roared on by 17,000 impassioned Reds, as another great performance inspired by an encounter with Arsenal. Or, even better, I might pick the game at Highbury in February 2005 when United came from behind twice, magnificently running out 4–2 winners. It will take a long time to dim the shine on the final nail in the coffin – John O'Shea's delightful chipped goal that seemed to leave even him gobsmacked.

Ken Ramsden: It is true that most opposing fans tend to hate Manchester United. I often travel on the team bus to matches and the reaction you get when you arrive at opposing teams' grounds is phenomenal – there is such anger and hatred on the faces of fans towards the players. Obviously, there are the gestures as well. But why? What harm are United going to do to you? We're going to play a football match. If your team are better, they'll win. If they're not, you won't. Perhaps I'm taking too detached a view, but realistically that's what it's about. It's not a war and players don't see it as a war. In the Fifties and early Sixties, if a youngster swore at a football match he took a clipping and would be told not to use that type of language. Nowadays it's common to see fathers and their children swearing together; I've seen children on the shoulders of their fathers when the team bus arrives and they have both been giving the team a two-fingered salute. That's one change that hasn't been for the better.

Sir Alex Ferguson: It's an incredible challenge that we now have from Chelsea. We have had a lot of meetings recently, all to do with how we get back on track, and we will get there. We can't match them for money but we can do it in a different way. One way will be in developing youth. We may have to wait a little bit but each year we will get better. One of the things that, when you have been a manager as long as I have been, you have to accept is that players will retire or move on. This is probably the fourth team in my time and it's not easy. You're dealing with emotions and players you admire but, unfortunately, you have to move on and do what is best to keep Manchester United where we should be.

Part Two:
The People

5

The Men Who Made United

Two visionaries have made Manchester United the club it is today: Sir Matt Busby and Sir Alex Ferguson. Their commitment to bringing through young players and to playing football in an expansive, entertaining style has established United as premier purveyors of top-quality football.

Both men initially proved themselves as winners with United through an FA Cup victory. Both ensured that victory would be built upon by ploughing time and resources into creating fresh, young, home-produced teams. Championships and success in Europe followed. The personalities of Busby and Ferguson are dissimilar in many ways, but there is an uncanny similarity between the types of teams they have created and the methods they have used to create them.

United's pre-war managers had struggled to produce sustained success. James Ernest Mangnall, who was secretary–manager for nine years prior to the First World War, is the only man other than Busby and Ferguson to have led a United team to a League title. He captured it twice, in 1907–08 and 1910–11. He also pushed hard, and successfully, for United to move to Old Trafford. Mangnall, a perceptive individual, was aware of the mystique of football even in those early days of the game, once stating, 'A great, intricate, almost delicate and, to the vast majority of the public, an incomprehensible piece of machinery is the modern, up-to-date football club. It is a creation peculiarly by itself. There is nothing like it.'

Mangnall was unusual for his time in that he took charge of team selection and tactics, and his departure was as radical as his achievements:

he quit Old Trafford to join Manchester City in 1912. A variety of faces came and went in his wake – J. J. Bentley, John Robson, John Chapman, Clarence Hilditch, Herbert Bamlett, Walter Crickmer and Scott Duncan – but Mangnall was not adequately replaced until the arrival of Matt Busby in 1945. When Busby won the 1948 FA Cup it was the club's first major honour since Mangnall's 1911 Championship.

Prior to Busby's arrival, directors had habitually fiddled in such matters as team selection. Busby was quick to wrest full control of the playing side away from the boardroom and to stamp his own image on the club. His successors – Wilf McGuinness, Frank O'Farrell, Tommy Docherty, Dave Sexton and Ron Atkinson – all struggled, in different ways, to live with his legacy. The occasional cup would come the way of Old Trafford but the League title and European success proved elusive. By the time Alex Ferguson arrived on the scene in 1986, the need for radical change was clear and the succeeding years have, many times over, borne testimony to the effectiveness of his approach to management and to the game of football.

Sandy Busby: At lunchtime on a Friday I used to go and get fish and chips for the family and then race back home and ask my dad, 'What's the team? What's the team?' He would go through it for me and he would tell me little stories. We had a player called Stan Pearson and I remember him telling me once, 'Stan wants to be left out because a corner of the crowd are getting at him.' My dad told me that he said to Stan, 'Don't you worry about the crowd. You worry about me. You're playing.' We had a brilliant inside-forward called Billy Whelan who was killed in the crash. He looked slow but he wasn't – he used to put the ball through people's legs and he had a tremendous shot as well. The same thing happened with him – part of the crowd were getting at him. My dad said to him, 'Just worry about me. Forget about the crowd.'

David Meek: Matt Busby and Alex Ferguson had authority in common, and then their principles of football, I think, are very similar. I think both managers believed in players being able to express themselves, personality players who are going to come on to the stage and not shrink – great individualists, but ones who can be moulded into the team ethic. Matt Busby did that right from his very first team. He had players of great character who'd been away, a lot of them, during the war, – very strong personalities – and he quickly encouraged those who had great skills and individual flair.

I think Matt Busby was very much a product of his age; I think he was a fairly simple, straightforward man. That's not to mean simple in the sense of daft because he was certainly not that. He knew where he was going. He was very strong, he was very resolute. Some people have tried to say he was ruthless – I don't think he was any more ruthless than any football manager has to be but he was certainly strong, and it was always said that if you crossed Matt Busby in a serious way he could be quite unforgiving. Certainly, if he decided that somebody's personality was on a collision course with the club he didn't hesitate to transfer him for the sake of keeping things right in the dressing-room. For instance, Charlie Mitten became a football rebel. When he came back from Bogota, Matt Busby put him on the transfer list and Charlie always resented the way that Matt – as Charlie would see it – failed to support him; but as Matt Busby would see it, Charlie went off to South America, made his bed and had to lie on it: there was no return.

Johnny Morris was transferred to Derby County on a matter of principle and he was arguably United's key man – it was almost like Alex Ferguson transferring David Beckham. I always remember Jack Crompton saying they would have won the Cup again if Johnny Morris had stayed but he had to go.

Sandy Busby: My dad had great principles and a great belief in doing things with dignity. I don't think there's a more dignified club going – but then I'm biased! My dad also used to look after himself. He was very wary of his weight and my mother would always make sure he went out of the house in a well-presented, well-dressed fashion. My mother used to look after my dad's appearance. If she ever thought he was going out looking less than smart she would call him back and tell him to change this or that. He had broad shoulders because of being down the mines at 14 years of age, and in those days they had no machinery like they have today. They used to do a lot of digging and pushing of wagons by themselves. So he was well-built and he never misused himself. He used to have a drop of whisky now and then and there is a good story about a party he gave back in his home village, Orbiston, to celebrate being made captain of Scotland when they were to play England. My dad had a cigarette in his hand and my grandmother, who was a very strong character whom he admired greatly, said, 'What do you think you're doing, smoking a cigarette? God, Mattha, I don't know what you'll be doing next – you'll be drinking next.' He looked down at the Scotch he had on the table in front of him and thought, 'I'd better not touch that again. She'll kill me.'

Bill Foulkes: I made my debut in '52, at Liverpool, and how the hell I was doing that I don't know. I hadn't played full-back, I was injured, and I got told to go up to the boss' office. I had been injured for three or four weeks and I thought I was being called up to get the sack because I was a part-timer at that stage and there were so many good players at the club; he had about 40 really good players at the club at that time. He said, 'How is the leg?' I said, 'It's OK.' He said, 'I think we'll give you a game. Just jump and let me see how you land.' So I jumped up – it killed me but I didn't say anything. So he said, 'It looks all right. We'll see how you are tomorrow and we'll give you a game at the weekend.'

I didn't know what to do. I was in a right state. I was injured, I wasn't fit, I hadn't done any training for a while, and I was playing right full-back against Billy Liddell. At that time he was one of the greatest, and I remember just before the game Billy Liddell came across and he shook my hand. He said, 'I believe this is your first game. Well, I wish you all the very best, son.' He meant it; you could tell. I stuck to him throughout the game. He scored, but we got two and beat Liverpool 2–1. My ankle was terrible. I'm sure he knew I still had the injury. He was testing me.

Ken Ramsden: Matt Busby was absolutely terrifying – but in the nicest way. He would get a ticket allocation and he would phone me and ask me to bring them over to his office. I didn't need to knock on his door because my knees did the knocking for me. Remember, I was a boy of 15, I was a big United fan, and this was Mr Busby. I can't describe how important he was to people; whatever he wanted doing got done, willingly, cheerfully. Not that long ago I was talking to his daughter and she commented, 'My dad would come in some days and tell me that he had asked you for some extra tickets and he would mention how surprised he was that you had found them for him, because he had thought there were none.' I said, 'Blimey, I wish I'd known that at the time because I didn't know it was an option.' If Mr Busby asked for something, Mr Busby got it! The aura that he had was one that had been created because of what he was. He had earned it. He didn't go out of his way to frighten people but you were frightened of him just because of who he was. He didn't rule by fear or by threatening people – I don't recall ever hearing him raise his voice to anybody.

David Meek: The avuncular image of Matt Busby was just his style – he was very strong underneath all that; not a sophisticated man; his hobbies and his interests outside football were fairly simple. To a certain extent they had to be, compared to a successful manager of today, because although Matt Busby was well-paid compared with his contemporaries, he certainly didn't move in the top financial world, which Alex Ferguson is well capable of doing with his financial background.

Nesta Burgess: Sir Matt was great – he was a father figure. He was the type of man who was always very quiet. He had strength in his own way. He treated us all alike and every member of the staff would join in everything. They used to take the whole staff to London for the weekend when we played there because Matt saw everybody as part of the team. We used to stay in Charing Cross. We all mixed. To me, it's too big now.

Ken Ramsden: Alex Ferguson is very demanding and Sir Matt was too. Sir Matt had this image of being this kindly gentleman, which he was in some ways, but my goodness he was tough: he was tough as boots. Tony Dunne was an international full-back, a great player. In his day he was classed as the best full-back in Europe. He was hardly ever injured and was very dependable. We had a big European game coming up and Tony was injured. The day before the game Sir Matt went into the medical room and said to the physio, 'How is he?' The physio said, 'He's struggling, boss; he won't make it.' So Sir Matt walked past him into the room where Tony was lying on the bed. He just put his hand on Tony's knee and said, 'All right son; I know you won't let me down.' He then turned round and walked out of the room. Tony said, 'What do you think happened? I played.' That was the toughness. Sir Matt wanted him to play because it was more important to Sir Matt that he played than the effect it would have on his injured knee, and he put it in such a way that it was not a conversation or a debate. It was a case of ,'You're playing.' Sir Matt wasn't a callous man; he would never have asked the player to play when he couldn't play, but clearly Tony would simply have to play through the pain. That typifies the toughness of the man – Tony never had the option of saying no and, likewise, when Sir Matt asked me for tickets I never felt I had the option of saying no.

Nesta Burgess: You didn't take advantage of Matt because he was kind. You didn't speak to him unless he spoke to you. You'd keep your distance – you respected him. There was something about him. Jimmy Murphy was a different type of person but they matched. I've served under seven managers but Matt was different. Alex Ferguson is kind, too. When I was given the UEFA award, he came down the tunnel shouting 'Queen of UEFA' and that sort of thing.

David Meek: I think the comparison between Sir Matt Busby and Sir Alex Ferguson is uncanny because they had a lot in common, not so much the nature of the men, because that's quite different, but in terms of football, in being both great figures of authority who were much respected, even feared, by players and those that came in contact with them.

Each man set about establishing his authority in different ways. For instance, Matt Busby's was more a headmasterly approach. If you were called to his room it felt a little bit like going to the headmaster's study to answer for your sins. I never heard him swear or really raise his voice, which is rather in marked contrast to Alex Ferguson, who establishes his authority in a totally different way – one of passion and losing his temper

– although I think the temper is not really as lost as it might appear. He's invariably in control and it's a controlled fury that he uses but of course different methods achieve the same result. Nobody took any liberties with Matt Busby just as nobody takes any liberties with Alex Ferguson.

Sandy Busby: The '68 side was great. They achieved what my dad had set out to achieve. The club would probably have won the European Cup prior to that if it hadn't been for the crash. He was 60 years of age and, being a strong-minded person, he decided it was time to bring in a younger manager because he was no longer getting on to the training pitch. He looked around and couldn't see anybody. At the time Wilf was coaching with the FA and my dad said, 'Right, we'll give this fellow a chance.' From being alongside the players and joking with them – and he was a real joker, Wilf – he was now manager and had to tell them what to do.

The people who say my dad left a team that had passed its sell-by date are wrong. You had 10 internationals in that side, including Alex Stepney, Shay Brennan, Tony Dunne, Nobby Stiles, David Sadler, Willie Morgan, Bobby Charlton, Brian Kidd, Georgie Best. I'll bet you a manager of today would love to have that side. Another myth is this business about my father's influence being to blame for the club's decline after he had stepped down, that it wasn't the managers who were to blame. Yet the managers were given the freedom to use their own judgement. He never interfered with them at all – what he did say to them was that if they ever wanted to come and talk to him in his office, his door was open.

Bill Foulkes: I think after the European Cup win Matt himself felt, 'That's it.' I felt that if someone as good as him had had a talk with him and said, 'The club still needs you. The players still need you,' like they've done with Alex, he might have stayed on as manager. I felt that if Matt would have stayed we would have progressed because we had a good team. Through replacing me, for a start, and one or two other players, there could have been another great team. He was 60 – he definitely should not have retired because he had so much to offer as manager.

Tony Whelan: He was very much the father of the club; everybody's father. I remember him as being extremely charismatic, extremely charming. As a young boy of 15, I remember him as a nice man, with an aura and a certain gravitas about him. Everybody at the club was in awe of him. I do remember him coming on our youth team tour to Switzerland in 1969 and he came out after we had been there two or three days. We won the tournament and he made sure that we all got an extra £5 bonus.

Sandy Busby: I think Old Trafford – the club itself – was my dad's nest. Two people have brought fame and fortune to Manchester United, two Scots; needless to say who they are. My dad was the foundation of Manchester United and Sir Alex has produced its resurrection.

Sammy McIlroy: I was the last professional signing by Matt Busby, in 1969. It was very much a transitional time at United. They'd won the European Cup in '68 and a lot of the players were getting on a bit and Sir Matt was just getting ready for retirement. When Wilf took over he wanted to bring new players in and it was very hard for him, with the team having just won the European Cup, to get rid of those players.

Nesta Burgess: I remember when Wilf was made manager and the press were here, Jimmy Murphy pulled Wilf aside and said, 'If you put a foot wrong they'll crucify you', which they did. It was a shame. It was too early for Wilf to have got the job.

Wilf McGuinness: Then the great moment came when Matt asked me – not asked me, told me! – I was to be the next manager of Manchester United. They called me coach at the start to take the pressure off me and he was to be general manager. They thought of continuity, and nobody could have had more United in their blood than me. The thing that was against me was my age because I had palled out with the players, but, in fairness to the players, they backed me to the hilt. That first pre-season we had people like Alex Stepney doing circuit training but we didn't get off to the best of starts in the League, although we played in three Cup semi-finals in my period in charge – and that was seven games. We played Manchester City, Leeds United and Aston Villa. Unfortunately we didn't win any of those games, although we drew a few.

Don't forget, Sir Matt Busby was there to help me, but possibly there were too many grey areas where Sir Matt didn't want to come to me and I didn't want to go to Sir Matt. I was responsible for picking the team and coaching, and Matt dealt with the board. It was the first time he'd been a general manager and the first time I'd been a manager, so there was a lot of learning to be done – unfortunately we didn't win games while we were both learning.

I was disappointed and hurt because I thought I'd get the three years instead of 18 months. It didn't happen either for Frank O'Farrell, a very experienced manager. He went after 18 months. Tommy Docherty's first 18 months would have been the worst in the history of Manchester United because they just escaped relegation and then they got relegated. Normally he would have been sacked, but fortunately they kept him and he got an attractive team together. He got Coppell and Hill on the wings and Stuart Pearson, Sammy Mac and Lou Macari – good players – and it was a good time, but his first 18 months was a nightmare.

I was very young and inexperienced. You don't come in and become a manager of Manchester United as a 31-year-old, just like that, because being manager of Manchester United is not like being manager anywhere else. Unfortunately, I didn't get the chance to become experienced here at United. If the results had gone well for us at the right moment it would have helped my progression as a manager but they didn't, because the team basically wasn't strong enough, and the managers that followed proved that.

Sandy Busby: My father, when he had first taken over at the club, had said clearly, 'I am the manager and no one interferes with me.' And that was his policy when the new managers came in. They made their own decisions. For the lads, though, going from Matt Busby to Wilf McGuinness meant that it wasn't too much of a happy camp. My dad saw that, although Wilf did take them to three semi-finals. So Wilf went and they brought in Frank O'Farrell.

Tony Whelan: I always feel that my time here was scarred by the fact that they had such a changeover in managers. I played under Sir Matt. Then Wilf took over, then Frank O'Farrell and then Tommy Docherty. So I had four managers and I was here just less than five years as a player. I remember the Frank O'Farrell era as being a particularly unsavoury one at the club. You could sense the discontentment amongst the first-team players with his regime. He wasn't close to the players, although his assistant manager Malcolm Musgrove was a decent man. He did all the day-to-day training and I think the manager only turned up for the games on the weekend. He wasn't the paternal figure that Sir Matt would have been. He certainly wasn't the energetic young coach that Wilf McGuinness was. Wilf was very dynamic and enthusiastic about the club. He was Manchester United through and through.

Sandy Busby: Frank O'Farrell blamed his sacking on my dad. Well, they sacked him around about Christmas time and I know for a fact that my dad asked the board to wait until after Christmas to see how it went in the new year and the board said 'No'. That's a fact. My dad had built the club, his achievements were second to none, so he did have a say in the club, but the sacking of Frank O'Farrell was a board decision.

Tony Whelan: I was released when Tommy Docherty came. The club had tried to loan me out to Doncaster, when Frank O'Farrell was here, and I didn't fancy going to Doncaster Rovers. Then Tommy Docherty tried to get me to go on loan to Blackpool and I didn't fancy that at all. I just felt that they weren't the right clubs for me at the time. So I declined to move and I think in the end he may have got exasperated. So I got released around about February. He just told me that he didn't think I was going to consistently make the first-team squad. He called me into his office and told me properly and I've always admired him for that because I don't think he needed to do it and he did it properly.

I was devastated. My formative development as a young player had been here and I had had a lot of happy times at the club. I've never been a drinker but I remember going into a place in town and having a drink… and having a drink… I do remember that.

Ken Merrett: He [Docherty] was a manager who knew his staff. He knew all the ladies and the groundstaff and he was very generous in giving of his time to the staff. If you talk to people inside the club, they will say he was well-liked. He did a good job for Manchester United in the time he was here.

David Meek: Tommy Docherty had to pick up the remains after Wilf and Frank O'Farrell had not been given very long to try and rebuild. Tommy started the rebuilding process with a hire-and-fire policy that saw players coming and going as if through a revolving door. He took United down but he brought them back up and I think he was unlucky – if you would call it unlucky – not to get a bit longer, but he blotted his copybook by running away with the physiotherapist's wife and it was inevitable that he had to go. The two of them couldn't have worked together and it would have been a bit unfair to sack the physiotherapist for losing his wife to the manager, obviously the Doc was the man responsible so he went. The club were unlucky to find him falling in love with the wrong woman, because I think he would have been successful had he stayed.

Sammy McIlroy: We went on a tour one summer that took us to Tehran and finished off in Los Angeles. One of the stop-off points was Indonesia for a tournament involving us, Ajax and an Indonesian side. In those days you would go on tour at the end of the season but you might be without some players to begin with, because of the Home International Championships and through national teams playing some other friendlies after that. In Indonesia we were missing some of the Scottish players, so Tommy Docherty named himself as a substitute. He always told us players to compete fairly and not to argue with the referee, so we were playing this Indonesian side and winning easily and the Doc came on, and with his first tackle he kicked this Indonesian guy up in the air and was booked immediately. He then said something to the referee and was sent off, creating a great commotion in the crowd. He never kicked a ball! I think the Doc had had a good bottle of red wine with his pre-match meal.

Lou Macari: Everybody had a dispute with Tommy Docherty! That was his way of managing. I had a scrape with Docherty when he asked me to play in a testimonial at Mossley. I didn't want to go and told him so but even though I turned up for the game and played he still fined me. I said to him that I had played in the game, so there was no need for him to fine me. He said, 'But you didn't want to play. That's why I'm fining you.'

Sammy McIlroy: It was a shock to the players when Tommy Docherty left. We didn't know anything at all about what was going on. We were confident that the following year we could win the League and the whole country was talking about us turning into a side.

David Meek: Dave Sexton was a brilliant coach and a lovely, lovely man but I don't think he was ever really going to quite do it.

Martin Edwards: Dave was a very straightforward, nice man. He'd had four years. We'd finished very well in the 1980–81 season, we'd won the last seven games, but after Tommy Docherty and the style that Tommy played I felt that under Dave we didn't go forward, we didn't improve. I felt that the football wasn't that exciting. Supporters were voting with their feet and I just felt that we needed a change.

David Meek: I think Ron Atkinson was unlucky because he's a very astute manager and in his five years his team always finished in the top four of the First Division. Now there are some clubs who would give their eye teeth for that kind of manager, one who could deliver that kind of consistent performance, and I think Ron just needed a break to get through and win the championship, but he didn't get that lucky break.

Paul McGuinness: Ron Atkinson is a likeable sort of guy and his teams played attractive football but he really didn't have a great interest in the youth policy, as far as I could see, being a player. He didn't really know your names that well; he wasn't so interested in what you were doing. There was a massive contrast when Alex Ferguson took charge. He knew everybody and knew what was going on all the time. You really felt as though you had a chance.

Sir Alex Ferguson: It was never my intention to emulate Matt at any stage. Most of my success was with young players, producing them at St Mirren and at Aberdeen. I also get great satisfaction from working with young players. You get good fun with them and you develop a certain loyalty with them. The other thing about young people is when you give them opportunity and trust, it's amazing how they can surprise you. Time and time again over the years, I've put a young player in and said to myself, 'Is he ready?' And they go on to tell you they're ready. They sprout wings. So that's always a satisfying part of the job.

When I came to the club I wanted to know what every manager coming here would want to know, which is, 'Where do you start here?' We were second bottom of the League and I spent a lot of time needlessly going through all the years when they had been losing the Leagues – Did they start well? Finish badly? whatever. I spent a lot of time uselessly looking at all these stats, including how their pre-season had gone and where they had travelled pre-season. But it was stupid because it was no use to me. I was just fiddling about, I suppose. The real focus is on what the future is to be.

Sandy Busby: Alex became good friends with my dad and a good friend of my family. When he first arrived, I was running the club souvenir shop. He introduced himself and said how pleased he was to meet me and I think he bought every book in the shop, history-wise. He came to the club in '86 and I finished with the souvenir shop in '87. I met him in the car park one day and he joked, 'It's nothing I said, is it?'

Paul Hardman: Alex came down from Aberdeen and it was just one of those things, really. Somebody had to deal with him and it ended up being me. I was quite a young kid at the time – early '87. I remember the first time I met him like it was yesterday. It was at The Cliff training ground on a Tuesday morning. Even then he had charisma; he's always had charisma. I didn't feel at much ease with him – it was one of those situations where the person's reputation had preceded them and the person turned out to be so different. You'd think you were going to get a strip torn off you even though you weren't.

Martin Edwards: Alex came in November '86 and it took Alex time. Coming from Scotland he probably didn't know the players as well as he thought and, of course, he had to get used to our squad and there were certain things he didn't like, so there were a few comings and goings. He didn't like the drinking culture and Whiteside and McGrath went.

Paul Hardman: He's different to what you would expect. Underneath it all he's very perceptive: he knows when somebody is uneasy, and that's quite a skill. As an individual he's been very loyal and he actually engenders that in other people. I think that's why he has been so successful with young kids. When I first met him I could say within 20 minutes that, yes, I would be very, very loyal to this person. I think Alex himself is very loyal and sets quite a store by loyalty. You know when you talk to him that if he says he will do something he will do it.

Sir Alex Ferguson: I wasn't overawed by United and Matt Busby because I was relishing the prospect of meeting him and he was terrific. I found him a great, warm man and very helpful. I think some managers used the heritage of Matt Busby being in the background as a reason for not doing well. I think that was an easy burden to put on Matt; to take away the pressure from themselves and make it somebody else's fault.

The fact that they hadn't won the League for 19 or 20 years meant you had to address some issues. One was the question: where are the young players? Every manager has his way of running the team and Ron Atkinson had his way, Dave Sexton his way, Tommy Docherty his way and Frank O'Farrell his way. I'm always careful about what I say about Ron because I have a respect for Ron Atkinson. He never, ever, when he left this club, criticized the club. He always spoke about it in glowing terms. In other words he relished and appreciated the opportunity of managing this big club, this great club, and he had great times. He won two FA Cups; he was in the top four all his time here and he lived up to the reputation of United – he made sure they played attacking football. But he liked seasoned players, proven players – although he gave Norman Whiteside his chance, he gave Mark Hughes his chance, so he was never altogether ignoring young players.

Because of the pressures on you as manager you have to make the first team your priority, but the more important thing which had to be addressed was, 'How do you build the football club out of this?' My comfort in dealing with young players meant that the obvious thing for me to look at was how to develop the youth. Archie Knox and I, every night, were working at The Cliff, indoors, setting up meetings with all these boys' clubs in the Manchester area.

It turned out that we actually had two scouts to cover Manchester. We had more scouts in Ireland than we had in Manchester. So I said it was pretty obvious that we were going to have to do something about that. So I invited all the boys' clubs down and I picked out one or two people I knew were United fans and I got them going right away on the scouting. There had been one or two people doing it in an unofficial capacity and I always think that when you do something unofficial there's nothing definite about it. You don't need to put a report in: you might just say, 'Oh, I heard there's a player down here and I heard there's a player in this park here.' Well, I think organization is important. 'What park?' 'Who knows the player?' Then, whoever is in control of your scouts says, 'Right, let's get down to that park.' Then they log it and there's a report.

Paul McGuinness: There were many times, when I was a player and when I had joined the staff, he would pull lads into his office and make them shave – or shave them himself. He would get the shaving cream out. Nowadays you'd probably get locked up for it, but at that point there was no messing about. He would drive people down to the barber's to make them get their hair cut, things like that. That showed what he wanted and you didn't go against it or, if you did, you didn't last long. All the young boys knew they couldn't step out of line, but at the same time they were treated well.

A massive part of Sir Alex's success is these young players who have come through and are now the heart of the club and are so attached to him. Part of the reason for that is that when he first came down he was hands-on with every aspect of the youth development. If a young player had done well, Ron Atkinson would have known them for a few months if someone had mentioned them to him and he had then maybe put them in the first-team. To put someone in the first-team you've got to have a lot of trust in them, but Sir Alex had the trust in the players because he had seen them since they were kids. He saw them improve – he was watching them closely. I think he did test them in youth games and so on – he would demand more from them. He would go into the dressing room and have a go at people if they weren't doing it, even in youth games, to test them and see if they would come back.

He had known them since they were 14, these kids, so by the time they were 18, he knew them inside out and knew they were ready to play. He didn't see it as a bigger risk. Another manager, who has known them only a few months, is not going to be so sure. The other thing about it was, not only did he trust them but they trusted him, because they'd seen him all those years. It wasn't just a guy saying, 'Trust me.' It was a guy saying, 'Trust me and I'm here every step of the way.'

Sir Alex Ferguson: At the end of that first season the main thing I did was to change my chief scout. It wasn't that I was necessarily disillusioned with the previous guy there; it was just that I wanted freshness, I wanted someone with energy who would show serious commitment to the club, and I got Les Kershaw. He has been unbelievable. He has played a role in youth development here far greater than anyone else because he's aggressive, he's energetic, he's decisive. He covered the ground – he scouted himself and he made sure the scouts all over England, Ireland and Scotland were working. He got them all together and that energy just went right through the youth part of the club. At the end of the following year we decided to bring Brian Kidd in to look after the scouting and he did terrifically. The thing Brian did was get about 17 people he knew in Manchester as scouts – schoolteachers and others – and most of them are still here. We were lucky to get good scouts who supported the club and Les Kershaw was organizing trials, with Archie Knox, all over the place. We started to get a semblance of a structure.

Once you get a foundation in you've got a future. The first team was a little bit different. That was a painstaking job of agony. I knew that the team we had couldn't win the League. In life, people get so many chances and then they get to the point where they haven't got the energy or the real desire and will to do it. That United team was just too old; there were just too many of them of the one age to continually go for it, so in '89 we brought in five new players and the likes of Lee Sharpe and Ryan Giggs came in and there was some energy about the club. We'd sold Strachan, Olsen, Chris Turner, Whiteside, Graeme Hogg; we had just gutted the place to finance five new players. We brought in Danny Wallace, Mike Phelan, Neil Webb, Gary Pallister and Paul Ince. We then knew that things would start to happen for us, either that year or the next year. Then Cantona came along. Bit by bit, you're building a football team.

Gary Pallister, Mike Phelan and Paul Ince proved terrific buys. Neil Webb suffered an injury to his Achilles and that prevented him fulfilling the potential he had shown at Notts Forest. Danny did well for one year but just lacked confidence at times. He also got a couple of injuries. Then we brought in Schmeichel and Kanchelskis after the '91 Cup-Winners' Cup final. At that time you had the likes of Lee Martin, our Darren, Robins, Ryan Giggs; you had some back-up of young players in the squad. So from '86 to '91 I changed the personnel. I also brought in McClair, Hughes and Donaghy, who was a good servant to Manchester United, a good steady player who could play in a few positions. It gave you a far stronger and much more durable squad. That's what got us the Cup-Winners' Cup in '91. We had a great run because we got to the semi-final of the League Cup that year after beating Liverpool, Arsenal and Leeds United along the way. Then we lost to Sheffield Wednesday in the final, which was crazy, but it had been a great run. We finished sixth in the League so it was a good, steady improvement. You felt that we had a chance. After winning the Cup-Winners' Cup in '91, I brought Paul Parker in and he was a good addition. We won the League in '93 and brought in Keane so the whole thing develops and you're trying to get better and better all the time.

David Meek: Alex Ferguson, certainly in the second half of his management career at Manchester United, has had to deal with a totally different animal. He is now dealing with showbiz cult icons, young men who earn a lot of money, and he's had to adapt and adopt a slightly more aggressive style, which suited his temperament anyway. While Alex Ferguson and Matt Busby had the same goals they chose different paths because although it's easy to say that Alex Ferguson had to adapt his personality to suit present-day needs he was just as fiery when he was at Aberdeen. When Gordon Strachan joined United from Aberdeen he brought with him tales of the tea-cups flying in the dressing-room etcetera, which was the Fergie style. Alex has always been an aggressive leader, whereas Matt Busby was more of a headmaster-type leader.

Ken Ramsden; Alex is very demanding. He wants the best; he expects the best. He will usually get into Carrington between seven and seven-thirty. I think only the chef and the cleaners get there before him. He has a tremendous work ethic. He has also, down the years, given up tremendous amounts of the thing of which he has had least – his time. He has carried out numerous hospital visits; he goes to more funerals than anybody I have ever met; not because he likes funerals but he recognizes how important his presence is. For instance, the former Manchester City groundsman died recently and he went to his funeral. Why? A lot of football people were there and it was important he showed his respect for someone who was, like him, a real football man. Alex is very much a traditionalist and that man represented the old-fashioned side of football, something of which Alex is very respectful.

Alex has a great work ethic, so he doesn't carry passengers. He is fiercely loyal and he expects fierce loyalty from those who serve him and I don't think that's really any different from the way Matt Busby was.

Sir Alex Ferguson: When I first came, the main aim was to get some substance about the team; to make it durable, because they were a cup team. They never really knew how to go for leagues; they would get to third or fourth but they were never in there at the finish. There was never a season when they came late to get into second position or anything like that. They were always there or thereabouts, but they never really showed a flourish when it mattered. So the durability of the team had to be addressed. You wanted to have players who could go the full distance and be able to keep it going all the way through to May. My training has always been designed to ensure that the team is still going strong in the latter part of the season.

Paul Hardman: Sir Alex is very charismatic. The public persona probably does him a disservice. He is a fantastic guy and there is a lot more laughing and joking about him than you would think. He has a great enjoyment of life, which doesn't really come across in the media. A lot of journalists are just looking for a story and are always writing about how Fergie blasts this or blasts that, and it creates a particular picture of him. The guy is also unbelievably loyal. He has a lot of time for people. All the time that I have known him he has been tremendous – I wouldn't have a bad word said against him unless I was saying it! He is fantastic with kids as well. We went to his house once in one of the years when we weren't playing in the Cup Final; I think it was the year Arsenal played Newcastle. He came to the door in his slippers, which played some kind of tune, and my kids loved it, seeing this man who is treated by people as some kind of god with these fluffy slippers that played 'Auld Lang Syne', and making a real fuss of the kids.

Rebecca Tow: Sir Alex has got such a stern exterior, but behind the scenes he is almost this huge, larger-than-life comedian. He's always singing at the top of his voice and having a laugh and having fun. I remember going into the canteen once and there were some youth team players, some coaches and Sir Alex there, and it was all very quiet and serious. Then a youth team player took the lid off the server where you get a plate and there was a plastic, singing lobster that Sir Alex had placed there to freak out anyone who pulled the lid off. His PA Lynne then opened it and screamed.

David Meek: I think in 15 years, Alex Ferguson has really seen great changes, summed up by the fact that when he came his backroom staff numbered eight and it is now 32, so that tells you how the club has grown. From having an ordinary training ground at The Cliff they now have got the magnificent Carrington, complete with every conceivable type of fitness aid, and the academy there, which will be a massive enterprise. That has all really come during Alex Ferguson's management career. Okay, the board of directors take on the development of that kind of thing, but I doubt whether it would have happened if it hadn't been for the manager spelling out just exactly what he required on the playing side. I think he pressed the club – that was his vision. He succeeded in persuading the board that they should provide the finance to build and develop it.

John Peters: Alex Ferguson's professional attitude and the way he knows and runs the club from top to bottom is exceptional. He really does know and remember everyone's name.

Paul Hardman: I'm sure that Alex, for his age, is a young person. For his age, he looks well. He's got plenty of energy and he would have known in his own mind that perhaps he had a couple of years left and that is maybe why he decided to continue instead of retiring. It does add something more knowing that Alex is still in charge. I would probably still have watched the games if he had gone, but probably not as many. A lot of it comes down to:'How can you replace Alex Ferguson?' I don't think you can. The sad thing is that it has taken so long for everybody to realize that. Anyone you got in as a replacement would only be different, not better. It's taken a long time for that to dawn on people; the fans and the press. For months it was: 'Who's going to be the new manager? Is it going to be Capello? Is it going to be O'Leary? Is it going to be O'Neill?' The debate continued until everyone realized that Sir Alex was irreplaceable. The warmth of feeling towards him is phenomenal and that's because 67,000 people feel he is doing something for them. The fans also recognize that a lot of hard work has gone into what he has done. He is passionate about what he does and he is very driven.

Paul McGuinness: Everyone has got a great respect for Sir Alex because of his hands-on approach and I get the feeling, through speaking to my father, that that's what Busby was like. Everyone was a little bit afraid of upsetting him, and that's the same now. Everyone realizes what the club owes to him.

Sir Bobby Charlton: He's unique because he has never been like other managers, who tend to go for about three or four years and then people stop listening to them and they have to move for whatever reason. That hasn't happened with Alex Ferguson. He is still the boss and it has never been boring. Players have always wanted to be in the team; they've always wanted to win; there has always been competition for places. They know that if they don't perform to their best, he is strong enough to make sure somebody else will be there. With his personality, he keeps them all happy. They are quite satisfied to wait on the sidelines; we've had very few rumblings about players being dissatisfied that they're not getting a chance. They do get the chance and if they're the best player they'll stay in.

Les Kershaw: As he's gained experience he hasn't softened but he's softened his approach. If a decision has to be made, he's the best bloke in the world to do it but he probably does it a little bit better now. There's no substitute for experience in his game and that's why he's a wise man; because he's had experience.

Sir Alex Ferguson: It was really after my wife and my three sons got together at Christmas-time in 2001 that I decided I would like to stay on. They said to me, 'Look; we all think you should be staying and keep on working.' It wasn't the potential of the current team that encouraged me to stay; I've got the respect of the players and I respect them because they're good people.

Yes, if we were bottom of the League and were about to be relegated, obviously, it would make a difference. Then they would say, 'You've had your time, you've done well.' My faith in the players has got a lot to do with it but the decision was really my family's and it was probably what I wanted to hear, because I was starting to worry about what I was going to do. You worry about things like not going to the training ground any more.

Sir Bobby Charlton: I just couldn't see what he could do. He's like everybody else: you like golf and you like going to the races, maybe, and you like playing a little bit of tennis, but at the end of the day the nitty-gritty is the football and the stadium and working with players and there's no substitute for it, I'm afraid. I think he realized that and I'm pleased he made the decision.

Martin Edwards: It takes away the uncertainty. It is so much safer, so much more comforting for us that he is staying on because he's done it all before; he's got the track record, the players respond to him – you don't know how the players are going to respond to anybody new. Whoever comes in, you don't know how they're going to cope with being manager of Manchester United because it is different to anything else. So I'm delighted. The board had approached him a few times and he was quite adamant that he wanted to go, but he clearly had a change of heart. I think he knew all along he never had to go and the board had never suggested he went. We had always said to him that he didn't have to go: we thought there was no way he would change his mind.

Greg Dyke: I tried to persuade him to let us put a film crew with him in his last year, or what was supposed to be his last year. He wouldn't do it, but what I want to know – and what nobody has ever captured – is: what does he do? What makes him the great manager that he is? What does he do in that dressing-room? What does he do with those players? What's that relationship? How does he do it? We all guess, but we don't know. In some ways he almost reminds me of Rupert Murdoch. People that work for Rupert Murdoch are totally committed and he's committed to them and at some stage he decides he wants a change and makes a change. Well, that's what being a really successful manager is like, and Alex is like that. You saw the anger he had with Hoddle over the World Cup in France when Hoddle was criticising Beckham in public. You'd never hear Alex do that. What he does in the dressing-room is one matter, but out there he supports them. I'd love to see what he does in more detail. It's clearly something he does instinctively. I'm not sure you could learn what he does, but it would be interesting to know: how he disciplines people; how he takes action.

Gary Neville: I think the manager staying is the best thing that's happened for the club. With a change, there could have been a period of transition and it would maybe have been unsettling in terms of the new manager wanting to bring in new staff, new players. The best thing is continuity – probably the one thing that has helped us as a club more than anything over the past 16 years is having the same manager. All right, the manager has changed the team but, if you look, he has been able to change it gradually rather than building a team then building another team. He's been able to do it through bringing in and losing one or two players every season, and that's the way to do that. If you do that, you're on to a winner.

Eric Halsall: I feel Sir Alex Ferguson performed as well as ever in the three seasons since he went back on his plan to leave the post of manager in 2002, which means doing most of what he does magnificently and, on occasion, leaving us scratching our heads in bewilderment.

A case in point was December 2004 when the Wizard chose to field a truly feeble side against Fenerbahce in Turkey. It won't wash to talk about how many internationals were on the pitch because it was an inexperienced team not used to playing together in a daunting atmosphere and it performed accordingly. It didn't matter that we'd already qualified for the knockout stages; the youngsters duly lost 3–0 – with even United's official magazine describing the defence as 'giving away more presents than a drunk Santa' – and thereby surrendered United's top spot in the group.

Other criticisms levelled at the gaffer, even by many of his most loyal admirers, have included the seemingly patchy quality of the scouting system, which has produced magnificent signings along with the acquisition of some curiously ineffective but very expensive passengers; a problem with the first-team coaching that left a peerless strike force with an apparent inability to score in the 2004–05 season; a continuing failure to provide the necessary strength that comes from having a top-class Number 1; and, finally, a weirdly uneven level of motivation that allows the team to hit the heights against the best teams in the Premiership but to leak points by the bucketful against its most dodgy strugglers – losing 2–0 to Norwich at Carrow Road in 2005 was a depressing example.

With such a talented and expensive team – in purchase price and weekly wages – it's hard not to wonder why so much skill, natural ability and obvious potential is not being brought to full effectiveness. I know that I'm just a punter with a very limited awareness of what it takes to weld a top-class team into an all-conquering one, but I believe that it's the quality of coaching, the work done on the training ground and in the teaching rooms, as well as the motivational skills of the football management team, that bear the responsibility for bringing everything together into ruthlessly winning team performances on the pitch.

They're only lads after all: the oldest in his mid-thirties. Most of them are bound, therefore, to need an awful lot of leadership, guidance, analysis, teaching and motivation. I know deep down that there is something not quite right when we are left to rely on the awesome natural ability of some and the wonderful attitude of some to compensate for the fact that there is clearly something missing. Sir Alex knows this and says so, and so does his brilliant team captain.

It's a fact of life that any football supporter considers himself or herself an expert, but, if we're honest, running any club, let alone one as huge as United, is a damned sight more complicated than it looks and, in the final analysis, no one has done it better than Sir Alex. You don't earn the nickname of the Wizard from a crowd like that at Old Trafford without the most amazing qualities and track record. Just look what happened to the whole set-up when he appeared to be leaving – it all went instantly pear-shaped. Now, a couple of years into his second wind, he's on course to build yet another world-beating side – and even God would have difficulty doing that without some of us telling him exactly how he was getting it all wrong!.

No, he can make us wonder what he's up to from time to time but there are very few who will admit in 2005 that they were among the 'Fergie Out!' brigade nearly two decades ago. I'm inclined to believe, like most of the Stretford Enders around me, that, even when he appears to have lost the plot, he probably knows something we don't and that he's been right so often that he's earned our loyalty more times than enough. We're unlikely ever to see his like again and, as we sing every week, 'Every single one of us loves Alex Ferguson.' That's almost true – so, long may he reign.

Sir Alex Ferguson: I'm just going to wait and see [*speaking on 18 May 2005 about his reaction to the change of club owner two days after Malcolm Glazer had gained more than 75 per cent of the shares in the club*]. I spoke to him last night [17 May 2005] for the first time; we just introduced ourselves to each other. There's nothing I can do. I'm not going to jump up and down. It could turn out to be good for the club.

Retirement is a big issue in this country; not in America. We're pigeonholed a little bit with it, with this retirment age of 65; I feel it should be taken out of the statute book of life. I'm very open-minded about it now, although I don't see myself carrying on until I am 70. When you get to 63, as I am now, or a similar age, you're not guaranteed your health all the time so it's subject to health. It is a question of if you feel fit you can go on and do it.

6

Star Attractions

Extreme entertainers have always found Old Trafford to be a welcoming home. Billy Meredith, an early rebel against players' conditions, was simultaneously a captivating winger for United in the early twentieth century. George Best made special demands on the club and in return rewarded United with guile and style. David Beckham has maximized his fame as a footballer to an unprecedented degree.

Rare flair has also been exhibited by a multitude of others down the years. The likes of Ryan Giggs, Ruud van Nistelrooy, Eric Cantona, Bryan Robson, Sammy McIlroy, Lou Macari, Denis Law, Bobby Charlton, Duncan Edwards, Tommy Taylor and Jack Rowley – all were great individual talents who understood the importance of the team ethic. Solid servants of the club, such as Gary and Phil Neville, Bill Foulkes and Charlie Roberts, have underpinned those players' magnificent moments while also contributing more than a few of their own to United's classic tale.

Meredith, Alex Bell, Sandy Turnbull and others formed a team of talents who lit up English football in the opening decade of the twentieth century. Joe Spence stood out in the 1920s and 1930s, becoming known as 'Mr Soccer' in Manchester. 'Give it to Joe' was the cry from the star-starved terraces, the focus on one player a reflection on the scarcity of talent available to the club in those decades.

The club began to revive in the late 1930s, but it was the harnessing of resources which took place in the years after the Second World War, when Manchester United was remade and remodelled, which led to an endless series of football maestros taking the turf at Old Trafford. At a club which relies heavily on its players to sculpt moments of blissful inspiration from their mastery of the ball, their artistry has not only been welcomed – it has been essential.

Leo Rocca: I could see my father sitting down below, close to the pitch. I called him several times but it wasn't until I put my hand on his shoulder that he realized I was there. He smiled and said: 'Hello. I was just thinking back to the earliest days out there. Billy Meredith on this touchline; Roberts, Duckworth and Bell in the middle; I can see them all.'

Mark Wylie: In our records, we have found at least three players who have died during United matches. There were two in Newton Heath times; both were in reserve-team games. A kick in the stomach in those times could result in death. Another reserve-team player headed the ball, collapsed and died in the dressing rooms. They put it down to natural causes. That was in 1907 – the ball was just so heavy, especially when it was soaked through with water.

I know that Charlie Roberts, during the close-season, used to go out on a trawler to supplement his income. Close-season wages dropped from what they had been during the season so they used to do things like that. He had a tobacconist's as well, and Billy Meredith had a sports outfitter's in Manchester. He supplied the shirts for the 1909 Cup Final. They weren't daft – they had their eyes on making a bit of money here and there because they had a maximum wage. The only way they could make extra money was through getting a benefit – they were slaves almost to the club, because the club could hold their League registration and they wouldn't be able to move to another club. They could then be left out of the team and would miss out on bonuses.

John Gladwin: My dad went to United in the 1936–37 season from Doncaster Rovers and he always said that he much preferred playing for Doncaster Rovers than for United because he had lived in Worksop and was a bit of a homebird. It's also worth remembering – and it might seem strange to people nowadays – but Doncaster Rovers and

Manchester United possibly were not that different as teams in those days. Doncaster had been promoted from the Third Division North to the Second Division when my father was with them and United had been in the Second Division for most of the 1930s.

A lad called Stan Pearson was an apprentice at Manchester United when my dad joined the club, and my father said he was a pretty good lad. My dad used to play with James Brown, George Roughton, Jack Breedon, Tommy Manley, Tommy Breen, Bill McKay, Harry Baird, Billy Bryant, Charlie Craven, Jack Smith, Jack Griffiths, Hubert Redwood, George Vose and Stan Pearson. Mr Curry was the trainer and Mr English was the assistant trainer. That would be in the 1930s. My father played against Matt Busby when Matt Busby was at Manchester City. He also remembered playing against Charlie Mitten. He said Charlie Mitten could only move one way – to his left – and that once you knew which way he went, you couldn't help but take the ball off him. My dad was a pretty hard player – a good, hard footballer.

On October 1, 1938, my dad wrote about playing for United in a newspaper: 'We play good football at Old Trafford, which has proven to be a success. We seem to have struck a right blend of enthusiasm and skill. I feel happy about my own share in the club's fortunes.' That was just after United had been promoted back from the Second Division into the First Division. He told me he got paid £6 a week if he was in the second-team and £8 a week if he was in the first-team and that he lived in digs in Manchester during his time at the club. My dad got shot in the war and that stopped his football career. He got shot in Burma – he got seven machine-gun bullets in his right ankle, but they managed to save his foot. United sent him £200 from the Manchester United Benevolent Fund and he also got some money from Doncaster Rovers, even though he had finished playing with them in 1937.

Jimmy Billington: I remember Georgie Vose, the centre-half, Jack Breedon and Tommy Breen, the goalkeepers. Tommy Manley was there and Tommy Bamford and Georgie Mutch. When I came out of the orphanage it was 1938 and I remember seeing United v Arsenal and Jimmy Hanlon scored the only goal when they beat Arsenal 1–0. Jimmy wasn't much bigger than me – he was about five feet five inches and I'm three inches – but when he scored he got between two fellows who were six feet.

Sandy Busby: My father came to United in 1945 and at that time in Manchester, United were the very poor relations because they were in the red up to their eyeballs. Also, the ground had been bombed so they had to go and ask City if they could use their ground, which they did up to about 1949. They had lads coming back from the trauma of war and, although some of them had great ability, they were all playing in the wrong positions and my dad could see this. The great Johnny Carey was an inside-forward in those days and my dad first of all put him back to wing-half so he was facing the game and eventually put him back to full-back where he became probably one of the greatest full-backs to be seen. Johnny Aston was a centre-forward: he put him back to left-back and he played for England. Jack Rowley was at inside-forward and my dad put him at centre-forward because of his shooting and heading ability; he was strong. Big Allenby Chilton was a wing-half: he put him at centre-half and he played for England. So the ability was there, but it needed the organization and management from my dad to see it.

David Meek: Matt Busby's introduction to management meant that he was dealing with, to begin with, slightly older footballers who had been away in the war, men in their own right, men who stood on their own feet and weren't little boys to be pushed around. They were mature. I'm talking of people like John Aston Senior, who was away in the war in the commandos, I'm talking about Stan Pearson, Jack Rowley, Johnny Morris, Charlie Mitten; players who had all been away in the services. So it meant a more mature management approach was required and I think that maybe cast Matt Busby's management technique, which suited his personality, because he was never a man to shout his head off.

I think when he started, with the young players, it was a more respectful age. The youngsters who joined came from humbler backgrounds than today. They weren't unduly well-paid – it was a modest profession in financial terms. After their careers they were going to take shops and post offices, pubs and betting shops and that kind of thing. So it was an age where you didn't require the same amount of discipline. I think it's true to say that youngsters fell into line much more readily. There was a greater sense of discipline in the parental home and in the workplace, and I think that took itself into a football club as well, so Matt Busby didn't have to raise his voice.

Jimmy Billington: Jack Rowley, who was in that '48 team, was a great player. There was one thing he did, when they were playing Middlesbrough and there was a bloke kept having a go at Charlie Mitten. Rowley told Charlie Mitten to go into the centre. Five minutes later this bloke was on the deck and after that Rowley told Mitten to go back on the wing. He was a tough lad, Rowley, as well as being a great goalscorer. They say that to practise he used to stand two bricks on the ground put the ball on top and hit it as he hard as he could. Johnny Carey was a very good captain and Jimmy Delaney, the winger, once put Frank Swift, the best goalkeeper City had, in the back of the net with one shot. Jimmy Delaney was a great winger and a really good bloke.

Sandy Busby: Jimmy Delaney was a very well-loved fellow. My father had this great side in the Forties but they were missing one player. In those days they played with wingers, forwards, half-backs and full-backs and he didn't have an outside-right. My dad had played with Delaney in the Scottish team. He was probably my dad's greatest signing at that time.

Sandy Busby: The '48 Cup-winning side were a great side and that showed through the sizes of the crowds that came to watch them. In the fifth round of the Cup in 1949 I went to see them play a non-League side called Yeovil Town and there were 81,000 at Maine Road watching this game. The shame was, of course, that the lads were getting to about 30 years of age but my dad, probably from his experiences as a boy playing football, had the idea of creating a family team, bringing young boys up as a family. This is what he achieved.

My dad set a youth team up that went on to be the great Fifties side that won the Youth Cup. My dad believed greatly in this team and they won the Youth Cup five times on the trot. He also sent them over to Switzerland to play in a competition where the big European sides used to send their youth teams, called the Blue Stars tournament. They were a great set of lads. I was luckier than Roy of the Rovers, me. I started playing a lot of football myself and I was allowed to train on Tuesday and Thursday nights with this youth-team set-up. I grew up with players like Eddie Colman, Bobby Charlton and big Duncan Edwards, and socialized with them. We used to go to the dances on the weekend, either the Plaza or the Chorlton Plaza. The great Bob Paisley said they would have won everything for the next ten years if it had not been for the crash.

Sir Alex Ferguson: I remember the Coronation Cup in 1953, when I would be about eleven and a half. It was in June. The English teams were Spurs, Newcastle, Arsenal and Manchester United. The four Scottish teams were Aberdeen, Hibs, Rangers and Celtic. There were games at Ibrox and games at Hampden Park. I remember seeing Spurs at Ibrox and Newcastle at Ibrox and I saw Rangers' first game, when they lost to Man United. I saw Celtic beat Arsenal 1–0 and then they beat United in a semi-final and beat Hibs in the final. I always remember Roger Byrne was outside-left in that team. It was the last days of the Pearson–Rowley partnership, Carey, Cockburn, Aston, Allenby, Chilton. They had won the FA Cup in '48 and they were coming to the end of that era. Delaney had gone by that time. That was my first knowledge of Man United. With Matt being manager and coming back to Scotland there was a great storyline there at the time.

United stood out because they beat Rangers! I was a Rangers supporter but my dad was a Celtic supporter and he took me to the Arsenal game, which Celtic won 1–0, and to the United game, which was 2–1 for Celtic. I always remember Roger Byrne playing at outside-left rather than at full-back. He caught my eye because he was really quick – he was this lightning winger. At that time, England used to be able to produce great wingers – they seemed to be the scourge of Scottish teams: Finney, Matthews. So I always remember that about Roger Byrne – his pace; he was a flying-machine.

David Meek: Busby's way became even more apparent in the team he built from recruiting his own youngsters, the Busby Babes. The Babes were a really talented bunch of individual players, but he moulded them into a team. We're talking here of Duncan Edwards and Eddie Colman; Tommy Taylor he bought, but there were just as many that he brought through, like Mark Jones, Jackie Blanchflower. He bought Johnny Berry, Dennis Viollet: he made Albert Scanlon, David Pegg. So many of them were killed in the Munich air crash, of course, but they were all very gifted individuals who had the ability to lend their skills to the team effort. Along with that, of course, came Busby's idea that if he got them young he could bring them up to play as he wanted them to play. Hence the Busby Babes, who won the Championship two years running with an average age of about 22. Most of them he had produced himself but of course he wasn't afraid to go into the transfer market if he thought there was a gap in his own production line.

Nesta Burgess: Duncan Edwards – I can see him now. He used to come on a bike; he didn't have a car. He was stopped once for riding on the pavement. He was coming here and the policeman stopped him. 'I'm going to work,' he said. Matt said, 'Now, don't make that an excuse – that because you work for Manchester United you can do what you like.'

Sandy Busby: Duncan Edwards was built like Charles Atlas – he was a great player. In those days my dad would have a meeting with his staff: Jimmy Murphy and Bert Whalley. They would go through how the players were getting on. Shortly after Duncan joined the club, they came to his name at their meeting and Jimmy said, 'I can't teach him anything. He's got everything.' If they were struggling to score in a match, they'd put him up front to get the goals they needed. He was just as reliable in defence. I remember one game at Maine Road where Allenby Chilton got sent off and my dad put Duncan to centre-half; he played City by himself.

Cameron Erskine: The first time I saw United was in the Fifties at Ninian Park. I can remember seeing Duncan Edwards, Rowley, Mitten.

You didn't particularly notice Duncan Edwards, strange as that might sound: you took it for granted that Duncan Edwards would have a good game. He had everything.

Jimmy Billington: Duncan Edwards was a great player in every way. He never hurt anybody, but when they ran at him they bounced off him. He was solidly built, like a tank. He'd go through three or four of them at a time. The other thing is, he was always laughing. Billy Whelan was another fine player – he could play about with the ball on the spot, then crack one in.

Bill Foulkes: I joined United as a part-time player and had a good job in the mines – I was earning twice as much as the lads at Old Trafford. I was picked for England in 1954 and Matt said, 'You've got a future in the game.' I stuck at it and kept myself in really good physical condition and learned a lot from the older players. I listened, I watched and practised hard. Jimmy Murphy was a big help to me in that respect. I then carried that on to the field and we learned as we went along in Europe.

Sir Bobby Charlton: My debut was against Charlton in '56. I'd played for a bit in the reserves and I was doing all right, scoring a lot of goals, and I kept thinking, 'Well, everybody else is getting a chance. They'll have to give me a chance.' It seemed like ages. Maybe I was just impatient, but he seemed to be playing everybody I thought wasn't as good as me. I thought, 'I can do that.' I played in the reserves at City and the centre-half and I hit the ball at the same time and a ligament in my ankle swelled up. That's probably the only injury I've had in my whole life: I was off for two weeks and Matt called me up to his office. Whenever he called you up to his office it was either good news or bad news. You were either in or you were out. I knew he couldn't be dropping me because I wasn't in the team. I was injured. He said, 'What's your ankle like?' I said, 'All right, boss, thanks. It's swollen a bit but I can run with it.' He said, 'Are you sure?' I said I was but I wasn't at all. He said, 'All right, you're playing tomorrow.'

I used to go to matches when the first-team were playing and the adrenalin would be flowing and I thought, 'That'll do me.' But I wasn't fit and I actually hardly used my right foot at all. I just stood on it, really. My right ankle is still bigger than my left ankle now. I never got over it fully.

I only played when somebody else was injured, either Tommy Taylor, Billy Whelan or Dennis Viollet. By the end of the season I think I'd played about 14 games and we won the title that season.

Nesta Burgess: I had some of the boys to lodge with me: Mark Pearson, Alex Dawson and some of the Irish boys. They used to come over for trials and some very poor boys came over. They were only young and Joe Armstrong, who was the chief scout, was great with the kids. He'd find them jobs and he looked after them because they'd have left home at 14 and would never have been out of Ireland or Scotland. He was good – he would keep them out of mischief if necessary but he didn't have much trouble with them. The only thing I didn't like was when they were on trial and they didn't make it. They used to send them up to my kitchen to give them a cup of tea and some biscuits. They used to cry and I used to hate that part of it. They were a young 14, not like today. They weren't worldly-wise. Joe was good with them – he was jolly. They had lots of fun – he didn't bully them to do anything.

Sandy Busby: United still had some very good players after the crash at Munich: Bobby Charlton, Harry Gregg and Dennis Viollet. A very good pal of mine, who died just last year, Shay Brennan, had been more or less in the third team and they put him in at outside-left because they were in crisis. My dad finished up putting him at right full-back and he won numerous caps for Eire. Some kids from the reserves were put into the first-team, such as Alex Dawson and Nobby Lawton. Then they had these forwards – Charlton, Viollet, Scanlon – who were exciting to watch. Scanlon was a flier on the wing and had a lovely left foot. They were getting results and my dad gradually put the jigsaw together. Five years later they won the Cup and he then went on to build his '68 side.

Ken Ramsden: One of Sir Matt's strictures to the staff was, 'Whatever you do, look after the players because the football looks after you.'

It was all about the football. Everything was geared towards the football. We still say now, 40 years on, that fundamentally we are what we are because of the football.

Sandy Busby: After a game against Huddersfield's youth side my dad went to Andy Beattie, their manager, and said, 'I'll give you £10,000 for your little fellow.' This was Denis Law and, in those days, to pay that for a kid was a fortune. Beattie turned round and said, 'Oh, no, no, no. We realize we've got something special.' After that, my dad became manager of Scotland and picked Denis to play at 18 years of age. Later, when Denis was in Italy, my dad heard that Denis wasn't happy, so he arranged with Torino for my dad and the chairman to go over and negotiate a deal to bring Denis back. The chairman at United at that time was Harold Hardman, of whom my dad was very fond. So they went over, even though Mr Hardman had not been very well. They were supposed to meet the chairman of Torino, Angelo Fillipone.

When they got there the Torino secretary said, 'The president can't make it today. I'm very sorry.' My dad went away fuming. So he took Mr Hardman out to a restaurant and who is in the corner but Fillipone? My dad went over to him and said, 'You so-and-so. You let this chairman of Manchester United Football Club come all the way over here to do business with you and you tell us you're not available. How dare you?' So Fillipone says, 'No problem, no problem. Deal done.' That's what happened.

Nesta Burgess: In the old days they used to have what were called transfers behind closed doors, because nobody knew they were taking place. I used to go home at the normal time and then I'd come back on my own later on. We had no restaurants here, as there are now, so I used to make sandwiches and a pot of tea for them. So I would be the only one outside of the transfer business who knew which player was being transferred. I remember Denis Law coming from Italy that way. He was brought in by a friend of Jimmy Murphy's and I remember him being in the boardroom and I can remember what Denis said: 'If I don't come here I'll go on the trawlers, like my Dad.' He was so keen to come here.

Denis was a great lad: they all were. It was like they were your brothers. Denis was my favourite. He lived in my kitchen, with his cups of tea. I had a little kitchen in the club and every morning Denis would be there and I would make a cup of tea for him. It was only a small kitchen, but before and after training the boys and the trainers would come in to have a cup of tea. They were funny. I didn't know much about football so I didn't talk football. That meant they weren't talking about their job all the time. We didn't discuss football. Pat Crerand and the ground staff used to have general knowledge quizzes. That sort of thing's important for players, even now. You've got to talk to them and get to know them. Some of them will sit in a corner – I got that with Andy Cole. It can be difficult for players when they come at first.

Cliff Butler: I totally idolized Denis Law. I'm not religious – I'm an atheist. Yet when Denis was put on the transfer list in 1966, I prayed every night and, sure enough, he was taken off the transfer list at the end of the week. That should have converted me. I just thought I'd do anything that could help so that Matt Busby didn't sell him. The way I looked on it was that Bobby Charlton was for the dads, George Best was for the girls and Denis Law was for the lads. Bobby was the senior of the three and the older supporters liked him. Denis came in on a transfer from Italy: a real sort of whizz-kid, Jack-the-lad, but in the way he played the game the crowd could identify with him totally. He was mischievous as well – they didn't call him Denis the Menace for nothing.

He really was a red devil, Denis Law. He was one of the first to celebrate a goal by thrusting his finger to the gods and wheeling away punching the air, all that sort of stuff. I think the scallies in the crowd identified with him. Then George Best came on the scene on the back of the pop culture, The Beatles and the rest of it. That's when you saw the first real influx of girls coming to matches on their own. Girls had always come to games on the hand of their father or their mother to watch matches, not in great numbers, but they still attended. I think George and his style and – I've got to say it – sex appeal had a lot to do with the influx of females into football. The Stretford Enders liked Denis and the season-ticket holders and the ones who went in the Paddock were

Bobby fans. That's generalizing, but to a great degree I think it's true. I've got to know Denis in the years since and he's a terrific person.

David Meek: Before George Best became famous, players would have been able to walk around Manchester but George Best was the turning-point. Towards the latter end of George's days was when football entered the cult era and George wouldn't be able to walk quite as freely around Manchester, but certainly more freely than David Beckham could. That's something that's changed.

Ken Ramsden: There was a photocall one day, a team picture, and for some reason I was down in the area of the players' tunnel. I had a four-button jacket on and George was telling me which buttons to fasten and which to leave open, for style. We were, in a way, all in it together as young people in those days. In the Sixties some players had cars, some had bikes and some would get the bus. Certainly all the young players went on the bus. So on leaving Old Trafford after training, they would call in at the corner shop, for some sweets or whatever. Then they'd cross the road and get on the bus. So the fans would see them on the bus and would talk to them, naturally.

Nesta Burgess: Georgie Best was 15 when he came over. He was a very kind boy. He would give you anything. He just mixed with the wrong people – it was a shame. I loved watching him play – he was great. I don't know much about football, but he was lovely to watch. I was very fond of George – he looked after his mum and dad.

Ken Ramsden: I lived in Sale at the time George was opening his first boutique, which was in Sale. One evening I was going out to the chip shop on my bike. I rode past his shop and George was in the window. This was ten o'clock on a Monday night. He was dressing the window, so I went in and we had a natter.

Bill Foulkes: George is the best player we've ever had here. He could tackle, he could head the ball, he could do anything. I remember once, against Liverpool, he got above Ron Yeats, about two feet above him, and banged the ball into the net with his head. Ron Yeats didn't even see him. After the goal Ron Yeats was saying, 'Who was that?' I told him, 'Bestie.' I signed him for San José Earthquakes from Hibernian and he was just superb. He played out of his skin for us and I think he only missed one game. I spoke to Ron Atkinson and said, 'You ought to take a look at him.' I think Ron was interested, but it was George who put the knocker on it.

David Meek: I think it's only with hindsight that you can put it into the scheme of things and become aware of how great the Sixties were – at the time I just took it for granted. The fact that we had three European Footballers of the Year in Charlton, Law and Best all playing in the same team is really pretty historical, but it just seemed the natural order of things at the time. When you have seen them grow from being boys to become so elevated, it doesn't take you by surprise. It just seems the normal way of things.

I thought all three were particularly gifted, with very varying personalities. Bobby Charlton was quieter, more studious, not aware of his great gifts, balletic and graceful; a Corinthian, sporting man. Denis Law, 'The King', had a streak of villainy that appealed to Stretford Enders, all fire and fury, razor reactions, a very dramatic player. George Best, for me, was the most talented all-round player I've ever seen – he graced the football field and had an extraordinary range of gifts. All different, all 100 per cent committed to Manchester United, which made them very special. I don't think Bobby realized how good he was at the time. He was an instinctive player who just enjoyed it. They all did to a certain extent – I think Denis was probably the more hard-headed man who knew his own worth, but Bobby just played for the sheer joy of it and George did so too, to a certain extent. Both of those players went on to play for other clubs because they didn't want to hang up their boots. I know Denis played after he left Manchester United but I don't think he played with quite the same joie de vivre.

Sandy Busby: My dad got hold of Denis Law and said, 'I've got to get a half-back. Who do you fancy: Crerand or Baxter?' Denis is supposed to have said something like, 'Can you get both of them?' My dad said, 'I only need one.' So Denis said, 'I don't think you'll get Baxter – I don't think Rangers would let him go.' So I think my father just plumped for Crerand. Now Veron is a lot faster than Pat, but Veron hits balls the way Crerand used to do; streaking passes that split a defence. Pat and Denis were great signings for my dad.

Sammy McIlroy: Since I came from Northern Ireland, when I arrived at the club George shook my hand and wished me all the best. It was very difficult at first, leaving Belfast; I was extremely homesick, but George and Pat Crerand and people like that always came and made sure everything was OK and that was brilliant, because George was my idol at the time and in the late Sixties and early Seventies he was shaping up as the world's greatest football player. So even to see him in training in those times was fantastic. Back in Belfast we would watch him on TV and then everyone would go out in the street and pretend to be him – and there I was training, and later playing, with him.

Sandy Busby: Martin Buchan, who is a very serious type of lad, told me that when he was at Aberdeen a whole host of clubs were after him. He said they would all come to see him with their accountants and talk money. Then Frank O'Farrell turned up and brought along my father. That sealed it – after a chat with my dad he signed on.

Nesta Burgess: There were double doors between the dressing rooms and the showers and Matt used to say: 'No ladies are to come through these doors for half an hour after training.' One day I said to the other ladies, 'They'll have finished now, the lads.' So we went in and there was an Irish boy, a goalkeeper – I won't tell you his name – who comes out of the dressing room stark naked and we all shouted,'Ohhhhhh!'. He covered his head with a towel!

Lou Macari: My first game as a United player at Old Trafford was against West Ham. The pitch was barely playable because there had been heavy snow. I'd come from Celtic two days before and didn't know what to expect. Playing against Bobby Moore in my first game in England was pretty memorable, the game ended 2–2 and I got the equalizing goal. So I was well chuffed with myself. I got a good response from the crowd; but when I first went there I was like any other player being transferred to a massive club – you just want to do all you can to stay in the team. I think if you then show the crowd that you are prepared to give everything for the team they will take to you.

I had a write-off with my car just a week after I joined the club. I wrote an Audi off near the training ground at Salford. I was very lucky. I went through a junction and into the side of a lorry. The car spun round, and the next thing I knew I was in a house with a little old lady getting a cup of tea.

Nesta Burgess: Lou was always up to something. I was running the players' lounge and one day more and more people kept coming in and I thought, 'Where are they coming from?' They had tickets and they were entitled to come in, but I wondered where they were getting them from. So somebody said, 'Lou Macari's on the front giving tickets out.'

Lou Macari: The story behind this is that with the players' lounge, some players didn't mind how many people came into it but others did. So Martin Buchan, who was the captain, said on the Friday before we had a Cup tie with Queen's Park Rangers, 'Right, I'm stopping all these people coming into the players' lounge. I'm issuing 40 tickets and there will be 40 people in the players' lounge. I'll be on that players' lounge door to make sure of it.' I got on well with Martin Buchan, really well; I thought he was a good captain and I used to room with him, but a lot of people couldn't really understand him and his ways of doing things. So the lads were a bit annoyed with the way he was laying down the law and wanted to stuff him.

On the day of the game he was still determined to see this thing through but the thing that Martin didn't know was that before the game I went and got 200 tickets from the office and was out on the front there handing them out to people. At 1.30 I was handing out tickets outside Old Trafford telling the fans to come in and get a drink. So we played this Cup tie against Queen's Park Rangers and we won 1–0.

The players didn't believe Martin would actually man the door, but after the game he didn't shake hands with anybody – he sprinted straight up the tunnel. At that time the tunnel was at the halfway line and the dressing rooms were at the top of the tunnel, and the players' lounge was up there too. One of our opponents pointed out to me, 'Look what Martin Buchan is doing.' He was standing at the door collecting the first of these supposedly 40 players' lounge tickets. Here's a Man United player collecting tickets! So we all walked past him into the dressing room, killing ourselves laughing, because there were going to be 240. Only after he got to 30 and a queue was forming did he start to think there might be something going on. The manager was congratulating us on our win but he noticed there were only ten players, not 11, in the dressing room. Ten minutes later Martin comes in with a huge bundle of tickets and throws all the tickets up in the air. 'Would I need two guesses to know who is the cause of this problem?' he said. He took it in quite good humour and slackened off a bit after that with his demands.

Sammy McIlroy: I left when I was 27 – it was a rush of blood from me. I'd been there 13 years and big Ron had just bought Robbo and Remi Moses for £2m, which was an awful lot of money in those days, and he had to balance the books a little bit. I have since heard that Arsenal, Everton and Stoke were in for me, but Stoke were the only ones that Ron told me about. Ron actually wanted me to fight and stay – he didn't show me the door – but when he told me about the bid from Stoke I thought he wanted me out. I should have listened to my father, who said that I should hang on at Old Trafford. Having paid all that money for Bryan Robson, Atkinson obviously would have to play him, so the manager wanted me to play wide left. It was my fault – I should have bided my time. I should have just moved further out to the left, but instead I got the hump.

Bryan signed on the pitch and I got three against Wolves that day. Obviously Bryan Robson was a tremendous player and there was speculation that Ray Wilkins and I would make way for him and Remi. You want to try to impress the new man and, with Moses and Robson being midfield players I just went out that day to try and impress Ron Atkinson that I could still play. Bryan Robson signed on the pitch and I went on to score a hat-trick.

Years ago we did a radio show and Ron told me he had been thinking of bringing me back from Stoke at a time when United had some injuries. I said 'I wish you hadn't told me that, because I didn't want to leave in the first place.'

Paul McGuinness: Frank Stapleton was great. On the pitch, he'd moan but off the field he'd give you lots of pointers – he was excellent. He would always talk to you about football. Gordon McQueen was a really funny guy – he had a great sense of humour. The reserves played a friendly at Chorley one time when it was absolutely freezing and Gordon, for the second half, put one of those big sub's coats on under his shirt and was running about like a Michelin man. He used to have a fag at half-time. In those days it used to be normal for the players to go out for a drink midweek and that was one of the things Alex Ferguson changed when he came. It was a massive thing for him to get rid of Whiteside and McGrath when they were two of the best players in the country at the time, but it really stamped the authority. It showed that nobody was going to mess with him, because it probably weakened the team for a period. I think that was vital to what he has done ever since – because he has been able to do those sorts of things he has kept a total grip on the whole thing. You've got to have control of the players and if you don't, anything can happen. By doing that, Alex Ferguson really laid down the ground rules and it was a big change from the regime that had gone before.

Jonathan Deakin: On the pitch, we haven't always been brilliant, but we've always had players that understood the club, its history and what it means to play in a red shirt. Players like Whiteside, Robson, Hughes, Eric, Giggs, Butt, Beckham and Keane are heroes because they are, or were, responsive to the fans. No players are more important than local ones, either.

Martin C.Y. Lai: I have a photograph of myself with Bryan Robson hanging on my wall. He was and still is my favourite United player: 100 per cent United, total dedication. The fans know what he was about.

David Meek: Spin on a few years to Alex Ferguson and you find exactly the same philosophy and policy as with Matt Busby, where the first thing he did when he came to Old Trafford was to restructure the scouting system to look for young players. Again, the word went out that he was looking for individuals, for athletes who had particular skills and who could be moulded into the team ethic.

The great equivalent, if you like, of the Busby Babes, was his team that won the FA Youth Cup in '92. We're talking here David Beckham, Paul Scholes, Gary Neville, Ryan Giggs, Nicky Butt and others who went to other clubs for distinguished careers. They form the backbone of the team today and are so good that they form the backbone of the England team as well. So there again there is a direct comparison between Ferguson and Busby in that he created his own super team, and I think the way they play attacking football is another comparison between the two teams; because Ferguson's teams and Busby's teams have always believed in playing with flair and great creative ability.

Sir Alex Ferguson: The trials at the time, with Beckham and all them, were quite amazing. The number of players we didn't take was amazing, and the standards we had ourselves meant that the ones we picked were players with outstanding potential. We seemed to have good players for every position. Les Kershaw was in charge of it all, and he had all that energy, and the scouts started working their socks off to bring the best players to our trials. You can't do that now; you're not allowed to, because of the academy status; I always wonder if the academy status was devised to make sure United wouldn't dominate the youth; because we were doing that for about eight years; everybody wanted to come here, but with the academy status you can only get hold of local players. You're not allowed to sign a boy outwith an hour-and-a-half's distance but there is a five-day window in June where you can invite a boy under 14 to your academy. One thing we have started to do now is have alliances in other parts of the world.

With Ryan Giggs, Knoxy and I went up to his house two or three nights a week to get him to come to this club. We worked on him, with his father and mother. Joe Brown, the youth development manager at the time, would come up with us and eventually he agreed to come down and I always remember he signed on his fourteenth birthday at Old Trafford. George Graham and I were having a cup of tea, and he came in and met George, and I said to George, 'He'll play for his country and he'll play for Man United. He's a great player.' George always reminds me about that. It's very difficult with a 14-year-old boy; you can never be sure, but we said about Ryan, 'If he doesn't make it, we may as well quit.' He had this wonderful lightness of foot. He just floated over the ground. He had courage and balance. He was the one real star at the time when we needed it, when we needed a bit of a pick-up.

Dennis Giggs: I played football until I was 40 and took Ryan to see Cardiff City many times. We would always go to see the Boxing Day match. Being a big football fanatic, when I first saw Ryan play for Manchester United I couldn't believe someone of mine was on such a big stage. It would have been a dream to see him play for Cardiff City, never mind Manchester United. It was only the night before that we heard he was going to make his first start, against Manchester City, so we dashed up to Manchester and of course he scored – the only goal of the game as well! He's fabulous to watch, as everybody knows.

Sir Alex Ferguson: I've still got scouts who say that they were the first to see Ryan Giggs and are still looking to get paid for that! It's absolute nonsense; rubbish. We got him through a club steward who told us about him.

Rebecca Tow: Harold Wood is a steward that has just recently left. He spotted Ryan Giggs. He remembers at the time that City were interested in Ryan and he kept telling the Gaffer that he really had to make a move on Ryan soon or someone else would get him and then, of course, we did. Harold had always given Ryan a pound every time he scored a goal and to this day he carries on paying Ryan a pound every time he scores a goal, which is quite cute.

John Peters: These guys are footballers first and foremost. Playing for Manchester United means they also have to be photographic models. They're inundated with requests to pose for magazines. Some take that in their stride and some would rather play football, which is, after all, the most important thing.

Bryan Robson was a true professional and Steve Bruce was a very good guy to have around. He had that wonderful north-east twang in his voice. You could have a good laugh with Steve Bruce. Brian McClair has a very dry sense of humour – he's a very witty man and it's been good to see him back at the club.

Dennis Giggs: Eric Harrison was running the youth team coaching when Ryan was there as a youngster. Eric's a lovely fellow and the young players also learned off other players like Cantona. When you've got that calibre of player beside you, then you can only learn from them. Ryan would stay on in the afternoons and of course Cantona did a lot of that – he stayed behind and practised. Others like Beckham and Ryan were doing the same, so players like that help the younger ones on.

Gary Neville: When you come through at United your character is tested in every single way. You're picked when you think you shouldn't be picked. You're dropped when you think you shouldn't be dropped. You're given contracts when you think you maybe shouldn't be given contracts. Contracts are held back from you when you think you should be getting them. They test you in every single way to see what affects you. That's the way you develop. They'll put you in a big-game atmosphere to see whether you sink or swim. They'll then maybe put you back down to the reserves to see how you handle that. There comes a time when they let you swim freely and they pick you all the time, but certainly when you come into the team as a young player at United you come in for four or five games and then the manager puts you back in the reserves to see how you react to that. All these things are to test your character.

You'll maybe travel with the squad a few times and then for no reason whatsoever you'll not travel with the squad for a month. Then there comes a time when he'll put you in a big game. My first really big game was the FA Cup semi-final against Crystal Palace and I remember being very nervous and thinking, 'This is the big game – the FA Cup semi-final. Wow.' These are the games that I had grown up watching. I did OK and I thought, 'I can handle that.' The manager sees that you can handle that and then goes on to pick you in other big games. Before that I had been playing in the sort of lower-to-middle games, if you like, where I'd been playing against the lower-half teams, some at home and a few away. Then the Liverpool game or the Arsenal game will come around and he'll tell you he's going for experience and you'll be upset, but you know that he's just bedding you in slowly.

You win the Championship, you get success, you maybe get a little bit more money and then your character is tested in other ways. Can you handle success? Some people can't handle success. It goes to their head and they go and do stupid things. You're out of the club – simple as that. Some people don't react well to failure, but some people don't react well to success as well. They think, 'I've done it.' I think that's what happened to Blackburn when they won the Championship. They never thought about what was going to happen the next year or the year after. Four or five years later they found themselves in the First Division because of that. They stopped. They stood still. This club doesn't stand still. We win the Championship and then go and buy three or four more players and get rid of two or three.

The most amazing thing was that the manager made way for us by getting rid of a lot of really good top players. You find out how ruthless the club is and how ruthless the manager is in getting what he wants. He sees that maybe they get to a peak and when they're dropping off he'll just get rid of them and bring in new players. He has to see that you're always wanting to do it. As soon as you're not, you might as well just go yourself because he isn't going to put up with that. When you've set yourself a standard – of work, of determination, of all those things – as soon as you drop below that, you just might as well go.

Over the past seven or eight years you've seen great players being let go by this club; you remember Paul Ince, Mark Hughes, Andrei Kanchelskis all being let go around the same time and there was uproar at the time. We forget now, but at the time there were petitions from local papers for the manager to be sacked. It was hard for us at the time because we were getting a lot of stick. 'How can Paul Parker be replaced by Gary Neville? Paul Parker's an England international.' 'How can Mark Hughes be replaced by Paul Scholes?' 'How can Nicky Butt replace Paul Ince?' 'How can David Beckham replace Andrei Kanchelskis?' And in time, we've not just replaced them; we've gone on to probably surpass their achievements, not as individuals but within the team group. I think that's something that only the manager saw at the time; we ourselves didn't even see it. Certainly none of the fans saw it: you don't get rid of one of the best midfield players in Europe to bring in a 19-year-old kid from Manchester. That's what happened: he brought in Scholesy and Butty and let the likes of Ince and Kanchelskis and Hughes and Parker and Mike Phelan go. Bryan Robson left and Steve Bruce left. All these players leave and before you know it, you're in there and you've got to go and do what they were doing – winning Championships.

You know you've got to perform to a certain level. It's constant. People talk about the pressure but I don't see it as pressure now in terms of playing because it's there – it's something that you have to do. You have to win; you have to go and play well; you have to give everything in every game, because if you don't you're out of the club.

Rebecca Tow: I've never been starry-eyed, which is helpful. I just treat the players in the same way as anyone else and I think they appreciate that. They don't want to be treated as superstars, in my opinion. I say I'm not starry-eyed: Eric Cantona does have a certain effect but he has an effect on everyone at the club, I can assure you. The last time he came over, it was to pick up an award to celebrate the magazine's 100th issue. We had asked readers to vote for their greatest-ever United player and it resulted in a bit of a two-horse race with George Best. Cantona pulled ahead and so we presented him with an award. I remember being at the training ground the day before and it was almost as if he'd left this trail of people that were beside themselves, just slumped in their chairs because they'd met Eric. I was thinking, 'Oh, come on; pull yourselves together. I'm sure he's not any different to anyone else.' Then me and my editor met him to do an interview and we were just a complete mess... the editor dropped his Dictaphone. He's just got such an aura about him.

Nesta Burgess: The good players now are millionaires. Our lot were ordinary boys. You don't see the players at Old Trafford now until the match day.

David Meek: The players have changed. They're much more disciplined than they used to be. It was much more free and easy in the old days. There was more likelihood of players, as young men do, kicking over the traces and behaving like a rugby team in the early days than now. Now it's like taking a Sunday school outing in terms of behaviour in an hotel. They never ever step out of line. The demands on them are much greater and they've had to respond. Otherwise they wouldn't last in the game. So the result is that they're much better-behaved. I don't mean that they were a wild lot before, but it was more free and easy.

Dennis Giggs: There's no one more dedicated than Ryan. He always wanted to play football, and once he got that taste of playing at such a high level it made him determined to stay there. He had his testimonial ball and nearly all the players and Mr Ferguson were there. Ryan said soon after the dinner, 'I'm going now. That'll give the youngsters a chance to let their hair down.' Not long after Ryan had gone, the younger ones went too. They were all gone at a reasonable hour. Ryan hardly drank anything all night – he doesn't drink much anyway. He's not a big drinker. Nowadays, the rule is that they can't drink in the 48 hours before a match, so if they've got a match on a Saturday, that means Thursday and Friday and if they've got a midweek match that means Monday and Tuesday. So there aren't many times when they can drink, and they're now doing less and less of it. The players have the odd Saturday night out but sometimes they don't even bother with that. Ryan can go for ages without going out.

Sir Alex Ferguson: At school level you look for ability and once you see the ability you say, 'What else have they got? Have they got the courage to play? Are they tough? Are they mentally tough?' You look for things like that. You can't really know that but you like to think that by looking at them you can see a bit of their character. In the main we have been all right in terms of the character of the boys we have brought here but in some we have been disappointed, and that's why they never made the first-team. That happens.

Nicky Butt and Scholesy were Manchester boys; you could see from the way they played the desire about them. They got stuck in. Butty was a great find; a terrific player, He was really tough and he got about, box to box. Beckham we got through Bobby Charlton. People will say that they saw David first, but it was Bobby Charlton who got Beckham from his soccer school. Bobby brought him down himself; he was a United fan – that was the secret. Tottenham, Arsenal and Chelsea all wanted him and I think he was training with Tottenham and Chelsea at the same time. They were offering him big money to sign for them and all the rest of it, but his parents were United-daft and the boy was United-daft. That's what did it; no other reason. If Bobby hadn't had his soccer school he would probably have been a Tottenham player, because his grandfather is a Tottenham fan. So there are a number of different ways in which people have arrived here.

Ken Ramsden: The thing about footballers is that they always want to play football. I've been in hotels on tours during the afternoon when the players should be resting and they'll have a skip down across the corridor as a net and they'll be lobbing the ball across it to each other as if it's a tennis game because they love football. That's the Nevilles, Scholes, the gang of '92. They just love to play.

Cameron Erskine: I think the players of the Sixties and the modern players are equally good. Having seen Charlton, Best and Law, and Giggs, Keane and Beckham, I think they are as good. It was a different type of football back in the Sixties – it's very rare these days to get three top goalscorers in the same team.

Dennis Giggs: Ryan can't lose at anything – he's dreadful. Whatever game you play, 'Millionaire' or 'Balderdash' – a word game – he even has to win at that. He'll sit and watch *Fifteen to One* in the afternoons and he's got to win at that too. His testimonial was fantastic – he was overwhelmed. He even wanted to win that and was disappointed they lost. He hasn't changed one little bit since he started his career at United – and he's marvellous with kids. I think he may do some sort of work connected with kids when he finishes. He's actually very shy – he's never loud when he goes out. I'd say he's a deep thinker. He'll come out with witticisms and quips, but a lot of the time he'ill just sit and take things in.

Cliff Butler: I think van Nistelrooy is the best striker we have had since Denis Law – and considering my feelings about Denis Law, that is some compliment. If he maintains this sort of standard he will go down as the greatest striker United have ever had. That's how good he is.

Adam Bostock: Ruud van Nistelrooy, the first time, when there were problems with his injury and the press conference never happened, on the day he went back to Holland and was training with PSV, following the collapse of the deal in Manchester, we had Radio Five on in the office and Radio Five were following our reports of the developments in the story on that day, when he broke down in training. The story shifted – again, that's the advantage of the website in that stories change throughout the day, so a story that's published in the newspaper in the morning may be dead in the water by 10 o'clock. On that day we followed the development of the story. We had David Gill, then deputy chief executive, on the phone to us, telling us what had happened. He had heard from Ruud's doctor, so the club were using us to set the record straight.

Sir Alex Ferguson: When I came down from Aberdeen to English football, it was a tough League. You had your Wimbledons and your Sheffield Wednesdays – they were giants. The ball was in the air all the time. You had to put your head in all the time. I remember playing Sheffield Wednesday when Howard was manager and Gary Walsh was carried off with a head injury and Kevin Moran played with six stitches and concussion right through the second half. I remember Bryan Robson getting stitches in his head. So I had to address the question of how we were going to survive in that type of football at that time. Now it's not the same issue. What we are trying to do here now is to provide a player who can add a percentage to the team.

Ken Ramsden: In the Sixties, players lived in houses in Stretford and in digs in Old Trafford. On a Sunday afternoon the players who lived in Gorse Hill would often go into Longford Park and play football. Kids would see them and join in. That wouldn't happen now. All that's changed because everybody's got a car now and they all live far away. There's far more security for them. On the other hand, we were in Rio de Janeiro a couple of years ago for the World Club Championship and UNICEF brought a load of kids to watch the players train. I wasn't surprised when the request came: 'Could the children have a kickabout with the players?' So I said, 'It's really hot and the players have been working hard and I really don't think it's such a good idea.' There also wasn't great enthusiasm among the players to do it. Then one of the kids went out on to the field where the players were and joined in. I turned round and all the children were on the field and all the players were playing with them. When you create the situation naturally, it still happens and you see that players are no different from the way they've always been, which I think is reassuring.

Simon Davies: The most positive thing to have happened for United in the past three years would have to be the introduction of some of the most exciting young players in the world. Cristiano Ronaldo really stood out when we played Sporting Lisbon in a pre-season friendly and it was genuinely thrilling when I walked past him in the club's East Stand reception a few days later. He's got the natural talent that can see him become one of the best players in the world.

Eric Halsall: I watched Cristiano Ronaldo's debut in the last few minutes of a home game against Bolton. I can't recall, in 50-odd years of watching United, any player having such an instant impact on the crowd. He's a legend in the making.

Sir Alex Ferguson: It's the history that means we have to have players with explosive talent. I don't think there's a club that's had more entertaining players than Manchester United and we've had more players capped for England than any other club. The fans love that kind of player and sometimes you get trapped into that yourself. Ronaldo can sometimes overdo it but he's got unbelievable courage and always wants the ball and to attack players and it is very unusual to get a player like that nowadays.

Simon Davies: Bringing Wayne Rooney to the club was also great to see, as a fan, especially having seen Chelsea buying up all the best players. His debut was the best I've ever seen and he was continually the highlight of an otherwise disappointing 2004–05 season. Sir Alex Ferguson insists that he has three of the best young players in the world at the club – he's including Darren Fletcher and Cristiano Ronaldo in that and, with the likes of Jonathan Spector, Gerard Pique and Giuseppe Rossi coming through the ranks, then the future for Manchester United looks pretty exciting.

Eric Halsall: Wayne Rooney has so much more than just breathtaking skill in front of goal; he has what is often referred to – only rarely with justice – as a natural football brain. That this is allied to courage, physical strength, skill and, apparently, the ability to learn and mature at a rapid rate, makes him another in waiting to join the long list of Red legends.

Simon Davies: I think we miss David Beckham more than we thought we would. The last time we saw him in a United shirt was when we lifted the Premiership trophy at Goodison Park – and I don't think that's a coincidence. I don't think Ruud has been the same player without the service Beckham gave him. Ruud thrives on pinpoint crosses and he's not getting anything like the number he used to get. Beckham's departure was the beginning of the end of an era. I just hope that the arrival of Rooney and Ronaldo is the start of a new one.

Eric Halsall: Gabriel Heinze is one who really had to prove himself, after keeping us waiting through the Copa America and the Olympics. It's a mark of his quality that he was as near to being an instant success as you will ever get at Old Trafford. He has exactly the mental and physical qualities to win the respect and affection of Reds. In addition, and something that is essential at United, he's a never-say-die warrior in the same way as, say, 'Sparky' or 'Robbo' were. The same judgement exactly goes for Alan Smith. If ever it took bottle to come to United as a career move, Alan Smith has it in spades, to cope with the loathing of the Leeds fans he left behind and the suspicions of Leeds-hating Reds.

7

Red-Hot Passion

There is a deep need among Manchester United supporters to display their attachment to their club. This need has at times been expressed in unusual ways, such as by the 'chewing gum girls' who for many years stationed themselves outside the Old Trafford dressing rooms to distribute their much-appreciated gum to players, or by the man who wanted to have himself stuffed and put on display in the club museum.

More widespread means of showing affiliation to United have been through scarves and badges, which proliferated from the 1960s and 1970s onwards. Those times were radically different from the club's early years, when mementoes were few and far between. Straitened supporters struggled to make ends meet and fun fripperies were far from their minds.

A jump to the modern era finds the United megastore packed on matchdays with the type of numbers that would provide a handsome attendance for a middle-ranking League club. Flat caps have been replaced by replica shirts as the de rigeur garb of the Old Trafford regular.

Souvenirs and memorabilia increase the feeling of belonging to the extended Manchester United family. Supporters' powerful attachments to their little pieces of Manchester United and their desire to get as close as possible to the players and their team demonstrate the exceptional role Manchester United has played in the lives of millions.

Mark Wylie: When you go further back, programmes become increasingly rare and Newton Heath programmes are very difficult to find. One of the rarest things we've got is a member's ticket and fixture list for Newton Heath, originally from 1881 but with the 1882–83 season's fixtures stuck on top. Obviously the guy has taken his ticket back, said he was renewing it and they have literally just plastered the new season's fixtures on top. That's one of our rarest items because, basically, it's from just three years after the club was founded. You've got to be really lucky to find anything from that sort of period.

If you look from 1878 until about 1905, there is a very slow rise in the amount of United material and memorabilia that becomes available. Then suddenly it rockets up and there's a lot between 1905 and, say, 1912, 1913. Then it tails off again because of the war, it rises slightly into the Twenties and Thirties and then it tails off because of the Second World War. Then it really rises again from the Forties onwards and keeps on rising until now. When you look at the Twenties and Thirties there are nothing like as many items as between 1905 and 1913. We've probably got more items from that eight-year period than from 1920 to 1940. People kept match cards, programmes, newspapers, scrapbooks, medals. They didn't have many big games during those two decades and crowds were a lot smaller, so there are even fewer programmes and other items of memorabilia around.

Ken Ramsden: People have always cared passionately about Manchester United. In the late Forties there was a group of young girls who were keen fans, who were known as the 'chewing gum girls'. Players have always chewed gum and in the days when sweets were rationed, players couldn't get chewing gum. These girls used to pool their sweet coupons, buy chewing gum and give it to the players. That went on until around 15 years ago. These three or four ladies, who were by now elderly, were still buying chewing gum to send into the dressing room. That's passion for the club.

Cliff Butler: When my dad used to go to games before I started going I used to love looking at the programme, the United Review. If I couldn't go to a game and my father was going I would say to him, 'Don't forget to bring me a programme.' My father worked in the newspapers in

Manchester when Manchester was one of the main print centres in Europe, and more often than not he would go to the match and then he would go straight on to work. He wouldn't come home until the early morning so I used to wake up in the morning and the first thing I would see would be the *United Review*, sitting there on my bedside table. So that was something I really used to look forward to. So I'd have my breakfast with the *United Review*, not the *Financial Times* or the *Telegraph*. I always used to look at the picture on the front, which was usually of the previous match, and if I'd been to that match I'd try and remember the moment in the game that was pictured and try to pick out the players in the picture. To me, at the matches themselves, the crowd and the *United Review* were almost as important as Manchester United itself. If we won, that was the complete package. In those days, if I didn't get a programme, that was worse than getting beaten.

Ken Ramsden: In the Fifties a lot of local youngsters would hang about the car park at Old Trafford looking for autographs because the players trained here. Even though my mum worked at the club I still wanted to be here, and if I was really lucky and she saw me outside she would sometimes bring me in and give me a cup of tea and I could sometimes see the occasional player going about his business inside the ground. As a kid of 12 or 13 I thought it was great just to catch sight of them. I was just drawn to it – it was heaven on earth to be inside Old Trafford. I remember I was taken into the dressing room one day and Tommy Taylor came in. He was lighting a cigarette and he dropped his box of matches and I couldn't wait to fall to the floor and gather up his matches for him. I can't remember who the other player was who was with Tommy but I remember Tommy turning and laughing to the other player about this little kid scrambling around on the floor trying to get his matches for him.

Chris Yeamans: Throughout the Sixties and Seventies, at every Christmas I'd get the new United kit for that year. I don't wear one any more; I've passed that ritual on to my son.

Cliff Butler: The image of the two figures shaking hands on the cover of the *United Review* did disappear from the front of the programme for about 10 seasons from the late Sixties through the Seventies. I've got to say I did have something to do with it returning. They were looking for a cover and I said, 'There's only one *United Review* cover and let's go back to it.' Everybody knows it – I know that image is on the banners of the mining unions and it's to do with unity, of course. I think the players' union also used that image when the union first started – I think they had it on the front cover of their publication. I think United probably modified it for their own ends from that. I've fought various regimes in the past who have wanted to change it – because, they said, it was old-fashioned. Of course it's old-fashioned – it's tradition

Roy Williamson: George Best's hairdresser's was called The Village Barber and was located next to his Edwardian boutique behind Kendals, close to the Crown Court buildings. The hairdresser's was very busy. I went in a couple of times hoping to see George but I never did. In the early 1970s my wife's mate Cathy paid for me to have streaks put in my hair at George's hairdressers as a birthday present.

Chris Yeamans: My dad had a mate called Tom Domville who was a bit of a 'Jack the Lad'. We used to drive to games in my dad's Ford Granada, and just before we got close to the ground my dad would put a chauffeur's cap on. We'd drive up to the policeman on duty and my dad would wind down his window and say, 'I'm just dropping these gentlemen off', while Tom Domville and his mates would sit in the back seat trying to look important. We always got let through. Then we'd drive up to a chip shop about 50 yards from the ground. Tom would jump out, slip the chippy owner a couple of quid, and he would then open these big double gates and we'd park in his yard.

Some time in the early Seventies, after we'd played Stoke City at home – I remember it because during the game the floodlights failed for about 20 minutes – Tom Domville beckoned us to a side entrance at Old Trafford and with a handful of little pink tickets (about six of them) managed to get about 10 of us past the doorman by creating as much confusion as possible.

Once past the doorman, we hurried up a flight of stairs, through another door and into the players' lounge. I thought I'd died and gone to heaven. After standing in a complete state of awe for about 10 minutes, I heard Tom Domville shout 'Chris, there's someone I want you to meet. Chris, this is Sir Matt, Sir Matt this is Chris.' He held out his hand and I shook it, and although I was a painfully shy 12-year-old at the time I can remember the benevolent smile on his face and the fact that he seemed genuinely interested to meet me. He asked me a couple of questions about my favourite players and that sort of thing before moving on. I didn't wash my hand for a month. Tom Domville used to work for Quicks for Ford and he sold Matt Busby a Jensen Intercepter, which is how, I presume, he got tickets into the directors' lounge. My dad remembers the directors' lounge, where I met Matt Busby, being full of Catholic priests! He also sold George Best his first Ford Capri with lots of flashy extras.

Ole Pedersen: I used to buy the club records, like 'Glory Glory...', up until about 1993–94. I think it was because you didn't get much information about United in those days, and the records were a way to fantasize about the club; you could play them in your living room and pretend you were at Old Trafford. Now, you just check their website.

Chris Yeamans: I used to have the album 'United, Manchester United', which I think is from '72. I used to play it to death every Saturday before we went to the game. I did have another United single but although I can't remember the 'A' side I do remember the 'B' side because it was Martin Buchan singing a song called 'Old Trafford Blues'. It was just him and a guitar, singing jokey, derogatory lines about the team – 'And then there's Alex Stepney, granddad of the team/He's been playing football since 1917', and other such lyrical gems.

Ron Snellen: The first United game I saw was the FA Cup Final in 1977. I visited Old Trafford that summer and ever since that day I've been totally hooked on United, but please don't ask me why. I can't explain that. My favourite souvenirs are the old ones: my first record from the 1977 FA Cup Final, my first pennant and scarf. And, of course, the new shirts which I keep buying. At home games I always wear a Dutch Mancunians shirt. For away games I never wear anything associated with United. I can't see MUTV every day but I visit the website – well, about every hour, really. Since the late Eighties I've visited United as much as possible. The average number of games a season for me is about 15 to 18, home, away and in Europe.

Voni von Arx: I think my supporting United has a lot to do with my Dad. In 1983, when I was seven, my Dad gave me a United shirt and said, 'Right son, wear it; you're a United fan now.' I never questioned my support for United and I knew that the first money I earned from my apprenticeship I would spend on a trip to England to see United. I saw United live for the first time in '92 and once you've seen United you can't go back. You don't want anything else. Since then I've spent almost my entire salary on seeing United in Europe and in Manchester. I never spent a second thinking, 'Couldn't it be easier to support FC Zurich, my local team?'

Martin C.Y. Lai: My son is called Trafford and I have a tattoo of a red devil and Manchester United FC on my chest.

Jonathan Deakin: I would never wear a replica shirt to a match now, as not wearing one separates me from the 'day-trippers'. I wouldn't call anyone for wearing one, but it is how I make my statement. I had them when I was 13 or so. The classic was the psychedelic blue United away shirt, worn over a paisley shirt with a matching blue sun-hat bought from a swag man, circa 1991. A classic combo.

Martin C.Y. Lai: On match days, I'll either wear a replica shirt or at least a shirt with Keano or Eric or someone on. Out here in Hong Kong in the pub I like to let people know who I'm supporting and fellow supporters can then join together. I don't like this idea that only nerds wear the shirts and that you have to dress casually to be cool.

Jonathan Deakin: I have only written around 10 articles for *United We Stand* in the past few years, but that is a big buzz because I am making a small contribution to our terrace culture. When lads who have read the articles say they enjoyed them then I am chuffed to bits that I have captured in words something about what it is like supporting United.

Roy Williamson: My favourite souvenir is undoubtedly my old red and white bar scarf, complete with the name of each member of the 1963 Cup Final team, lovingly sewn on by my mum. 'Old Faithful' comes out rarely – only in times of need. It was present in '68 at Wembley and, of course, in '99 in Barça.

Martin C.Y. Lai: I subscribe to the United magazine from Hong Kong. It's still a very good read. Most importantly, though, to me for the last few years has been the internet for updated news. I browse for around an hour a day on United sites.

Adam Bostock: One exiled Mancunian who used to live in Gorton and now lives in the Bahamas e-mailed us to let us know that he follows the match through our live text-commentary service and our live audio commentary service. This guy is out there in the Bahamas and the only place he really wants to be is at Old Trafford in the wind and the rain. He can sit in his apartment overlooking the beach and follow the match by the miracle of modern technology. As a website we have to try and deliver a site that represents Old Trafford. Sometimes you take it for granted that Alex Ferguson may occasionally walk past your desk; Bobby Charlton walks past once or twice a week. To the fans that is incredible and you have to remind yourself of that and if you think that interests the supporter then tell them. That makes the website a more entertaining read than just delivering news.

Angus Deayton: I remember being in Sri Lanka and it was the Oldham match at Wembley where Hughes scored with that volley in the last few minutes, and it turned the season round. They do follow English football to a degree there so I managed to track down a channel that was showing it. Unfortunately the hotel that we were staying in didn't have any TV so I had to check in to another hotel and found this rickety old black-and-white television set in the corner with a set-top aerial and if you held the set-top aerial in a certain position you could just about watch the game, although there was an Indian musical drama that seemed to be on roughly the same frequency. So from time to time you would suddenly find yourself being sung to and at times you weren't quite sure whether you were watching a game or whether it was some kind of dance routine. So it was kind of tricky but if you stood in the corner of the room on a desk with the set-top in a certain position you could just about follow it. When you are abroad it sometimes takes weeks of preparation to find which bars are showing English football and trying to work out the time differences. It generally proves completely futile but I always go through the motions in the hope that I'll eventually see it.

In Italy, I managed to discover that one channel would be showing a United Champions League game so I phoned up this restaurant that I knew had a television with lots of different channels and asked if they would show the United game. They said they would so I arrived there on my own to find that they had actually set a table with a knife and fork for me on one side of the table and a sodding great television on the other side. So I sat there having a cosy meal with a television showing the United match. Everyone else thought I was slightly strange, I think.

Chris Yeamans: I subscribe to MUTV. I can't afford Sky Sports or ITV digital, so MUTV is a good way of seeing all the games – even if it is a day late. Also, the thing I love about MUTV is that it's so biased; Paddy Crerand – what a guy. I love to hear the commentators and interviewers say 'we' when they talk about United.

Martin C.Y. Lai: I'll tell you a funny story. When I was 18, my girlfriend split up with me. I was devastated. I drove a total of 320 miles on a round trip to look at a closed Old Trafford at night for five minutes, then got on with my life.

Chris Yeamans: There's a little silver birch tree on the way to the ground that my fellow Red Chris Ward calls his 'lucky tree' and we have to touch it for luck. This lucky tree is at the Salford end of Sir Matt Busby Way. I've no idea how it started or when it was started by Chris, but I started touching it about four to five years ago, the first time I went to a game with him. It's just a scrawny little thing that looks like it's on the verge of being blown down or removed to make way for more concrete.

Greg Dyke: I was brought up in a working-class family in Hayes and to suddenly find yourself on the board of Manchester United was exciting, really. It was more exciting than becoming Director-General of the BBC in its way because Manchester United players were my childhood heroes.

Barry Moorhouse: The day of the Omagh bombing, a presentation was taking place after the game to Andy Cole from the Omagh branch of the supporters' club. Now it could well have been that if those people hadn't been at Old Trafford, some of them might have been caught up in the bombing. As it turned out, while we were in the throes of doing the presentation to Andy, a mobile phone rang and we heard of the news of the bombing. I said to Andy, 'There's been a bombing in their home town.' He was really taken aback. So I allowed everybody into my office to use as many phones as we could get access to, but obviously a lot of phones in Omagh were cut off. It was a really sad occasion; some of their families were involved. The nicest thing is that Andy Cole was very obliging and went over and the club played a game out there. So the sadness was softened a little by the fact that Andy Cole took it upon himself to go over there and say hello to all the people, which I thought was a good thing.

Angus Deayton: For some reason I've got Jaap Stam's boarding card from coming back from Monaco. I don't know how I ended up with his boarding card. I was flying back with the team so maybe the boarding cards got mixed up so I just hung on to it. I thought, 'This'll be useful because he'll be with United for many years.' Little did I know...

Chris Yeamans: I'm not a huge memorabilia collector but there are two items I'm particularly fond of. One is a United rug that I got for

Christmas 1968 and that has a picture of the European Cup on it. The other one is a packet of grass from the turf of the Nou Camp after the '99 European Cup final. I couldn't get tickets for the match, but it's still got to be one of the greatest, most memorable nights of my life.

Eric Halsall: Much as people may whinge about it, the club's marketing strategies have succeeded in capitalising on the basic appeal of the club's history; the more recent collective success of the 'kids'; the individual appeal of stars like David Beckham and Ryan Giggs; the magnificent renovation of the stadium as the 'Theatre of Dreams' – and everything else. The advertising and marketing men have ensnared a generation that has not only supported United but has also invested hard-earned cash in its allegiance. Once you've spent a fortune in the Megastore, you don't really want to admit you might have been better off supporting City or Milton Keynes FC – now do you?

Mark Wylie: One chap offered that when he died he would like his body stuffed and put on display in the museum. He wrote to us in 1994 and the letter actually said, 'I'm serious about this. When I die, I want to have it in my will that my body is stuffed and donated to the Manchester United museum to go on display as a United fan.' I think we wrote back and said, 'Thanks for your kind offer but I'm not sure if we'd be willing to do this at present.' You have to be careful because you don't want to upset somebody but we didn't want to start a trend like that.

Tony Whelan: The importance to the club of the youth system is never stressed in an overt way – it's taken for granted in the nicest possible way. The fans have always been supportive of players coming through the youth system. Sir Alex has always supported the academy and comes down and watches whenever he can and that's a big inspiration.

Our football academy moved to the Trafford Training Centre, the new academy facility at Carrington, in August 2002, although not all the programmes moved. The 9–10 year-olds are still based at The Cliff; the 11–16-year-olds at Carrington. I would say retention of the link with The Cliff is important because it has meant that the 9–10s have stayed low-key and it also helps retain the heritage of youth development at The Cliff.

The facilities are excellent for the youngsters – we have 11 playing pitches, an 80m by 60m gym, which must be one of the biggest in Europe, an outdoor pitch the size of Old Trafford, physios' rooms, meeting rooms, viewing galleries for parents – it's a massive investment.

The work we do at United with the young boys has always been a vitally important aspect of the club's existence and I am sure that will remain the case in the future. It goes back, really, to the Busby Babes and Matt Busby's decision to go with youth in the 1950s. I got interested in how the club signed Bobby Charlton from the North-east when that was the equivalent then of the Far East nowadays. I wanted to know how they managed to attract all these players from all over the British Isles to dark, damp Manchester and how they won the Youth Cup five times in a row – something no one has managed to equal. It even led me [to] write, over many years, a book called *The Birth Of The Babes: Manchester United's Youth Policy 1950–57*.

It is fantastic to see the tradition that was started with the Busby Babes continuing to the present day, especially when our youth teams capture the trophies to prove it. Our Youth Cup win in 2003 was our first in the 21st century and our first since we had been based at Carrington. It meant so much to Brian McClair and everyone involved; it has also been nice to see players from that team, such as Kieran Richardson and Chris Eagles, go on to play in the Premiership.

Then, in 2004, on the 50th anniversary of United's youth team winning the Blue Star tournament in Switzerland, which was really the beginning of Sir Matt and Jimmy Murphy launching the club's European ambitions, we won that tournament again; not only that but we retained it in 2005. It still remains vital for the experience of our youth team players. Wilf McGuinness, who had been in the team in 1954, was in Switzerland as our guest of honour and the whole thing provided lovely symmetry with the past and provided us with plenty of optimism for the future.

8

Background Detail

The staff at Old Trafford have always been happy to stay in the background but they have played a leading role in the club's rise to prominence. Everyone at the club, from the tea-maker – a key responsibility at any football club – and the groundsman to the chairman and the chief executive, plays a vital part in creating the right type of atmosphere away from the action. A family feeling has always been engendered at Old Trafford and that hidden strength has been one of the less heralded aspects of the club's success.

That feeling has continued into the modern era, during which United became a public limited company and a huge commercial success. So much so, that it became in 1998 the target of a £623 million takeover bid by BSkyB, which was eventually blocked by the Department of Trade and Industry after an investigation by the Monopolies and Mergers Commission. That takeover bid was unpopular among highly vocal sections of United fans who mobilized against the move and two years later United suffered serious adverse publicity when the club withdrew from the FA Cup to play in FIFA's World Club Championship in Brazil. Government pressure was exerted on United to play in that tournament in support of the Football Association's bid to win the right to host the 2006 World Cup.

It is all very different from a century ago when a St Bernard dog belonging to club captain Harry Stafford saved Newton Heath from bankruptcy and the club was relaunched under its new name, Manchester United. It was rescued from financial problems again in the 1930s by James Gibson, an old-style autocratic chairman, but he soon found Matt Busby to be more than a match for him when Busby was arrived in the 1940s. At that time, only a handful of staff served the club.

United now employ a sizeable, sophisticated staff to project the best possible image of the club. The football staff have also changed considerably with the demands of the modern game and sophisticated technology is used to monitor players' fitness levels and development. Overall, however, the natural warmth which characterizes Mancunians and which made Matt Busby grow to love the city, remains an essential, unchanging feature of Manchester United.

Mark Wylie: The team had a mascot, which was a St Bernard dog called Major and he had been instrumental in the saving of the club. It was Harry Stafford's dog and it went missing with the collection box on its back when they had a fund-raising bazaar in 1901 to obtain funds for Newton Heath, because the club was about to go bankrupt. The dog was found by a friend of one of the directors who happened to know John Henry Davies who saw the dog and said, 'Oh, my daughter would love this dog!' He found out whose dog it was and he and Harry Stafford got chatting about saving the club, it seems. Harry Stafford knew that John Henry Davies was a wealthy man and asked for his help to save the club. So John Henry Davies and two or three others contributed the money to cancel Newton Heath's debts and start the club up again as Manchester United. You can actually see Major in a picture of one of the team groups.

Sandy Busby: A lot was done by the directors. Mr Gibson was the chairman who signed my dad as manager and I think Mr Gibson had quite a say in team selection. When my dad first went to Old Trafford the club was in dire straits and then he started changing things round and getting big gates and big money coming through the turnstiles. Mr Gibson used to pick the papers up in the morning and phone my dad up and say, 'Hey, so-and-so's for sale. He's a good player. We'll have him.' My dad would say, 'No, he's not my type of player. I don't want him.' The following week Mr Gibson would say, 'Oh, so-and-so's for sale. Are we going to buy him?' This was when the money was coming in at a fair rate. My dad would say, 'No, I've told you. I'll tell you when I am going to buy a player and who I'm going to buy. You'll know before anybody.' So that was that.

Sir Bobby Charlton: Matt Busby was always aware that you had to have a long-term policy, not a short-term-one. So he concentrated a lot on youth. He got Jimmy Murphy as his number two, who, in terms of youth teams, produced the best that there's ever been. They won the FA Youth Cup in the first five years of its existence, here at Man United, and it was Jimmy Murphy and Bert Whalley who spent all their time on that. The philosophy was to entertain people and express yourself. Jimmy Murphy used to work on you as a coach and Matt Busby encouraged you and saw the overall picture.

It was the most exciting time. The club were winning the Youth Cup regularly and were starting to win championships. There was a real boom at Man United. At that time Man United, like today, were the team that everybody wanted to beat. Every ground you used to go to, it was tough.

Sandy Busby: First of all, my dad got an assistant called Jimmy Murphy. He saw Jimmy Murphy coaching a set of army lads and he thought, 'Right, that's the fellow I need as my coach.' He had fire in his belly, Jimmy, and my dad wanted Jimmy to put fire into the young lads. In those days the coaching staff was my dad, the manager, and two trainers: Jimmy, the first-team trainer, and Bert Whalley, the second-team trainer.

Nesta Burgess: Before I joined the club I used to bring home the wool socks the players used to wear and darn them, ready for them to play in. I used to bring 50 pairs home to darn at night for the team because their studs used to rip the socks. That's how I started. United came and asked me if I would do it because I don't live far from the club. They knew of me. Then Mr Olive came to me and said, 'Why don't you come in and join us full-time?' So I did. That was just before Munich.

In those days there wasn't a big staff and they were great days. We did everything. If the laundry girls were off I used to go and do the laundry, I'd clean the office, anything. I'd go home and then, if there was an evening board meeting, I would come back and serve the directors their dinners and all this sort of thing. It was a family, really, because we lived with the players. They trained here, and they were here all the time.

Sir Bobby Charlton: I went to play in a match for East Northumberland Boys and little Joe Armstrong, who was another really important person here, he was the Chief Scout, came to see me play at Jarrow and Hebburn. It was a frosty day in January. Our Jack's headmaster, Mr Hemingway, was a Man United fan apparently, and he wrote to Man United and told them to come and have a look because I was playing for my school and scoring a lot of goals. Joe Armstrong came up to watch me play for East Northumberland Boys and said to me after the match, 'If you'd like to come and play for Man United when you leave school we'd be delighted to have you.'

I might have gone to whomever it was that came first, I just wanted to be a footballer. But as soon as you knew Manchester United were interested, you started reading about the youth teams winning things and people always talked in glowing terms about how they made players better players and I just thought, 'This is just what I want. This seems to be right for me.' So I left school at 15 in the summer and I came down here. Jimmy Murphy met me at the station to take me to my digs and he told me about all the young players that he had here that I would be playing with: Jeff Whitefoot, Duncan Edwards, Billy Whelan, Eddie Colman.

I learned a lot from Jimmy Murphy. From being an amateur to thinking professionally, he was responsible, nobody else. He would tell me things like I mustn't use crossfield passes because if it got cut out you'd be working against your team and not for your team. A long, crossfield pass might look great but if it goes to their man and not ours you put three or four people out of the game. He used to just push things like that into you all the time. He always stressed that you had to work and that you can't carry passengers.

Wilf McGuinness: We all called Joe Armstrong 'Uncle Joe'. The other scouts from other clubs thought they had no chance of signing us because they thought he was a relative! They thought he was somebody's uncle so they had no chance.

Jimmy Murphy was the one who polished us and knocked off the rough edges. He either made you or broke you. It was, 'You've got to go through me to be a star. Now, come on. If you can't handle what I give you, you're not going to make it anywhere.' He was that sort of man.

Not a lot of clubs in the country really worked hard with youth players straight from school. They let you go where you wanted and thought you would develop late. There wasn't that continuity of coming from England Schoolboys into a football club and continuing to become an England player. Manchester United was the first club to really start that off.

Ken Ramsden: My mum and her sister were asked to start a laundry by Walter Crickmer, the secretary before Munich. I would guess that would have been around '54 or '55. They were known as Omo and Daz, although no one ever knew which was which.

Nesta Burgess: I used to love coming to work here – I couldn't get here quickly enough in the morning. You never knew what they were going to do next. There was always something going on and we used to have lots of fun. All the laundry used to get done here and the boys used to call the laundry ladies 'Omo' and 'Daz' . The lads would put the two laundry girls in the basket and run round the stadium with it, with the girls screaming. Matt never bothered about that.

Sandy Busby: The biggest influence on my dad was my mother. She was an incredible woman – she was an orphan, went through the war with my sister and I, lost four kiddies who all died after a couple of days. My dad was in the war so she had that worry too. There had also been the worry, previously, that my dad might not make it as a footballer. Then there was the crash. One of the first things my dad did was to introduce the players' lounge as somewhere they could take their wives

Passing on the mantle: Sir Matt Busby congratulates Sir Alex Ferguson on his first international trophy with the team, the 1991 European Cup Winners' Cup. Manchester United beat Barcelona 2–1.

Devoted following: Fans of Manchester United have always been willing to support the team anywhere, but it also has one of the largest followings across the world – from Asia to Australia and the USA.

Coming through the ranks: Under Sir Alex Ferguson's guidance the club's youth policy gained fresh impetus and with the help of various additions to the scouting ranks, the new policy paid dividends as the success of those recruited showed in the winning of the FA Youth Cup in 1992. Look closely above and you can see Gary and Phil Neville, Nicky Butt and, tucked away at the back, David Beckham.

Icons: As the charismatic Eric Cantona came to the end of his playing career, so David Beckham was beginning to establish himself as 'one to watch' in the first team at United.

State of the art: As the stadium at Old Trafford has changed and expanded over the years, so it has reached the stage where it is the envy of many clubs with its immaculate facilities and imposing façade.

Sign on the dotted line: United players always like to give something back to the fans – none more so than Denis Irwin who was happy to spend time signing autographs for legions of devoted Reds.

Are you Beckham in disguise?: United fan and TV presenter Angus Deayton dons the red for a charity match.

Home and away: Ole Pedersen of Oslo is one of United's many Scandinavian fans and goes to see them play whenever he can.

Memories of Barcelona: Where were you on 26 May 1999? It was certainly a night to remember as Manchester United completed the Treble. (Left) Nicky Butt, Sir Alex Ferguson, Peter Schmeichel, Teddy Sheringham and Denis Irwin celebrate with the trophy. (Below) Ole Gunnar Solskjaer scores the winning goal.

Wayne's World: Rooney goes down on his knees before the Old Trafford faithful after scoring the second goal against Fenerbahce. He scored a hat-trick during what was an unbelievable debut.

FA Cup winners: Mikael Silvestre, John O'Shea, Darren Fletcher, Eric Djemba-Djemba, Ole Gunnar Solskjaer, Gary Neville, Roy Carroll, Tim Howard and Ruud van Nistelrooy after beating Millwall in 2004.

Wing wizard: Cristiano Ronaldo takes on Paulo Ferreira and Tiago during the Carling Cup semi-final second leg between Manchester United and Chelsea at Old Trafford in January 2005.

Landmark moment: Before the Champions League game against Lyon, Sir Alex Ferguson is presented with a commemorative bottle of wine by Chief Executive David Gill to mark his 1000th match in charge.

and kiddies after the game. He started encouraging the wives. In addition, young players used to come and stay in our home until they found digs.

Bill Foulkes: I remember after Munich he still played me at right-back. He made me captain but I had always wanted to play at centre-half. That was my position. I had played for St Helens' Schoolboys at centre-half. The team was struggling for a centre-half and were thinking they were going to have to buy this one or that one and Jimmy Murphy said, 'You've got a lad here who can do the job for you.' So Matt listened to him. I think he listened to Jimmy quite a lot actually.

Wilf McGuinness: Jimmy Murphy taught us simple things. They might seem simple now but on that field they work. David Pegg, a winger, wasn't fast but could dribble. Jimmy Murphy used to say that if he couldn't get round a full-back there must be a reason for it. So he told him to try crossing it early instead of trying to get round him because then the centre-back would be telling that full-back to dive in because too many centres would be coming in. The full-back would then be diving in and David would then have the opportunity to get round him. Little things like that were really new in those days. There was a myth that Matt Busby only said, 'Go out and enjoy yourselves; entertain.' He didn't only say that: that was the final thing he would say on a match day but a lot of hard work had gone on before that. On a Friday Matt Busby would go through the opposing team and tell you their strengths and weaknesses. He would have a good half-hour to an hour team-talk. He was a tactician but he also encouraged players to play with fantasy and flair. You had already been taught a pattern of play: get out and play the Busby way, and the Murphy way and the United way.

Ken Merrett: A man called Jack Irons was the Manchester United mascot. You had adult mascots in those days, the late 1950s; it wasn't just for kids. He dressed in red and white, he had a red bowler hat on and a red and white umbrella and used to walk round the track. Quite a few clubs had mascots: Everton had the lady with the sweets, a lady dressed up in a crinoline who used to take sweets round. Blackpool used to have the fellow who looked like a magician, with a duck.

Sandy Busby: My dad was very fond of Harold Hardman, the chairman. First of all, he had been a footballer himself; he played for England. They did have a big bust-up early on when my dad first started at the club but they respected each other after that had happened. The bust-up was about team selection. Mr Hardman was a solicitor and was quite well-off but he travelled everywhere by bus. He never used a taxi. My dad would suggest to him that he should take a taxi but he was quite happy. They used to meet every Thursday lunchtime at a coffee-shop in town called the Kardomah and discuss the situation at the club: players, team selection and other such matters.

Ken Ramsden: I came to Manchester United in 1960 as an office boy. I lived in the same street as the then secretary, Les Olive. My mum and my aunt worked here at the time in the laundry and at that time the club were looking to take on somebody to be trained to help with the admin because there was a very, very small staff at Old Trafford.

It was a family business in every way in those days. Excluding the playing staff, there were probably about 12 or 13 people on the staff when I joined. Everybody knew everybody else – it's a bit different now. It wasn't a business – everything was just geared around playing football matches. For instance, you had one groundsman and two lads who swept the terraces. There were no maintenance staff or anything like that – you called in a local contractor when required. In those days the club was terribly poor. Anything we bought – office furniture, typewriters – was bought second-hand and you really had to make a strong case for buying anything at all. There was no money in the club at all. It was make-do and mend and if you couldn't replace something you would have to manage without it. Everything was manual: ticket sales, the payroll, the whole lot. Life at the club was a lot slower than it is now. The war had only been over for 15 years and while lots of people came through the turnstiles, gate receipts were not high. So there wasn't a great deal of money swirling round.

Everything was manual, so if you had a ticket sale on a Sunday you would have 20 or 30 gatemen on the turnstiles doing it for you because we had nowhere else where we could sell tickets. The hours were very long – on the day of a cup-tie ticket-sale we would be open from nine in the morning until eight at night. That was because everything was manual and took time; counting the money, counting the tickets.

Matt Busby was the manager at Manchester United in the sense that he managed the staff as well. Directors came into board meetings and decided policy but it was Mr Busby who ran the club. The club secretary referred to him as 'Boss'. He knew everything that was going on at the club; with a small staff it was easier. With Sir Alex, he is probably as close as you could get to how Sir Matt was because I have seen them both in operation but realistically the club and the business has grown to such an extent that no man could ever control the whole lot the way Matt Busby did.

From the age of about 18 I was in the ticket office and we had a situation once, in the early Sixties, when we had had a game and there had been some confusion over tickets. We had undersold by a small number of tickets – I hadn't sold as many tickets for one section as I should have done.

The secretary spoke to me about it and then Sir Matt sent for me and he used a series of short, sharp words to address me, 'I don't want to see this happen again. I don't expect this to happen again.' He did it in a quiet way but it was very upsetting to me. Forty years on, I can remember that interview very clearly and I went out and sat for a few quiet minutes on my own because I was so upset by it all. That's because if you let him down you felt dreadful. You felt terrible.

Ken Merrett: I got an interview to come and work here. I was interviewed by Les Olive, who was the secretary, and Matt Busby, before he was Sir Matt. The manager got involved with the interviewing because I would be doing a sensitive job, working with wages. So I was interviewed by them both. Matt Busby asked me if I was interested in football and I said I was. He said, 'Who do you support?' I told him I supported Manchester City and he laughed. Of course, he used to play for City so he said, 'I can't hold it against you.' He did say, and it's always stuck in my mind, 'We're a family at Manchester United and we all work together. I hope you're not one of these who's here today and gone tomorrow because we expect people to come to United and stay.' So that was his input really; the fact that he wanted to impress on me the fact that I'd be dealing with sensitive information about the players and because of that he wanted to make certain that I was of the right character for the job and that I would not pass that information on. I was quite in awe of him really, as you would imagine.

The majority of the players got paid by cash, weekly. I remember some, like Harry Gregg, being regular visitors, querying the wages. There was a lot of querying the wages, bonuses and tax. Some players seemed to think it was a personal thing, taking tax off them, and used to complain about it, Harry being one of them. One or two other players very rarely looked at their payslips. When I came, in '66, I don't think any player was earning £100 per week. I was here when the first player went over that amount, around '66, '67.

Tony Whelan: There was a very happy atmosphere at the club when I was a young player. The football philosophy that I learnt when I was here as a youngster I certainly carried with me right the way through my playing days and certainly now back at the club as a coach. That was that football should be artistic, aesthetic, and that as a player you should enjoy playing and you should express yourself. It was understood; it was unwritten. It was transmitted through the coaching, no question, through John Aston, who was the senior coach, and Wilf McGuinness. That's not to say that you didn't work hard, that there wasn't a work ethic. There was – you worked hard but not at the expense of playing what was considered attractive football, to express yourself when you got the ball. We still try to apply those principles now in our coaching.

United has been a launchpad for a lot of players to have good careers in football, not necessarily at United. I would be a good example of that because I was 17 years a professional, which I think is a testimony to the upbringing and coaching I had here. The club are still doing that – you just have to look around now to see the number of players who are playing first-team football around the various Leagues.

Sammy McIlroy: Bob Bishop, a scout United had in Northern Ireland, signed me. An absolute football man through and through, Bob walked everywhere – he very rarely got a bus – he had the overcoat and the walking boots and he was obviously a very fit man from all that walking. He got hold of me when I was nine years old and sent me to Old Trafford when I was 14, for a trial. He was one of the main reasons why there was such a concentration of Irish players at Old Trafford in the Seventies. He had a little holiday place at Helen's Bay, on the coast, and he'd take the lads there to play football from Friday to Sunday in the summertime. We'd all go down there and bring our own bread and beans and Bob would dish it up. It was tremendous fun to be playing football all weekend and running free through the woods.

Nesta Burgess: Louis Edwards was very good with us. He always used to give us a little bonus at the end of the season, a gate bonus, as a thank you. When we went down to the Second Division he put a letter in our wage packets saying he was sorry that he couldn't give us the bonus but he did give us an extra week's wages. All the directors knew you. You must know your staff – that way you get more out of them.

Lou Macari: It was a great club, that was obvious to me right away, as soon as I joined. Louis Edwards was great fun when you were away with the team. James Gibson, another of the directors, was also great company. He was one of these old gentlemen with thick glasses who could only see about five yards in front of him. Denzil Haroun is another director I remember well from that time. So we had a good board of directors who mixed with the players. When The Doc was here he used to call the chairman 'Chop Suey' because it rhymed with Louis. Whenever he saw him he'd say 'How's the Chop Suey?' Can you imagine nowadays calling the chairman something like that?

Nesta Burgess: Les Olive was a churchman and every Christmas he used to gather everyone in the players' lounge to have a drink. He then used to hand out hymn sheets, get us all to sing along and then afterwards he would collect them in again.

Mark Wylie: When we started the museum in '86, probably about 20,000 people came round. By 1991 that had risen to 75,000. We extended it in 1991 and had got the numbers up to well over 100,000 by 1997. We moved over to our new site in 1998 and peaked around 1999–2000, just around there.

Winning the treble and having it on display for around a year from 1999 until around March 2000 was when we were at our peak. We were getting something like 200,000 in a calendar year. Considering we're a paying attraction, that's pretty good, I would say, and we've also got restrictions in that we can't do tours on matchdays. The museum manager deals with the tours of the ground – it's all run from the museum because you can get one ticket for both the museum and the tour.

The museum draws people into the club on non-match days. We are a magnet to attract people to the club. We also provide people with things to do – the ordinary supporter can see trophies on display, which they can't do at some other clubs, where they are kept in the boardroom.

Sir Alex Ferguson: I brought the scouts in in my first week and I said to them, 'I don't want the best boy in your street. We all know who he is. I want the best boy in your town. So don't be sitting on your backsides – get out and work or you won't be here.' They all sat up.

Scouting is like everything else; scouts need back-up too. You need to get the arm round them and encourage them and let them know that they're doing their job and that it's respected. If they keep watching players and the management don't do anything about it, then quite rightly they're going to get disillusioned. So it was a matter of picking them up and saying, 'Look, you've got a job to do here. We're behind the times; we're behind the rest of them.'

Paul McGuinness: Alex Ferguson would be in, coaching, at the Centre of Excellence at nights, or observing it. So that established the work ethic. Everyone then thought that they couldn't drop below his standards and so everybody else has become used to working at that level as well, with the same sense of discipline.

Barry Moorhouse: In the 1980s, after the disaster at Heysel, Margaret Thatcher, the prime minister, suggested that clubs should introduce a membership scheme whereby the whole of the ground was given up to members in the interests of safety. There was a lot of opposition to that but we gave 50 per cent of our stadium over to members' sections. It has grown and grown. In the first year in which we operated it, '87–88, we enrolled 20,000 members into this scheme and on top of that we had around 20,000 season-ticket-holders so we brought them into the scheme without any extra payment.

From there it has just escalated. Nowadays we're looking at a figure of 170,000 members, of which 40,000 nowadays are season-ticket holders.

Keith Kent: I was pretty fed up with working for Leicester City and somebody came into the Leicester City training ground with a magazine and said to me, 'There's a job advertised for a First Division groundsman and it's a PO box.' So I said, 'Fine, I'll apply for it. I don't care where it is, I'll apply.' The PO box was London, so I went home and discussed it with my wife and I said, 'If it's Tottenham or Arsenal we'll go and have a look. If it's Wimbledon we'll forget it.'

About a fortnight later I was at work and my wife phoned me. She was whispering and she said, 'You've had a reply.' I said, 'What are you whispering for?' She said, 'You'll never guess who it is. Manchester United.' The hair on the back of my neck stood on end so I went home; I just had to go home and have a look at the letter.

Cliff Butler: I think it was in '89 that I got a call from the club secretary, Ken Merrett. It was like going to see the headmaster – it still is. I was wondering, 'What does he want me for?' At the time I was the curator

135

of the club museum, club statistician and club photographer. Ken sat me down and said, 'If somebody had said to you 25 years ago, perhaps longer, 'What would your ideal job be?', what would you have said? So I said, 'I suppose it would be to be the editor of the *United Review*.' So he said, 'This is the day. You've got it.' The first thing I did was ran back to the office and rang my dad to tell him and it was a fantastic moment that – it meant a lot to me and I'm still very proud of that fact. I remember thinking back to all those days when my dad used to bring the *United Review* home for me.

Mark Wylie: We're steadily acquiring something like 2,000 objects every year. We buy things – we recently bought a big collection of programmes to fill gaps in our youth, reserve and first-team away programmes since the fifties. We buy at auctions, normally medals, caps and shirts, things like that. We also get given items from players and from relatives of players, from supporters and we get items just from doing a bit of contemporary collecting. If, for example, we play in Europe, we get the programme, the ticket, the gift, the pennant, a shirt from the away team, so it goes like that. All these things steadily build up so we're getting at least 2,000 additions to the collection a year, sometimes a bit more, depending on some of the collections that we buy in. We've now got something between 22,000 and 25,000 objects in the collection.

We're quite strict in what we collect. We turn down 90–98 per cent of the offers we get either because it's something we already have or it would be something we would never use or it would be in very poor condition. Those are the main three reasons. Sometimes they all come together. I've lost count of the number of times we've been offered the programme for the 1968 European Cup final – over 100,000 were printed and everybody kept them. They're very common but don't get me wrong – if you were at that match or you are a United fan it is probably of great sentimental value.

Paul McGuinness: In my second spell at the club I had two years playing but wasn't going to get in the first-team so I wanted to make my own way and joined Chester, which proved not such a good move for me. As I was leaving United, Alex Ferguson said, 'Make sure you get your coaching badges.' He saw I had a future on that side of the game. At the end of the next season I was looking for a club and the manager said, 'I've got a job here – a welfare job off the field.' He saw how important the youth side was, looking after them in their digs, the education side and so on. Now, with the academy, that has gone a lot more in-depth and you've got education and welfare officers and so on. So that was my first job – welfare officer – to start with. It was the year they won the Youth Cup – Beckham, Butt, Scholes, Gillespie, Savage, they were all in their YTS years and in the youth team. I did some media training with them, things like that.

About 18 months into that there was a change around. Nobby Stiles, who was the director of the Centre of Excellence at the time, left and they sort of threw the job at me, really. It was a big thing because just at that point they changed all the rules. Rather than have the kids for just an hour a week, you could have them for virtually unlimited time and have teams. So it meant setting up a whole programme with coaches and teams and organizing all the fixtures and all the facilities. So it was as if a mini-club developed underneath. I was also in charge of the local scouting for the schoolboys, so it was a massive job. Now, nearly ten years later, there are six or seven staff doing what one person was doing at that time. From just running it one hour a week in the gym, with the boys all playing for different local clubs, now their training and playing is run by us, at the Academy. So that has been a massive change.

Les Kershaw: The greatest satisfaction from being chief scout – and maybe you dream a bit – is that you like to think that you've had a little bit to do with the success that's been going on here, that somewhere along the line, little bits that you've done for the manager have maybe helped him to get the odd point or couple of points or get a player in that has been successful. I like to think I did all right in that respect but I also think that I was smart enough to get a good staff. I regularly, all the time, communicated with the scouts. I wanted them to feel that they were a responsible part of what went on here. I used to have a list of all the scouts and I used to tick them off when I had spoken to them every week. I always wrote them letters, telling them how the stadium was being developed and what was happening with the junior teams and so on and they like that because they feel part of it. I still write to them because, although I'm the academy director, now most of the scouts who were the pro scouts do scouting for the young players as well. We don't get a lot of scouts leaving and that's because of the stability, which comes from the top – the manager.

John Peters: Edward Freedman, who was in charge of marketing and merchandizing for the club, wanted photos of United celebrating with the Championship trophy after the Blackburn match in 1993. He was pleased with what I did but then the pics would be good because the players were very happy with having just won the trophy. That first match, against Blackburn, was a little bit strange because I'd actually previously done some freelance work for Manchester City. I was just hovering in the tunnel waiting for some dressing room scenes, but one thing you find from the start about Manchester United is that it's a very welcoming place considering it's such a massive club. There is still very much a family aspect to it and they approach everything with a very professional attitude. That's the secret of the club's success. They are very approachable people.

After the Blackburn game, Edward Freedman then asked me to take pics on the bus, which was an unusual angle because normally the photographer would be outside looking up towards the bus to take photographs. When the players are on a bus displaying a trophy to the supporters you find that they are very reluctant to turn round and pose for a photographer. So I found myself hanging off the side of the bus to get the pictures I required.

Edward then asked me to photograph all the games, home and away, so off we went. The work has increased gradually over the years, with two magazines, the programme and six to ten books every year. So the need for pics just grows and grows. I'm very much a United fan. It's become my life. You get to know the players and people involved and when they don't win you really hurt.

Sir Alex Ferguson: Tom Corles was fantastic, a real scout from the old school. We were playing Blackburn and Shearer was doubtful. So I said, 'Do you fancy going up to Blackburn and finding out if that Shearer is playing?' So he said, 'Right, no problem, leave it with me.' Now there's a hospital beside Blackburn Rovers' training ground. So he goes up there with his slippers on, the pipe and the bunnet, walks in the door. He says, 'I'm in the hospital next door. I just wanted to see the boys. I'd love to meet Alan. I'd love to meet the boys.' So they let him in and not only does he see the training but he is talking to Graeme Le Saux who tells him the team. So he says, 'I've loved Blackburn Rovers all my days. Hope you win on Saturday.' That's what a good scout does – explores every angle for you. Tom died of a heart attack at Old Trafford. He was a good man, a terrific man.

Greg Dyke: When I was chairman of sport for ITV I started getting involved with football. The old BSB were trying to buy up football rights, I had just become Chairman of ITV Sport, and I decided to fight to get live football on ITV. So we went and dealt with the five big clubs, which was quite a controversial move, and that's how I first met Martin, Maurice Watkins and the guys from Manchester United. I always stayed in touch with them after that. That was in the late '80s and early '90s and in '97 they asked me to become a director. I was not in broadcast television at that time – I was at Pearson Television – and Martin and Roland Smith asked me to become a director. I became non-executive director of the holding company, which is basically the board that runs the club, as opposed to the football board, whose major aim is to spend the money!

An executive director works full-time for the organisation; a non-executive director is there basically to look after the interests of the shareholders. I was probably the only person who was construed as an independent, non-executive director. They asked me to go on because I knew about television and so much of their income came from television. I was independent in the sense that the view of the city is that if you are on for too long you become captured by the organisation. My job was to be separate from the organisation, to scrutinise the role of the management and what they did to make sure that the shareholders' interests were being protected.

Anyone who gets four tickets for the directors' box through being a director is likely to enjoy it! I enjoyed it. I had not been involved in sport in that way previously. I was coming from the entertainment business and you don't want all your directors to be financial people; you want some people who understand about the market and their customers and all the rest of it. So I did that from '97 right the way through to when I got the job at the BBC and it was clearly a conflict of interests for both the BBC and Manchester United. So I had to give up being a director, for which my children have never forgiven me! They don't think running the BBC is a good swap for four tickets in the directors' box at Manchester United!

John Peters: We've built up an archive of images which the club never had before, with pictures of matches, press conferences etcetera and I believe that one day that will be seen as a very valuable asset to the club. My favourite picture in the time I have been working at United would be the obvious one: lifting the European Cup. It still gives me goosebumps on the back of my neck when I talk about it. One of the most photogenic players at the club has been Ryan Giggs – he is a natural. You can take a picture of him when he doesn't know you're taking it and he will still look good.

Martin Edwards: I felt that Manchester United as a public company had done exceptionally well since flotation. We'd competed well but I just felt that if Sky had owned us that it would have given us more security, more wealth, ultimately more spending power and therefore I felt that it would have consolidated our position. That was, funnily enough, the year that we went on to win the European Cup but up until then we hadn't won the European Cup since '68. We'd done extremely well domestically but I just felt that with the spending power that the Italian and Spanish clubs had at the time it was always going to be difficult to compete at that level without an influx of cash. I felt that Sky would have given us that extra protection and extra security. Sky is a big company. It was well-capitalized and I just felt that it would have put us in a much stronger position than we were in or than perhaps we even are now.

Don't forget that, as directors of a public company, we have a duty, whenever we receive an offer, to consider that offer. We have to decide whether it's in the best interests of the shareholders and the club in general to accept or refuse that offer and it was the general decision of the board, having weighed up all the facts, that we should accept that offer. It wasn't just my decision; I concurred with the decision of the rest of the board. The offer came to me and I brought it to the board and discussed it with the chairman, Sir Roland Smith. Maurice Watkins, the club solicitor, was with me also when the offer was made; it was made to both of us. The three of us discussed it and said that we must put it to the rest of the board, which we did, and don't forget it was the unanimous decision of the board to accept that offer. So the directors felt that offer was in the best interests of the shareholders and the club.

At that time I was Chief Exec so, yes, I had an influence, but at that time I had about 13 per cent of the shares so 13 per cent is not substantial when you are thinking that you need over 50 per cent to accept the offer. As Chief Exec people would listen to me but I think in a situation like that, directors have a duty to make their own minds up. There are certain guidelines and Stock Exchange rules that directors have to abide by when making the decision. So whatever I felt I don't think it was a question of me influencing the rest. It was a question of putting the facts to them and professional advisors putting the facts to them and then they have to make up their own minds whether that offer should be accepted. Very often it's the price that dictates the acceptance, in other words people say, 'Maybe we ought to accept this but we'll accept it at a certain level' or 'If it gets to a certain level we have no option but to accept it.' That's really what happened in this case. The first offer was refused and we requested a certain figure, which Sky accepted, and at that level the deal was done, subject to shareholder approval, which, of course, it never got because it had to go to the Monopolies and Mergers Commission.

We floated in '91. If you look at the success of United since the flotation, I think it's difficult to be critical of what has been achieved or what the board has done. If you are running any business you have to please your customers and your customers are the supporters. Likewise, if you float, or you become public, you float in the knowledge that you have a duty also to your shareholders and to shareholder returns and everything else. Now, our meat business was a public company so I had worked in a public company before so I pointed out to all the other directors what it would mean to float and the disciplines that would be imposed and it was the board's decision at that time that that's what they wanted to do. In a way, through the flotation we raised money to build the Stretford End and subsequently we have had a very strong shareholder backing. Some people would say we could maybe have done it without that support but what would you rather have? Would you rather have a public, structured company where 70 per cent of the shares are currently owned by institutions, 10 per cent by the board and 20 per cent by supporters or would you rather have the club run by an individual? If we hadn't floated then the club was always subject to an offer by an individual a la Michael Knighton. Now I think at the time the board felt that they would rather go public and have a spread of shares.

Don't forget that when we floated the supporters could have taken a lot more shares than they did but they didn't and the institutions took up the slack. In other words, the offer was underwritten by institutions. Any shares that weren't taken up by supporters were automatically taken up by the institutions. So the supporters did have the opportunity of getting involved as shareholders of the club at the time but they didn't actually take it.

So I would say that Manchester United has flourished as a public company. Whether it would have been better off with an individual running it, I don't know. You don't know what an individual is going to do with the club, whereas, as a public company, you do have constraints on what you can and what you can't do with the business.

I think had it been Granada or somebody else then I don't think there would have been the same reaction as it being Sky. I think it was the Murdoch influence that got the supporters' reaction but, then again, whether it was Granada or Murdoch we would still have had to go through the same process and we would still have reached the same decision. Whether it would still have been referred to the Monopolies and Mergers Commission had it been Granada, I don't know. Maybe it would have been. I think the whole thing got a bit political as well. So, again, how much was it the political influence that stopped it? I don't think Sky were flavour of the month with the government. In fact, it got very, very political in the end.

Having recommended the offer to shareholders and then gone through the Monopolies and Mergers panel and all the rest of it, the offer having been voted out, that didn't bother me at all. I believed that we had done our duty in recommending the offer. In fact, I think that had we not recommended the offer, we could have been sued by shareholders for not recommending it. So you can't always win in these situations. You have to do what you believe is right and it is laid down as to what your responsibilities are as a director.

Greg Dyke: In the first year of my time there we won nothing. That was a disappointing year. In the second year, of course, we won the treble, which was also the same year in which BSkyB were trying to buy the club. So I lived through all of that. That's when it's quite difficult if you are a non-executive director representing the shareholders' interests. I personally wouldn't have sold my shares in the club to anybody. I saw no reason for it at all. I didn't see any reason why the club couldn't carry on being an independent organisation but I took my own separate legal advice – and it was quite clear that I didn't agree with the other members of the board, who wanted to sell – and my legal advice was that if you are representing the shareholders' interests and if somebody offers you a price that you think is a very good price then you have to sell. So I just sat there and said, 'I don't think the price is good enough.' Of course, they kept putting the price up and in the end they put the price up to what I'd said was a good price so then I had to recommend it but I was always unhappy with it and I made that pretty clear when I said that I was going to give the profit I made on my shares to charity. I didn't want to be seen to be profiteering from something that I didn't actually agree with.

I took legal advice on my responsibility as a director at that particular stage. The advice was that if I got a price that was a very good price then I had to accept it. Company law is very clear. You have no responsibility to the fans, you have no responsibility to the customers. Your responsibility is only to the shareholders as a non-executive director and if you think you're being offered a very good price for the market conditions at the time, you have to take it.

I didn't want to look at it in a hard-headed business-like way. I wanted to look at it as a Manchester United fan who saw absolutely no reason why the club should be owned by anybody else but I was on the board to represent the interests of the shareholders. So I had to go through that process.

I remember the Manchester United merchant bank telling me that I had to accept it a lot lower and I said, 'You must be joking.' So when everybody else was going to do a deal at around £2.10 or £2.15, my price started at, I think, £2.50 and came down to £2.40 and initially there was no deal at that price. Roland Smith, who was the chairman then, was of the view that if he hadn't got a unanimous board he couldn't do it. I was quite happy to say, 'You all do it and I will register my vote against because then I can campaign against this.' However, he insisted he either had a unanimous board or he wouldn't do the deal. So the deal was just about to fall apart when Sky decided to up the offer to the price I'd said I was willing to accept. I put a price on it that in that market at that time I thought it was worth. It was a good price, it was a high price but so it should be if you want to buy Manchester United. The thing I kept saying was, 'You don't know what you're selling here. You might be selling the television rights to Manchester United for ever. Now that's worth an awful lot of money. Just because the Premier League is organised in such a way at the moment where it is sold collectively, you don't know that's going to continue to be the case. It could well be that Manchester United at one stage gets the rights to sell its own television rights in which case this club is worth an awful lot more than £2.40 a share.'

I didn't want the club sold at all. People kept saying to me all through that period, 'Oh, they'll bring money in.' I kept saying, 'No, you don't understand. If you pay a very high price for the club, for a business, you don't do it to bring money in. You do it to take money out, to give you back your return on the money you've put in.' Secondly, Manchester United was not short of cash. It's a cash-generative business. So I didn't think you needed anybody else to bring cash into the business.

Also, on the day that the bid got announced, I said quite clearly to the people at Sky, whom I knew, that I never thought it would get through the competition authorities because the intent was quite clear. It was to ensure that BSkyB would continue to get the football contract by owning the best club and that's clearly anti-competitive in terms of BSkyB's relationship with other pay-television operators or free-to-air television operators. It would give BSkyB a lever in any negotiations because they had the best club, the club everybody wanted. I never thought it would go through because there were real competition issues. I think that when the Monopolies and Mergers Commission got some 600 submissions and only two were in favour – the one from BSkyB and the one from Manchester United's board – I think they realised that this was quite a political hot potato. It was quite interesting that the politicians walked away from it completely. In the meantime, we won the treble. It was funny; in the discussions earlier in that season there were some members of the board who said they thought the team had peaked and in the end we went on and won the treble!

Adam Bostock: The website was launched as manutd.com in August '98. I was fortunate to get the position of editor. I was approached internally because I had worked on the Manchester United magazine for four years. Through the club media we can offer access to players through their thoughts and comments. It's an information channel, channelling key information from the club to the supporter. Crucially, with the website, it's a two-way channel so if the supporter wants to talk back to you they are perfectly entitled to do so. We had a record 1,400 fan messages submitted after the Chelsea defeat in December 2001 when the team lost 3–0 at Old Trafford. Some were supportive, some not so. We had one fan calling for Ferguson's head, saying he had lost the plot and that he should be sacked before the team lost any more games. Now, that view looks entirely ridiculous but at the time some fans genuinely felt there was a problem. Perhaps the email was sent just a minute or two after the final whistle, in the heat of the moment, but although we are an official website we didn't feel that we should silence that view; we balanced it with some views that presented the counter-argument, but that person expressed his view well and we put it across.

Martin Edwards: My first reaction when Tony Banks rang me to talk about the World Club Championship was to say, 'There is no way that we can go off to Brazil in January to play in a World Club Championship.' I said it was just not possible. As European champions we had to go and play that game in Tokyo against the South Americans. We also knew we had to go and play Lazio in Monaco so that was an extra two games we had to play anyway. We just knew that we would run the risk of destroying our season if we had to take two weeks out in the middle, particularly if we had to play in the FA Cup. I discussed it with everybody in the club, the manager and all the rest of it, and we talked about playing a weakened team. The club's reputation was at stake in the FA Cup by playing the youth team or whatever else because we had to take a full squad to Brazil. We spoke very carefully with the management and the coaches as well and discussed the effect of playing a youth team in an FA Cup match. We took Arsenal as an example and said, 'If they go to Highbury and get hammered 6–0 what is that going to do for their confidence and future professional careers and everything else?' So we took all sorts of things into consideration. It wasn't a five-minute decision; a lot of thought went into it.

So we weighed up all these things and said that in the end we couldn't do it. In the end, we decided that if the government and the FA wanted us to go that badly they would have to give us dispensation to withdraw from the FA Cup. So, in the end, that's what we put to them.

We didn't want to go to Brazil. We would have been quite happy not to go but we also thought that if we didn't go to Brazil and England didn't get the World Cup, what were they going to say about Manchester United? We're already hated anyway. They would say, 'Manchester United jeopardized England's bid for the World Cup.' We wished that the whole situation had never arisen and that we had never been asked to go to Brazil. They kept on pushing and pushing and pushing and in the end we said that the only way we could go was by them helping us and the only way they could help us was by giving us dispensation to withdraw from the FA Cup, which is what they agreed to do. It was an impossible situation for us.

Then, when we did go it was said that we had destroyed the FA Cup. You've got to bear in mind that because of the success we've had there are a number of newspapers that will criticize United at every available opportunity and this was a golden opportunity for them to rubbish Manchester United.

Paddy Harverson: There is a deliberate misrepresentation of Manchester United in certain elements of the media. Now I don't want to get paranoid, I don't want to retreat into the Old Trafford bunker, but I can tell you now, having worked here on this side of the fence, it comes across loud and clear that there are people who deliberately want to portray us in a negative light and that's difficult but, that said, we weren't always doing the right things, communications-wise, in the past. Even when we were doing the right things we certainly weren't communicating them properly. I think that was a reflection of the fact that the club had just not reached that point where it understood that it needed to evolve further and that communication was part of that. they thought, 'Why do we need it? We get all the publicity in the world. We don't need someone to go out there and ring around asking, "Can you put our names in the paper?"'

The thing that they didn't understand was that you need to manage this, you need to have proper communications structures, skills, systems and individuals to make it work and I think the Brazil trip for the World Club Championship finally brought that home to the management here. I was a fan and follower from afar so I wasn't around but I think in the context of the withdrawal from the FA Cup it was already a negative story that we had to manage and I don't think, perhaps, enough was done to explain the predicament that United had been left in over that decision by the FA and the British government, which had put enormous pressure on United to go to Brazil.

Rebecca Tow: The magazine is an avenue through which you can hear what the players are thinking about things. I think its player access is extremely good. A lot of other times when players are in interviews it's through sponsors and I think it's quite neutralized. I like to think that in our club magazine we try to get those characteristics of the player that people don't often see and try to bring out their humour and bring out their views a bit more because we are privileged enough to have that little bit of extra time with them. We've all got different strengths on the magazine and I think we all try and bring some of those interests and strengths into it for the reader. For example, for some reason I have always taken a special interest in the youth set-up, in the youth teams, and I can tell from the feedback that I get that people really do want to read about these young kids. When I'm writing about them or interviewing them I know that probably one of the dozen lads I've talked to this season is going to make it, if that, because that's the ratio now at Manchester United. It's so, so difficult but, nonetheless, people are interested to hear their story; how a 17-year-old has made it to Manchester United and what he thinks and feels and I'm interested too.

David Meek: Reporting on United has become different. I wouldn't say harder. A lot of present-day journalists would tell you access to players is more difficult. On the other hand, the manager devotes far more time to press conferences and to media relations than Matt Busby ever did. So it's swings and roundabouts. In the past, you would just go down to the ground and wait for a player after training, ask for a word and off you would go. Sometimes the player would be like the present-day players and say, 'Sorry, I'm in a hurry' or if he didn't like what you'd written the previous week he'd say, 'Bog off!' You can't do that now. It's controlled now – at a press conference, Roy Keane, for example, will be brought in and will talk openly and freely. We didn't have anybody paraded like that in the old days, so to a certain extent a certain amount is handed to you more on a plate but by the same token you can't just go where you like and talk to whom you like.

Rebecca Tow: You've got to spend a lot of time hanging around and hovering around, waiting for the person that you need to see but I've made a lot of friendships with people at Carrington so I'm very comfortable being in that environment. When Carrington was first built, there was a huge question mark for the press people over whereabouts in the training facility they were allowed to go to because no one can watch training. I just basically went over to Sir Alex and said, 'You tell me where I can go. You understand the job I've got to do.' It isn't just big interviews, it's little interviews as well: a quick five-minute chat with a coach, a five-minute chat with a youth-team player. It's a real headache if you're having to book people all the time so I just said, 'Where can I go?' And he said, 'Come into the canteen with all the players and myself and if you need to see us just address us that way.' A lot of people go through the press office but because we're the club magazine I was allowed to do that. I checked if that was OK with Roy Keane as well and he said it was fine. So that's what I do. I kind of just exist and have a presence at Carrington so that I can approach players for these small, extra things that we need to do to fill up the magazine.

Carrington is amazing. I spent so much time at The Cliff, sat on the wall outside, and The Cliff seemed great when we were there. The Cliff is a fantastic facility but Carrington is so modern, with the gym, the pitches, the swimming pool – it's all so spot-on. It's an amazing place, it really is, and you can tell the players love it. There is just a freedom there for them. The gaffer has split the building in two and there is a half that no outsiders go to. I do well by getting into the canteen because I'm really an outsider; it's essentially purely for the players and the coaches. It's like a haven, really: no press, no one looking over their shoulders, no strange faces around. There is just a very comfortable environment there, you can tell.

Adam Bostock: Living in the north-west, there is a wealth of information about Manchester United and I think the further afield you go the more difficult it is to get that information. So the website is an ideal means for people who are at a distance to keep in touch. It is also an immediate vehicle – we break stories as and when they happen. That sounds very clichéd and cheesy but that's our job. If we didn't do it, we'd be out of a job. So if we sign Ruud van Nistelrooy, we're there, we report the press conference and the choice quotes from that press conference within a few minutes of the press conference coming to a close. So fans outside the UK can log on and get the very latest news from Old Trafford. A lot of our readers are based outside the UK – the countries where the website is popular are the countries that have traditionally been hotbeds of support for Man United: Scandinavia and the countries of the Far East.

In May '99 we had six million page impressions – that is one page being read by one user – in that particular month and that was only nine months after we had started the website. What a great first season in which to start a website – the treble season! We have around half a million different individual users of the website in an average month.

The gentleman who writes the press releases, Patrick Harverson, is literally based right next door to me, and as soon as that press release is written we have it, sometimes half an hour prior to everyone else. So we have the advantage of speed because we are literally here where the news is being made. We are always likely to be informed first of events happening so we are always the first website to confirm the hard facts. You know you've got to deliver because people expect you to do so – if you get it wrong once you run the risk of losing those users.

Having worked on the magazine as well, I have been in that sometimes difficult position in the past where we have known full well what the supporters have been talking about, we know what the buzz is in the pubs and around the ground. We know what the rumours are: are we signing this player or that player? And unfortunately, when you start to discuss those rumours on an official website or in an official magazine, the view can be taken by people that perhaps there is something in it. We have to be careful in what we publish because we don't want people to assume there is truth in what might only be a rumour. The vast majority of transfer rumours don't come off. We actually logged it one season, when United were linked with 120 different players and we didn't sign any of them. It was staggering.

•

Tony Whelan: It's an enormous club now. Even within our academy we have 120 players aged nine to 16 and we have probably about 10 or 12 full-time staff; academy directors, assistant directors, physiotherapists, scouts, European scout and youth development coach. We put seven teams out on a Sunday; they all play at The Cliff or Littleton Road. We also have a programme of training four nights a week, Monday to Thursday from six o'clock until nine o'clock. We have seminars for parents, we have player education programmes, we have a child protection officer and an educational welfare officer. If you think of it as being a part-time school, that's what it's like.

Les Kershaw: The manager inflicted the job on me of running the academy – and 'inflicted' was the word because I was the chief scout; I was quite happy with that, I felt I was doing all right. The club were doing well. The manager wasn't keen at all but he, I, we all realized that we didn't really have an alternative to an academy and so, almost reluctantly, we decided we would have to put an application in to have an academy.

That was when I went to the board and I said, 'Look, we've got this fabulous rehabilitation and training complex here and we don't have anything for an academy.' And the board said, 'We've just spent £14m here on Carrington. What have we got?' I said, 'You've got what was designed but an academy needs an indoor centre by demand. It has to have a full-sized outdoor, floodlit, artificially surfaced pitch. We don't have that. We have the indoor centre at The Cliff but surely we want the site to be integrated, so we need to develop Carrington.' Eventually, to be fair, the board backed the idea and the manager was extremely supportive and bit by bit they did see the vision that was required. At least I was able to explain to the board what was necessary, and I'd been here a while so I did have some respect from the board.

At first, they wanted to put up this indoor hall that was of minimum dimensions, 60 x 40m. I said, 'No, no, no, no. At Manchester United we have to be an icon. People have to say, "That's Manchester United."' And so I got the indoor centre built with a floor area of 80 x 60m. So it's appreciably above half the size of a football field and it's a magnificent structure. It's built to the same sort of specifications as the training centre at Carrington. It will be a magnificent addition; the bulk of the academy boys will train here at Carrington. It will be a hive of activity.

Academies started in the summer of 1998. A boy joins the academy in the school year in which he takes his ninth birthday. So all the boys are eight the first time they come into an academy. At 16 the big career decision is made as to whether you make them a junior pro. If they are doing all right, they stay in the system up until they are 21 years old. The only way they come out of the academy system is if they go in the first-team squad on a regular basis. Giggsy would not have stayed in the system very long; David Beckham would have stayed in the system longer because he was a little later with the final development that made him a great player. Some of the others who are in the first team would have stayed, theoretically, in the system until they were 20. The idea is that this five years as a junior pro is based as much as anything else on educational development so that the ones who, at 19, are not doing well, if they've done well at school they could take a university entrance exam.

We're now in football getting very much brighter players than we did because they see the mega-rewards. We've got a boy that joined the club in the summer of 2001 who got 10 GCSEs; all were As, of which six were A-starred and those are absolutely top of the pile.

In years gone by, that boy, would never, ever have ventured into football. It would have been the old adage, 'Get your education done first', but it's too late then. He's come into football but at the same time his education is continuing and he will be encouraged and pushed because we have a partnership with a top school.

At the end of his initial three-year spell here he will have university entrance qualifications, unless he falls by the wayside. Now, if he does that, we'll be asking questions because what we're trying to do is prepare them for football but also prepare them for the 30 or 40 years they live after they've been footballers, because if he has £20 million in the bank at 35 years old, he'll still want to do something. Some will do studies that will give them business acumen; some will do studies that will make them a joiner. So it's a good system now and it's designed so that lads are not just left with nothing.

Leo Rocca: My father would have been appalled by the money in the game nowadays, the huge salaries and astronomical transfer fees. In all other respects, though, the present squad would have had my father smiling approvingly. He was a great believer in two things: producing home-grown talent – that was his job – and playing exciting, attacking football.

Sir Alex Ferguson: We are trying to change our vision of the club. What we've tried to do is make ourselves as international as possible, principally through the development of alliances. We have, for example, 60 scouts in England and one in Brazil; now, there are close to 60 million people in Britain and 320 million in Brazil so there's something wrong there. Who produces the best players in the world year after year? Look, for example, at the Brazil team that won the World Cup in 1994. Who were the substitutes? Ronaldo, Roberto Carlos, Cafu, all young lads then. They've just got this incredible way of producing players. We are aware, though, that we have got to be careful that we maintain the balance of home-grown players with those from other countries.

One thing about the modern game is that, generally, players are bigger than we were and their kids are going to be bigger than them. Patrick Vieira is six feet three and playing in midfield. You wouldn't have seen that 25 years ago or, if you did, then a player of that size wouldn't have been getting a touch. It doesn't faze me. Some games you have to deal with it. Sometimes smaller midfield players are better.

We knew about Ronaldo [the Brazilian] when he was 16 – we knew about all of them – but it is difficult sometimes in this country to get the work permits, whereas other countries, such as Germany or Belgium, allow them in.

9

Solid Support:
The Republic of Mancunia

Manchester United supporters have, like the club, changed radically down the years. The days of rolling up, paying at the gate and standing on packed terraces are long gone. Those well-loved customs have been replaced by sophisticated ticketing systems and safer seating. The scarcity of away fans prior to the 1960s meant there was no segregation of supporters, something that was ended by the hooliganism of the 1970s. That, in turn, has now been replaced by a more tolerant atmosphere, in which rival fans may often mingle peaceably before and after the game. When the match starts, though, the language and chanting in the stands can be as salty as ever.

Prior to the Second World War, United supporters would be content merely to stand and watch the match. The modern era has seen greater supporter participation through identification with particular sections of the stadium, singing and chanting. Supporters are now much more aware of their role as part of the spectacle on match day.

Increased opportunities for travel and greater awareness of the club abroad has created for Manchester United a support that is drawn from all corners of the British Isles. That, in turn, is supplemented by a multinational blend of supporters from the continent and beyond. The images of Mancunian manual workers leaving work of a Saturday lunchtime to file into Old Trafford are part of the club's cherished history. They built the base for the club to now have one of the most disparate, unusual and interesting supports in world football.

Jimmy Billington: I was mad on football and we used to get the football on a Saturday night in the orphanage when one lad would read out the results from the pink or the green evening paper in the dormitory. We would all be in bed and had to listen to one lad reading them out. What got me bad was when Villa beat United 7–0, around 1930 or 1931, but that didn't bother me – I still decided I would support United. My father was supposed to come to see me every month but he didn't because he was a drunkard. He came sporadically – even in July at my birthday I don't ever remember getting a present – but in 1934 someone must have leant on him to get some tickets – complimentaries they were – and he took seven of us to a United match.

There were some crowds in those days. There was a lot of shouting but no disturbances. At Maine Road they used to pass the kids over their heads down to the line and the kids didn't half enjoy it. I would get behind two big fellows but I could still see the game. All the time I was there there was no trouble at all.

At Maine Road I once got into a big crowd when the police started chasing people on horses to get them all dispersed. I think they were frightened of them fighting but it was just bawling and shouting. I never saw any fights. After the game they would immediately drive people away by using their horses – you would not be allowed to stand around outside the ground.

Eric Halsall: When I first went to watch United, I wasn't really watching a real United team – it was during the war and teams were made up from whoever the club could get to perform in matches in the wartime league. It really was all very drab – as anyone of sufficiently refined vintage will tell you, before the '70s and '80s the hundreds of thousands of chimneys, domestic and industrial, which had been pumping out smoke from coal fires for a century and a half, had made most buildings black. Also, since football was the winter game, Saturdays in those days had more than their fair share of fog and smog, in addition to

Manchester's own special brand of rain. People the scene with a crowd that was almost entirely male – my Auntie Annie, my mum and a couple of girlie cousins being honourable exceptions – and you're on your way to an accurate picture. The majority – grown men – were dressed in black, grey or brown coats and flat caps, unless they were in uniform, during the war. The young lads still wore shorts until the age of about 13 or 14, usually with a raincoat and maybe a school cap, and the colours of their clothes were like their dads': dull. Scarves and rattles added a bit of colour, but not much! The sound outside the ground, once you were off the bus, tram or trolley, was of thousands of feet clattering along streets that were either cobbled or laid with stone or wooden setts – often shiny and slippy with rain. Very few people had cars and even fewer car-owners spent their Saturday afternoons at football matches. The crowd of memory seems to have been pretty quiet on the way to the match, if not downright grumpy. They were probably knackered from working a 50- or 60-hour week for some gruel and a beef-dripping butty. Afterwards, they frequently seemed to be hopping mad about something or someone – usually the ref. So Maine Road – before the return to Old Trafford – in those days wasn't much like a Club 18-30 holiday venue.

Ken Merrett: Why do we kick off at three o'clock on a Saturday? It's because people used to work on a Saturday until one o'clock. This was the biggest industrial estate in Europe, Trafford Park. You can see pictures of it in the Fifties. They came out of work at one and they walked into the stadium and all you could see was heads and cloth caps.

Angus Deayton: I'm from the Home Counties, so naturally I support Manchester United. I was from the Croydon area and my dad didn't support any particular team so I wasn't integrated into any particular following – in fact he was really a rugby fan. So I had to strike out on my own and find my own team. At the grand old age of seven I watched United beat Leicester City in the FA Cup Final on television and that was it, really.. I think you tend to pin your colours to the team that wins, at that age, which is possibly why United have so many fans now. I guess the fact that they had glamorous players and tended to keep winning through the Sixties didn't hurt – I'm sure that's one of the other reasons why you stick with them. If you're not from a footballing family you can follow a team through TV and I think that's what kids do more and more nowadays, and certainly did then if they weren't taken to football matches by their parents.

I don't really remember getting any particular stick for it until the Nineties, which either coincided with when I started to become slightly higher-profile or it coincided with their purple patch; their run of Championships. So I'm not quite sure which of the two is the catalyst but, for some reason, from the beginning of the Nineties onwards there has been no end of flak for being a United fan from anywhere but Manchester. Every major team has no end of fans who travel from Cornwall and Norfolk and all ends of the country in order to watch them, but for some reason it's United fans who get the stick for it.

The Nineties were the first time I remember receiving any degree of flak for it because most of the time being a United fan meant being a fan of that team that always lost out to Liverpool and it was endlessly frustrating – 26 years without winning the Championship was a long time. Some of us even remember the days when they were in the Second Division so I don't remember getting an enormous amount of stick in those days. It's only really the combination of two things: firstly them winning, and secondly there probably were people who then attached themselves to the club and they were celebrities so, simply because you are a celebrity, you tend to get lumped in with other people who maybe are only fans because of United's success. I'm very happy to take questions on United from 1963 onwards if anybody has any doubts about my allegiance to them.

Cliff Butler: In October of '68, for no reason of my own, I got slung out of the Stretford End and arrested. They actually said on the charge sheet that I was being arrested for causing the crowd to sway. Now, if you know football crowds of the 1960s you know how ridiculous that sounds but you had no chance in those days because hooliganism was growing and people were frightened of it and every football incident meant you were a hooligan. I wasn't a hooligan – that was the last thing on my mind. I just wanted to see the match and be involved in it inasmuch as being in the Stretford End and singing my heart out for two hours.

Early in the 1969–70 season, Bill Foulkes, one of the greatest servants this club has ever had, was booed – in that match against Southampton when we lost 4–1 and Ron Davies scored all four goals – and I'd never heard that before. I'd been coming here to Old Trafford ten, twelve years and I'd never heard the crowd boo United before. I was absolutely astounded by it. I was shocked. They were picking on Bill Foulkes because he got laced three or four times by Ron Davies, who was a young fellow then. It was Bill's last game – he never played for United again after that. I think that was a day on which an era ended. Bill Foulkes had seen it all, from the early fifties right the way through Munich and to the new successes. For him to suffer that, to be booed by his own fans... I couldn't believe it.

I remember turning round to people who were doing it and saying, 'What are you doing that for? Why are you shouting at him? All right, he's had a bad game today but just think what he's done for this club.' I can't repeat their responses. You know, they were just so fickle and short-sighted and narrow-minded about the whole thing, as though all that mattered was that one game. We'd lost before, you know, and I thought it was awful to see him suffer that. Bill's career should have ended with him being carried shoulder-high from the pitch, not being jeered by his support. It wasn't a good moment that, for me, as a supporter and as a student of football. I thought it was really sad.

Eric Halsall: I can't tell you how much of a downer it was, being torn between joy in the performances of Doc's United and disgust at being surrounded by nasty little prats in bell-bottomed, half-mast jeans with tartan turn-ups, scarves round their waists and wrists and far more interest in kicking seven bells out of visiting fans than in watching the footie. That's as close as I ever came to giving up on the beautiful game.

Jonathan Deakin: As a Mancunian, the terrace culture and awareness of the city is special to me. My early years supporting United coincided with a great time for music in the city and that sense of Mancunian swagger has prevailed. Currently, the 'siege mentality' is something I love. Others clubs' fans hate us and we are reviled in some quarters, but it is great to be part of the 'clued-up' element of our support.

Swallay Bandhoo: Manchester United is so special – it's simply the best team in the world, having won all the honours in the history of English football and in European football and even world-wide. The winning spirit adds more spice to the Manchester United specialities and the campaign against racism encouraged by Manchester United makes them even tastier. I really like the very secure atmosphere when attending matches at Old Trafford. I think that we are the best supporters in the world; we have acquired a lot of experience and we have learned a lot from the ill-effects of hooliganism.

I think the aggressive campaigns against hooliganism and racism encouraged by the club have considerably helped to make people feel very secure at Old Trafford and, as a foreign fan, I fully recommend people from abroad to attend matches at Old Trafford. Every time I've been there, the fans sitting close to us have been very friendly and supportive. I've been able to express ideas, views, share the happy moments when United score and even discuss things positively if something is going wrong on the pitch. I also witnessed the same atmosphere at Wembley in August '97 and May '99, for both the Charity Shield and FA Cup.

Roy Williamson: The football we've played in the last ten years was better even than anything we played in the Sixties and as an old-timer you tend always to look back on your younger days as being the best of times but this last ten years' football has been out of this world. I would never criticize any of the players or teams we've had. If anything, I'd criticize the fans for not giving them the backing the previous teams had.

The '94 team was probably one of the best teams we've had but they didn't quite make it in Europe for a number of reasons, such as the international player rule and all that kind of thing. I thought they deserved to win it – they should have won it. That's United isn't it? They've won the European Cup twice, they could have won it another two or three times but they haven't. This is the cavalier thing – anything can happen with them, can't it? But I wouldn't change it – I'd rather watch United and the way they play than guaranteed, dull European campaigns. There are times when they stretch your patience a bit, particularly in recent years, but that's what watching United is all about.

Ken Ramsden: I think the fans are at their best when you're struggling in a match but they know that the team is good enough to come back and do better. If they come to a game and they expect the team to win they almost sit back, fold their arms and say, 'Entertain me.' It's the 'How many will we get today?' syndrome. Now that we're winning things so often it can be hard for fans to get motivated. The opposite to that occurred when we played Juventus at Old Trafford in a Champions League game, a very important game, and we went behind. We went behind early on and the place just erupted, and that was to do with the fans recognizing that the players really needed them. They lifted the team – there's no doubt about that at all, but the conditions have to be right.

Swallay Bandhoo: I have always been very impressed by the full support the fans give to the team, the encouraging songs for each and every player. Personally, I haven't seen anyone doing crazy or unusual things while at Old Trafford, but I can say that I'm really very impressed by the fact that the fans anticipate almost all the actions in a match, they can read the game easily.

Voni von Arx: I don't call myself a fanatic – I wouldn't die for the club. I'm married now and I'm 25 years old but I just hope the day never comes along when my wife asks me the question, 'United or me?'

James Marshall: It's still a friendly club and they still care about the fans but it used to be that you could talk to the players. Now they are like superstars but that is something that has grown with the club and the success on the pitch. When I started going it felt like there weren't many fans from London and all over the world. They had the support but not as big as now – the fanbase has just grown and grown and grown. In some ways I like that, in others I don't. Some people call them gloryhunters so you then get City fans saying you are a gloryhunter because you support United but I started supporting them when they weren't so good. It is only now that the club has grown that everyone thinks you are a gloryhunter.

Swallay Bandhoo: In Mauritius, each victory of Manchester United is welcomed by firecrackers, even if it's very late at night, and opposition fans celebrate United defeats by using firecrackers. More and more local fans follow live matches in public places. As chairman of the supporters' club, I receive several phone calls every day or on match days to give the latest news on the club, squad, scores etcetera.

Martin C.Y. Lai: In Hong Kong we now see more live United games on cable than supporters in the UK see. When I first came out in the early 1990s only the Cup Finals were live – if we were lucky. We had to rely on BFBS [British Forces Broadcasting Service] radio. To be honest, I think I miss watching United live more than I miss my parents! I get back as much as I can to watch them, but they always seem to lose when I'm there!

Angus Deayton: It constitutes the perfect day for me now to go up to Manchester, watch them play and then fly down again. I'd be very happy doing that every day and wouldn't be at all bothered if I never had to set foot in a television studio again.

Voni von Arx: To me, being a United fan is really something great. People always question why you are a United fan from abroad and suggest that you are a gloryhunter. You read it all the time. We have a good fanbase at the Swiss Devils – about 100 members – it's small but it's cool and we support the team as if it is our local team. We don't mind the cost of travelling around to support United. Even though I am just 25 and am one of the youngsters, I have fantastic memories. I really started following United at the beginning of the Nineties when everything really started to be successful, and even when we don't do well I still enjoy myself. There are two sorts of people in Switzerland – some people think it's cool because I've been in I don't know how many European countries thanks to United. Others think I'm stupid. It's as simple as that. They wonder how I can follow a team that is miles away in a different country.

Ron Snellen: You don't think in terms of money or distance when you follow United. Indeed we will follow them to hell and back. No other club in Holland or the rest of the world is of any importance. The Dutch Mancunians have about 600 members and we are indeed one of the best foreign branches in the world. We're Man United! We'll never die!

Part Three:
The
Triumphs

10

Title Deeds

There have been four title-winning bursts for Manchester United. The team of pre-First World War days finished on top of the League table twice, winning the championship in 1908 by nine points and then winning it on a nerve-racking final day of the season three years later. Billy Meredith and his team-mates were then split up soon after the surprise departure of manager Ernest Mangnall in 1912.

The twentieth century had reached its middle years by the time United won their next League Championship, under the tutelage of Matt Busby in 1952. Again, this team would soon go their separate ways – Busby had managed to coax the final drops of footballing goodness out of experienced players such as Jack Rowley, Stan Pearson and Johnny Carey. This time, though, a new set of stars were ready to regenerate the club's credentials as title-winners: the Busby Babes. They would surely have triumphed in many more championships than those of 1955–56 and 1956–57 had it not been for the Munich disaster.

George Best, Bobby Charlton and Denis Law were the figureheads as the club claimed two championships in the 1960s; fine achievements but they seem scant reward domestically for a team that is rightly regarded as one of the finest in the history of British football. The club missed out narrowly on clinching the two or three further titles which would have done greater justice to their reputation.

The decade which began with United winning the first Premier League title in the 1992–93 season has seen Alex Ferguson establish United as almost the natural possessors of the League title. As each season starts, the question is less whether Manchester United can win the League title and more whether any other club can wrest it away from them. The answer has usually been a positive one for United.

Second Division Champions 1905–06 and
First Division Champions 1907–08 and 1910–11

Mark Wylie: We're quite lucky in the fact that the families of the players who got those medals have generally kept them and have loaned them to us. So we've got the captain Charlie Roberts' medals, Alex Bell's, some of Dick Duckworth's, some of George Wall's; some of the quite famous players from that era. I wish we had more from Billy Meredith, but I'm not quite sure what happened to his collection. He did have family spread all over the country and they may still have them. We've got League Championship medals from those players. They also got a promotion souvenir in 1906, which was commissioned by the club.

They also got things like Manchester Cup and Lancashire Cup medals because it wasn't quite like nowadays when there was a chance to win European medals. Local cup competitions were of quite high status, so United always put in quite a strong team for the Manchester Cup and had a lot of success in it during the opening decade of the 20th century. They'd come up against teams like City, Rochdale, Oldham; sometimes teams a bit further away, like Crewe Alexandra, who sometimes played in the Manchester Cup. The medals from the Manchester Cup are absolutely fantastic: lovely golden medals with beautiful enamelling. They actually put a bit of effort into getting a nice distinctive medal, which looks really attractive. So things like that are really nice to have on display.

First Division Champions 1951–52

Jimmy Billington: United were playing Arsenal and I think United were at the top of the table and Arsenal needed to beat United by six clear goals to win the title, but United won 6–1. Arsenal's centre-half got taken off so United ran rings round them and got the title. It wasn't a bad tackle on their centre-half, not a dirty tackle, but in those days there were no substitutes, so if you took a player off you were down to ten men.

First Division Champions 1955–56, 1956–57

Ken Ramsden: I remember when we won the League in '56 I went to a match near the end of the season with an older lad and at the final whistle we all ran on to the pitch because we had won the League – that must have been one of the earliest pitch invasions, albeit a friendly one.

Bill Foulkes: I was in the Army doing my national service at Aldershot for two years and during that time we won the Championship two years back-to-back: '55–56 and '56–57. Eddie Colman was in the Army, Duncan, Dennis Viollet, Jeff Whitefoot. I actually lost my place in the United team to Ian Greaves for a spell just at the end of the 1955–56 season because I couldn't get off duty.

I thought those teams were absolutely fantastic, I tell you, players like Eddie Colman. Nobody talks about Eddie Colman but he was a brilliant player. He was short, looked a little bit dumpy, but you would never believe he was so quick into the tackle, he was so fast, running. Roger Byrne was the only guy who could beat him and Roger was like lightning. Big Duncan had everything – he would have been the greatest player of all time if the crash at Munich hadn't happened. Roger Byrne was a brilliant full-back. Mark Jones and Jackie Blanchflower, the centre-halves, were top-class. We had Johnny Berry and Kenny Morgans, who was only 18 but was already a Welsh international, playing on the right. Johnny Berry was another international and an experienced player.

Tommy Taylor was the best header of the ball ever and one of the best centre-forwards ever. Dennis Viollet was a brilliant player and never got the credit he deserved. Albert Scanlon would have been a world-beater but for the crash. It ruined it. Ray Wood was in goal. That team would have taken over Europe, there was no question about it. We were confident.

Wilf McGuinness: The '56 and '57 teams were brilliant. I was the youngest player in that squad, Bobby Charlton was the next. I'm very proud that I was the youngest one of those great, great players. Duncan Edwards would have been the greatest all-round player that Manchester United had ever seen. Tommy Taylor was quite outstanding; he would be on the end of any ball down the flank. He led the line so well. Dennis Viollet had a great touch and was a brilliant finisher. Liam Whelan was a tall lad, with brilliant technique on the ball. He would keep a ball for ever. His and Tommy Taylor's goalscoring records – there are not many better ever than those two. Eddie Colman was just developing – most of these lads had been in the Army for two years. They would have developed into the best in the world and, believe me, I'm not exaggerating. They gave Real Madrid a run and they were only 20 or so then. Bill Foulkes and Ray Wood were supposed to be our weaknesses and Bill went on to play 700 games for United! He was supposed to be one of our weaknesses!

First Division Champions 1964–65, 1966–67

Bill Foulkes: Matt brought in people like David Herd, Denis Law and Pat Crerand, distributing the ball from midfield. It changed everything because before then we had been a team that was going nowhere fast, and it turned it right around and, again he had a League- and European Cup-winning team – and it was a really good team, although not in the same manner as the Busby Babes. It was different to the Busby Babes in that we had players who had not played much together and we also had players who were stars – Denis Law, at that time, was the best player in the world and we got him. Matt paid a record fee for him, quite rightly, and we got him. Matt did a fantastic job in getting together a really good squad of players.

Paddy Crerand had come in '63, Denis, David Herd, and then, the biggest of the lot, George Best came along. He just emerged from the ranks and Nobby Stiles came in. All of a sudden, players were springing up again and Matt had got it going again. We should have won everything, that team was so good. I was getting on and Bobby was getting on, although both of us were playing well at that time so age really didn't matter. We should have won the European Cup and FA Cup more. We got to so many semi-finals it was becoming a joke.

Everyone talks about the attacking players in that team and we did have three of the greatest forwards of all but it was the defence that held the whole thing together. Tony Dunne was a really quick left-back who quite often went forward, and Shay Brennan was a very cultured right-back. Then you had David Sadler floating across the front of the defence. We were a really good unit but the funny thing was that if one of us was out of the team, for whatever reason, the whole thing collapsed.

Wilf McGuinness: I broke my leg in December 1959 and they took me on as a coach when they realized I couldn't play, but I was also still a signed player with the club, with the opportunity of coming back. I did make a comeback in '67. Having trained with the World Cup squad in '66 I felt sure I could do better than Bobby Moore and Bobby Charlton and these players! I thought, 'If Nobby can get a game, surely I can!' But I did make a comeback in '67. I played a season in the reserves and it was the year we won the Championship and Paddy and Nobby were outstanding, as well as everybody else. So I put it down to me pushing them as a wing-half or a midfield player in the reserves.

Second Division Champions 1974–75

Chris Yeamans: I was obviously upset by relegation in '74 but I think we'd been expecting it for a while, and funnily enough there was an air of optimism around, because I think we all knew The Doc could turn it round for us – rightly, as it turned out. The season in Division Two was actually a great season to watch the Reds because we stormed the League and played some refreshingly exciting football.

Sammy McIlroy: From the first game in the Second Division, at Orient, we went on a hell of a run. We played attacking football, with two wingers and attacking midfield players. The country was talking about us and it was great to play in that side. We had to come back as champions and we did. That was on our minds, that we had to come back quickly. We felt that if we didn't get out in the first year it would be very very difficult to get out after that. We felt embarrassed at letting everyone down and that was another reason why we felt we had to get back right away. There were some great young players in that side like Steve Coppell and Stuart Pearson and Alex Stepney was there with his experience. I had some marvellous years at Old Trafford. The only regret was that I never won a First Division Championship medal.

Lou Macari: After I had been at United for a year we started to grow together as a team. When we went into the old Second Division we were winning a lot of matches, so we became a lot more confident as a team. The goals were going in and we had grown into a side that was maybe a bit too adventurous. We were not consistent enough to win the League but we were a good side for the cups.

Premier League Champions 1992–93, 1993–94

David Meek: The team that Eric Cantona came into and got hold of by the scruff of the neck and led to the Championship in 1993 would be my favourite Championship-winning team. Eric was the right man in the right place at the right time. Without Eric I think the team would have given a good account of themselves but it would have taken the young boys longer to mature into a team.

Chris Yeamans: Obviously, the '92–93 season was amazing after a 26-year wait. After our capitulation to Leeds the year before, I was wondering if we were ever going to win it.

Ken Ramsden: There's no doubt about the most memorable Championship-winning season; the first one after 26 years. That was just incredible because we had waited so long and you do seriously think, 'Will I ever see it?' Martin Edwards said afterwards, 'If I'd have known we were actually going to have to wait for 26 years I don't know whether I could have put up with it.' Each year before that you would think, 'Well, this might be our year.' So when it did happen it was just unbelievable. We won it by not playing – Villa lost at home to Oldham. We had made some plans with the Premier League to bring the trophy up here quietly in case it happened because if I remember correctly, even if Villa had won against Oldham on the Sunday, and we had beaten Blackburn on the Monday night we would have been champions anyway. So the trophy was brought up here and hidden away just in case everything did fall into place for us. Every minute of that day and night was just so memorable.

Phil Neville: I became a professional with United in '94 so although I had not been involved prior to that, when we had not won any League titles, you could tell there had been a bit of negativity surrounding the place in the years when we'd not won that League title. We'd always done well in cup competitions but the League was always the albatross around the club's neck and it was important that we got rid of that and built on it. After winning the FA Cup in 1990, the boss bought some outstanding players and they played a vital part in us winning the next couple of League Championships.

For me, the '94 team was one of the outstanding teams that this club has produced. If you look at the back four of Parker, Irwin, Bruce and Pallister, it is so solid. In midfield you had Ince, Keane, Robson and McClair and Kanchelskis and Giggs or Sharpe on the wings. Hughes and Cantona were up front. It had everything, that '94 team. It was a brilliant team and it had Peter Schmeichel, the best 'keeper this club has ever had. So I think the team had everything: pace, power and experience as well. That's probably something that was missing from our team a couple of years later, that little bit of experience, but that '94 team had everything, international caps, everything. It was a pity that

that team couldn't play in Europe because it had to be broken up because of the foreigner ruling.

Martin Edwards: The thing about the '93 and '94 sides was that Cantona was absolutely at his peak then, and I can remember you had Hughes and Cantona up front, who complemented each other. Cantona was feeding Giggs and Kanchelskis with the ball inside the full-backs and the two wingers were running riot, absolutely running riot, and I don't think anybody could quite cope with them.

Gary Neville: That was a really good team; it probably had as many strong characters in a team as Manchester United have ever had in the sense that you had the power and strength of Schmeichel, Bruce, Pallister, Keane, Ince, Robson, Hughes, Cantona. These were all really big figures in the history of Manchester United, and for one team to have so many powerful people – strong-minded as well as physically strong – created a real air of confidence around that time. To watch those players play and to watch them be successful was something that I think spurred us on and around that time, because of the European three-foreigner rule, we were actually getting opportunities to travel with them away in Europe, because you needed a lot of English players. We travelled with them many times, even in the UEFA Cup before they were in the Champions League, and we were lucky enough to be substitutes and to come on the odd time. It was a real experience for us to actually watch them play and to travel with them and see the way that they worked. To play with them was an experience in itself.

Premier League Champions 1995–96, 1996–97

Phil Neville: The first of those seasons probably stands out for me because it was my first season in the first team. At the start of the season we'd been written off by everybody because we'd sold Hughes, Kanchelskis and Ince in the summer and the young players had come into the team. Before Christmas our form had been a little bit patchy.

We'd been up and down. We'd produced good performances and then let ourselves down and people were writing us off. Then in the second part of the season we went on an unbeaten run. It was fantastic. There's no better way to win a League than to come from behind to pip a team, and that's what we did to Newcastle.

Martin C.Y. Lai: The title-winning season I enjoyed most has got to be the one when Newcastle had already 'won' it, as they were so far ahead.

Chris Yeamans: The '95–96 season was particularly special because we beat Newcastle to the title and I live in Newcastle. It was also the 'You'll-never-win-anything-with-kids' season and the emergence of Beckham, Scholes and the Nevilles. It was also a brilliant season for Cantona, when he seemed to win loads of 1–0 matches for us, the one at Newcastle being particularly memorable. Keegan loosing his cool is also a great memory. The best bit, though, was the final day of the season, when we played 'Boro away and Newcastle were at home to Spurs. I didn't have tickets for the 'Boro game so I watched the game on Sky. Thing was, I was watching it in a bloke's flat that was about 100 yards from St. James Park, so we could hear the despair of the Newcastle fans from the ground as our own joy got greater and greater. After the games ended we could lean out of the window and see thousands of Newcastle fans walk past, blubbing their eyes out. The whole town was subdued for weeks, while we were on cloud nine. Since that season, though, it has become particularly dangerous to go to a pub to watch a match and cheer for United.

Phil Neville: In '96–97 we had learnt from the season before and people weren't surprised by our performances. We won the League a little bit easier than the season before. We were leading throughout the season so it was a little bit of a smoother ride but, in saying that, it was still as enjoyable to win the competition.

When I first broke into the team and we won the double the first year and the League Championship the year after that, the quality was probably the same as the '94 team but we were probably missing the experience that the '94 team had. When the going got tough they had great mental strength because they were all probably four or five years older than us. That's probably something that we're getting now because of the experience that we have gained over the years, and hopefully we can go on to better things as well.

Premier League Champions 1998–99, 1999–2000, 2000–01, 2002–03

Voni von Arx: The best United team I've seen is the '98–99 team, the one that won the treble. I do mean every player, even the substitutes. Everyone stuck together. There were no black sheep and nobody had a bad run. That was the best team ever. The success in that season gave that team the right to be described as the best team United ever fielded.

Ken Ramsden: I remember the day after we won the Championship for the first time in 26 years. I remember walking across the car park the next day – actually, I didn't walk; I floated. I looked up at the flagpole and the Championship flag was there, and I felt so thrilled and so excited. The next year, when we won it again, I was still feeling good about it but by 2001 it was just another day and I'm ashamed to say it, but seven in nine was great and I'd love it to continue for years, but it can't have the same effect as the first one had. I think that shows you the manager's mentality, because his job is to make the players believe that every Championship they are going for is as good the first one. How he manages to do that goodness only knows, but he does because the record books show that. That's a measure of his success and it's something that even Sir Matt didn't have – he didn't have that consistency of success that Alex Ferguson has had.

Phil Neville: I think one of the secrets of our success has been that we've been able to sustain our success. That comes from the manager and the players that we have got at the place. Every season that we have won the Championship, in the following summer the boss has always gone out and bought two or three players. That has kept everyone on their toes and it sends a message out, not just to people in the Premiership but to people in the club, that we need to get better and we need to improve and every year the team has shown some kind of improvement. You need to do that to keep winning because people are there to knock us off our pedestal and still, to this day, the boss has stressed to us that we need to improve and get better and that is what we have kept doing over the last seven years. Hopefully that will continue because it needs to: teams are catching us up and teams are trying to become better than us. We need to keep improving.

After winning the two Championships in 2000 and 2001 quite convincingly, it was important that the manager went out there and bought some world-class players, especially for European football, where we'd been disappointed to go out in the quarter-final two years running. He went out and spent £48m, which was a signal to everyone in the team that your place isn't a certainty. He's bought two world-class players and they certainly helped keep us on our toes. I think the rest of the Premiership have also improved. They've spent big money and they've improved. They would have had to have done, really, because in those two years the Championship had been over by March. So they have had to improve and that has helped us improve.

Gary Neville: You look at clubs like Blackburn, who won it in '94–95, who haven't been able to sustain that level of success. They haven't been able to come back the year after, and that's the sign of a really good team; that they can come back the year after and do it again. People say, 'What motivates you to do it year after year?' Well, there's no other option at United. You either do that or you're out of the team or you're out of the club. Players have found that in the past. You have to win Championships and I think that it's something that the manager passes down to us, his determination. We go out on the pitch and try to do what he wants us to do and that's win every single game that we play.

I think that it is difficult to win a Championship for a second successive time because other teams haven't found it easy to do. If you look over the last 20 or 30 years, United and Liverpool are the only teams that have done it. So you'd have to say it takes a lot of character. You have to remotivate yourself at the start of each season and the manager always says that as soon as you've won a trophy you enjoy it that night and maybe the next day and the day after, but then your thoughts should start to switch towards what's going to happen next rather than maybe going through the summer thinking about what you've previously done. Instead, you should be thinking about what you are now going to do. I think that's something that's important, that we're able to do that. I think the first one's the big one and when you get your second one you think, 'Well, I want three. I want four.' I think probably we were lucky that when we first came there were still a lot of strong characters left from that '94 team that helped us through. So I think it's about remotivating yourself as soon as you win the last trophy.

Sir Alex Ferguson: I've always thought that the '94 team, character-wise, was the strongest; powerful guys, mentally strong, not as talented as the present squad, but what the present squad are adding and developing is that toughness. You need players with a bit of character who can get themselves out of a hole and I think a lot of them have acquitted themselves well that way. I think that the present team can continue for a long time, for a few years, at this level but I also think we have to address little areas. You start to nit-pick a little bit, actually, because everyone's trying to catch us up and they're all spending fortunes to catch us up. So therefore we have to be one step ahead.

If you built a sandcastle when you were a kid, there was always somebody trying to knock it down out of jealousy or whatever, after you had spent all that time building a beautiful sandcastle. My young brother used to do that – he'd build a beautiful sandcastle and I used to break it down, just out of devilment. So the name of the game is not to let anybody near your castle. That means you have to get the drawbridge up so that nobody gets into the castle. When you're at the top, it's "repel all boarders". That's what we have to do; that's why we always have to address improvements.

Simon Davies: At the time we won the 2002–03 championship title, it was tremendous to overtake Arsenal the way we did, having been written off by everyone but, with hindsight, I think it was a case of them losing it rather than us winning it. Yes, we went on an amazing winning run but we could only win it if Arsenal started losing, which they did. I think the win papered over the cracks to a certain extent, leaving us thinking that everything in the garden was rosy, when, in reality, it wasn't.

Eric Halsall: My memories of the 2002–03 title win take me first to that horrible day when City stuffed us 3–1 – although it probably provided the necessary wake-up call for the rest of the season. Even some of our more pampered and undermotivated 'stars' must have realised in the aftermath of that humiliation what it would have meant to real Reds. Speaking for myself, I was just glad to be a long way from all those 'Bitters' [Bitter Blues] exercising their bragging rights on the Monday morning. It was bad enough down here in the British Equatorial Midlands, where no one could understand why I didn't want to go out of the house to hear idiots making jokes about it all.

That the backlash was so comprehensive was vintage United – a 2–0 home win over Arsenal then, after an obligatory blip around Christmas time, the overhauling of Arsenal's lead – six points at the beginning of February – with wins like the 4–0 walloping of the Scousers at Old Trafford and then, within the week, the Bar Codes 6–2 at St James' Park. Running like a golden thread through it all there was Ruud's goalfest; with a club record of scoring in 10 games on the bounce and an incredible total of 44 strikes in 50 appearances in all competitions. To think that in the last couple of months of the 2004–05 season there were those halfwits – the worst sort of spoilt, Johnny-come-lately glory hunters – calling for his head because he didn't immediately start scoring after a long absence through injury.

That championship had all the ups and downs necessary for real drama – the best route to eventual triumph, for the eighth time in 11 Premiership seasons. It provided much more satisfaction than just leading from the front all the time – and was so typically United.

11

Cup Wizardry

Each of Manchester United's FA Cup Final victories has been of wider significance than of simply capturing the grand old trophy itself.

The club's first FA Cup Final triumph, in 1909, established United among the coterie of leading clubs at the time by virtue of the fact that, in many eyes, the FA Cup was still a more prestigious tournament than the newer competition for the League Championship title. Four decades later, a thrilling victory in the club's first Wembley final landed Matt Busby his first trophy as a manager and gave him credibility as a man with the ability to bring silverware to Old Trafford. His other Cup Final victory, in 1963, marked the end of the period of reconstruction after the Munich disaster and the beginning of United's Sixties successes.

Tommy Docherty's Wembley triumph over Liverpool in 1977 prevented Merseyside from gaining English football's first Treble – it also brought United their first major trophy after winning the 1968 European Cup. That FA Cup victory was expected to herald a period of great, renewed success for United. Instead, flush with victory, Docherty was prompted to reveal his affair with the United physiotherapist's wife and was dismissed by the club. Ron Atkinson was also expected to go on to build on his two exciting FA Cup victories in 1983 and 1985 by taking the title. When he failed to do so, he too left Old Trafford.

Alex Ferguson's first trophy in English football was the 1990 FA Cup. He built on that landmark victory so well that his visits to Wembley for FA Cup Finals in 1994 and 1996 brought United the first two doubles in the club's history. By 1999, when United brought home English football's first-ever Treble, the FA Cup had become a palate-freshener in advance of the more substantial fare offered by the European Cup final. It was still a grand day out for the thousands of United fans who were present, many of whom were able to cast their minds back down the years to other memorable and dramatic Wembley occasions in the club's history.

Bristol City 0 Manchester United 1

Crystal Palace, 26 April 1909

Mark Wylie: They wore a white shirt with a red diamond around the neck, like an Airdrieonians shirt, in the 1909 final and I've spoken to family representatives and said to them, 'I'm glad you've kept hold of the 1909 final shirt.' They'll reply, 'Oh yes, I used to go to bed in it. I used to use it as a nightgown.' Seriously, granddaughters and daughters would end up wearing some of the football shirts, including the Cup Final football shirts, as nightdresses because at that time there was no value attached to them. They were just football shirts.

In 1909 the club had a goat – it had been presented to Charlie Roberts by the Benson's Theatre Company. Sir Frank Benson was quite a well-known theatrical type and he presented this little pygmy goat, no more than two feet high, to Charlie Roberts and it became the club mascot. They used to take it to the pub and it would drink. After the Cup Final in 1909 it drank too much and it actually died. We've got its stuffed head because the Roberts family kept it at home – Charlie had kept the goat in his back yard when it was alive. Once it died they had the head stuffed and it's on a shield and we've got that for the museum.

Blackpool 2 Manchester United 4

Wembley, 24 April 1948

Jimmy Billington: When we won the Cup in 1948 United won every game away from home to get to the final – because they were playing at Maine Road at the time. That was what we used to boast about. We beat Villa 6–4 that season in a match that was up and down but we should have beaten them 6–0 because we were that much better than them. There was one bloke called Anderson in that team – he played at right-half. He had been on his way to play Middlesbrough reserves and they'd called him back to play Middlesbrough and from then on he didn't look back all season. He got right through to the final and got the last goal.

I went all the way down to Wembley in '48 and in '57 but didn't get in either time. The first time, I remember the Londoners called us all the names under the sun. We went through Petticoat Lane – we were just strolling through – but when they heard our accents they gave us such stick. If we'd started anything I wouldn't be here now. They didn't like us northerners. I went to Wembley Stadium on the day but I didn't have enough money to buy a ticket.

Aston Villa 2 Manchester United 1

Wembley, 4 May 1957

Jimmy Billington: In '57 we started off saving up to go to the final in the pub and if we won any raffles we gave the winnings to the treasurer. We had tickets to go down on the train and enough money for two nights in a big hotel in London and all we needed to do was find tickets but we couldn't get them anywhere. So we watched it on television at our hotel. That match, when they played Villa in that final in '57, was so bad. They played all in white and when I saw them come out all in white I thought, 'These fellows are not angels.' It just didn't look right to me – and, sure enough, they lost.

Wilf McGuinness: If we had won the Villa game we would have won the double and I came away from that game in tears, honestly, because we were so great that we should have won the Double and if the goalkeeper hadn't got injured we almost certainly would have. Don't forget, there were no substitutes then, so we had ten men. Ray Wood broke his jaw. I thought it was a foul on him by McParland. That was the first time I saw Duncan Edwards nearly lose his temper. He took three steps forward and then stopped and I'm sure he was going to hit him or tell him what he felt. Duncan was such a mild-mannered player but even he nearly lost his temper when he saw that challenge. I was in tears after that because we should have been the first team since the war to win the double. We deserved it, so I was very upset when Villa beat us.

In those days you did push into people, so I don't think McParland meant to break Ray's jaw. I think he meant to flatten him because he had no chance of getting the ball, but in those days you could charge the goalkeeper. Without that challenge they definitely wouldn't have won the Cup and Manchester United would have done.

Bolton Wanderers 2 Manchester United 0
Wembley, 3 May 1958

Sandy Busby: It was great for the club to reach the final but it was a sad situation on the day. I don't think there was a person in the place who wasn't in tears during 'Abide With Me' because of the lads that had died. It wasn't a good game. Greggy was definitely bundled into the back of the net at the second goal but Bolton probably deserved to win it. I think it was there and then that you realized just how much work had to be done if the club was to recover fully from Munich.

David Meek: My first final in 1958, when they lost to Bolton, was so dramatic that that left an indelible impression on me. It was so full of incident – that was when Nat Lofthouse scored by bundling Harry Gregg into the back of the net. That sort of thing was not particularly exceptional in that day and age; that's how goalkeepers were dealt with by centre-forwards. It wasn't the greatest performance, and obviously they were beaten, but in terms of a Cup final being great in impact I would pick that one because of the drama of Munich and rebuilding and getting to Wembley with a makeshift team and, during the final, watching the tide of emotion, that had sustained them all the way there, drain out of the players. That's why they lost the match – they were just spent, physically, mentally, emotionally spent, from the start. After all the build-up, when they got out there it was too much for them.

Wilf McGuinness: 'Fifty-eight – what a shame! I was a bit unlucky: I was just getting back to fitness after a cartilage operation. Stan Crowther played and, in a way, he held back to allow the first goal. If you see it on film, Nat would have been offside. The second goal was the bundling-in that should never have been a goal.

I think the occasion might have got to us there as well. We'd done so well, we'd played on the sympathy, but that's football. That was a sad moment for Manchester United – we deserved to win something that year as a symbol but unfortunately we didn't. We had done well enough, with Jimmy Murphy, to survive.

Leicester City 1 Manchester United 3

Wembley, 25 May 1963

Ken Ramsden: George Best was a contemporary of mine. I had been at Old Trafford for a year when he came to the club and he was a very, very quiet boy when he came. He was messing about one day on the concourse just before the Cup Final in '63 and my mum bumped into him. She said to him, 'If you do that one more time I'll tell the secretary and you won't go to Wembley.' He got a bit upset at the thought that he might not go – he was just a young boy.

Nesta Burgess: We went to all the Cup Finals. I remember in 1963 when we played Leicester we got the train down to London with the directors and somebody threw a brick through the window when we stopped at Leicester.

Wilf McGuinness: Well, we had nearly been relegated. I was one of the coaches at the time and we had had a bad season. Leicester were actually favourites – they had Gordon Banks in goal – but United showed such flair and imagination. Denis Law and Paddy had a blinder and Banksie didn't and that helped. It was a bit of a surprise because we were second-favourites for that one. So it was a thrill.

Bill Foulkes: That was a big year. That was it – we were back in the big time. We were back on top. We played some great football in that particular match. We had a really good team. We had a lot of players playing out of position, like Johnny Giles on the wing, but we had really good players who played to their best that day.

Manchester United 0 Southampton 1
Wembley, 1 May 1976

Lou Macari: It was a massive let-down – we were overwhelming favourites that year and ended up losing. Looking back, there was so much pressure on us to win. Then you have Southampton's winning goal, which some people still to this day think was offside and where the ball bounced just over Alex Stepney's hand. We didn't really have enough time to get back from that and we had lost – it was a horrible day.

Sammy McIlroy: I remember we got a corner and there was someone in front of me. Someone got a flick on the ball and it came to me so quickly that I just stuck my head out. It was just a reaction header and it hit the underside of the bar. I thought it was going in the net but the Southampton defenders got it away. They came away and then scored to win 1–0. We didn't really play on the day. We were playing magnificent football at the time but we were a young side and Southampton had a lot of experienced players – their experience helped them win the game.

Liverpool 1 Manchester United 2
Wembley, 21 May 1977

Chris Yeamans: I had broken my leg a month before the 1977 FA Cup Final – playing football, of course – and we managed to get a special pass so that we could park right outside the ground and go through a special entrance into the stadium itself. Once inside Wembley, we walked into the trophy room and there was the FA Cup itself, gleaming away in a big glass cabinet. I missed seeing our two goals in that Cup Final, because as the ball got near to the goal everyone would stand up. With me being on crutches, it took me an extra few seconds to get to my feet, by which time the ball was in the back of the net. It was the first trophy we'd won – apart from the Second Division Championship – since 1968, and it came after the huge disappointment of losing it the year before to Southampton. And, of course, it was against Liverpool and it stopped them winning the Treble. After the game, my dad and I returned jubilantly to the car. My mum had come down with us and sat in the car listening to it on the radio. When we arrived at the car my mum was stood outside it with a couple of policemen, looking a bit shocked. The car bonnet and roof had huge dents in them. Some over-excited Man United fans had decided to stage a celebration on our car while my mum was still in it.

Lou Macari: Twelve months later it was a complete reversal. We were not expected to win but this time we had the good fortune on the day. The winning goal was really bizarre. I remember it being chipped on from the midfield and I flicked it up over Emlyn Hughes and then made my way into the penalty box and struck it and I couldn't have told you where the ball went because everything all happened so quickly, and next thing I knew it was in the back of the net. At full-time I expected to collect the golden boot for the player who scores the winning goal in the Cup Final. You see, back then there were no big loudspeakers or anything booming out the name of the player who scores a goal so I thought I had scored that goal. I couldn't believe it when Jimmy Greenhoff got it. Every time I see Jimmy I keep asking him for that boot back.

Sammy McIlroy: Liverpool were going for the Treble and everyone thought we were just going along to make up the numbers. Liverpool were a fantastic side and beating them made up for the disappointment of the year before. When you think about Liverpool, there was always a great rivalry between them and us. They had won the Championship, were in the European Cup final and had all the experience in the world. They were on a great run and we were still a young side and just becoming experienced. When they equalized I thought they'd get stronger and go on and win it, but we got the bit of luck with Lou Macari's shot coming off Jimmy Greenhoff and flying into the net.

Arsenal 3 Manchester United 2

Wembley, 12 May 1979

Martin C.Y. Lai: Unfortunately the 1979 loss to the Arsenal is the most memorable Cup Final for me. I wasn't there as I was only nine but I remember it clearly. At 2–0 we were down and out. Suddenly it's 2–2 and for sure we're going to win it. Next minute we're 3–2 down. My plate of boiled potatoes, ham and beetroot went everywhere! I climbed the apple tree in the back garden and cried for the next two hours. Mum was close to calling the police as she couldn't find me!

Sammy McIlroy: In that game we were out of it with three minutes to go. When we equalized I thought it was going into extra time and when I saw the faces of my Northern Irish friends on the Arsenal side – Sammy Nelson, Pat Rice and Pat Jennings – they were all dejected. I thought that in extra-time we could do it. We had a couple of attempts to bring Brady down as he went up the field and Gary Bailey made a hash of the cross that Alan Sunderland put in the net. We went from joy to absolute deflation. It was like winning the pools but forgetting to post your coupon.

Brighton and Hove Albion 2 Manchester United 2

Wembley, 21 May 1983

Brighton and Hove Albion 0 Manchester United 4

Wembley, 26 May 1983

Martin Edwards: It was very exciting because the last trophy we had won before that was in '77. So we had gone six years before winning the Cup in '83. Ron had bought very heavily in his first season and I think it was exciting because you could actually see the fruits. You could see what was happening; you could see the team taking shape. He'd bought some very exciting players. Stapleton had come in, Gidman had come in and Remi Moses and Bryan Robson and Arnie Muhren. Wilkins had come in at the back end of my father's time with the club. So actually we had quite an exciting team. Norman Whiteside was just coming through as a junior then. So I was pleased when we beat Brighton because I felt we had an exciting team and I could see a rosy future.

Everton 0 Manchester United 1

Wembley, 18 May 1985

Martin Edwards: It was a very, very close game and then, of course, Kevin Moran got sent off and I thought at that stage that Everton were favourites. They had already won the League that year and they won the Cup-Winners' Cup that season. The thing I remember about that was that when Kevin got sent off it didn't seem to affect us at all. If anything, we started to flow a bit more and it was a great goal by Norman that won it. So I think there was great satisfaction in beating the League champions and in the manner that we did it. I thought we showed a lot of guts on the day in coming back to win it with ten men.

Crystal Palace 3 Manchester United 3

Wembley, 12 May 1990

Crystal Palace 0 Manchester United 1

Wembley, 17 May 1990

Sir Bobby Charlton: Alex was long-term from the start. He said it would take three or four years and the directors never doubted for a moment that he was right. Even though the odd ones started screaming when Man United weren't winning and that his job was in jeopardy when we played in the Cup at Nottingham, it was nonsense. It was never even mentioned by any director because it was going to be right. As it turned out, he took the club to victory in the Cup Final that year. Once it happened, then you just build on it and the past dozen years have been just magic. Over this last dozen years I've never watched a team that has thrown the towel in; they go at it all the time.

Greg Dyke: When we drew with Crystal Palace in the FA Cup Final and then won 1-0 it was the weekend my father was dying and I couldn't go to the Cup Final. I stayed with my dad, who was then unconscious, and I remember vividly rushing in and out of the room next door to watch the Cup Final. Then he died, and I remember going to the replay and feeling pretty sorry about the world, and we won 1-0.

Chelsea 0 Manchester United 4
Wembley, 14 May 1994

Keith Kent: At that time the head groundsman at Wembley was a guy called Steve Tingley, who was a big friend of mine, and he was a Chelsea fanatic. We were playing Chelsea for the double and he rang me. I didn't go to the Cup Final because I was working. I know that sounds daft but my pitch means more to me than the Cup Final. About two o'clock my phone rang and it was Steve Tingley and he said, 'You're going to win.' I said, 'Why?' He said, 'It's belting down with rain.' He said, 'You're going to win, aren't you, because it's wet?' If you remember, it was so wet the lines were almost washed out. It just threw it down and we absolutely battered them 4–0; pass, pass, pass, pass, pass.

Ken Ramsden: I really enjoyed the Chelsea Cup Final because it was unusual for a big match. Football fans are so perverse, aren't they? At any big match football fans can't wait for the match to start and then they can't wait for it to finish. At that game, when we got to 3–0 I just turned to my family and I said, 'Right, relax. Just sit back and enjoy yourselves because we've won the Cup.' You can't often say that during the game. For those few minutes it was bliss because at 3–0 so late on in the game we had won the Cup. Even at 2–0 we might have worried about them scoring a goal but at 3–0 it was over. The fourth goal was a bonus.

Liverpool 0 Manchester United 1

Wembley, 11 May 1996

Jonathan Deakin: At the 1996 Cup Final we hardly watched the match – we just sang and sang 'Down by the Riverside', knowing we'd already won the League.

Ken Ramsden: The '96 final was memorable, perhaps because it was against Liverpool. It hadn't been a good game and you couldn't really see a goal coming and then when it did come it was an absolute pearl and it was scored by the man himself – Cantona. His execution of the goal was just perfect. It was a double-winning year so that added to it.

Martin C.Y. Lai: Since I have been in Hong Kong the most outstanding Cup Final is the one in the '96 double season. We were watching it in a sports bar with about 1,000 people inside, of whom about 800 hated United. My mate jumped up on stage and kissed Eric's face on the huge projection screen that we were watching it on. He got pelted with glasses and stuff – plastic ones, fortunately. Wild celebrations followed.

Manchester United 2 Newcastle United 0

Wembley, 22 May 1999

Angus Deayton: The whole end of that season was kind of astonishing. People forget that we were drawn against top-five opposition in almost every round. We beat Arsenal and Liverpool. It was a really tough FA Cup campaign that year and then there was the Arsenal semi-final: it was extraordinary as well that we should ever have won that, and with such a goal. So that whole season was like someone had sprinkled fairy-dust over those three cups.

Wilf McGuinness: Keano getting injured and Sheringham coming on; it was the best 11 days in Sheringham's life, I would have thought, what he did for Manchester United.

Paul Hardman: The FA Cup Final in the year we won the Treble was almost a formality. We had won the League and we had the European Cup final to come and if we were going to win the Treble we had to win the Cup Final as part of it. Normally I would see the Cup Final as a big day out, but because of the circumstances it was not an FA Cup Final in its own right any more. You weren't really interested in it for its own sake but because it was part of a bigger picture. I went down with someone who was at that time involved in MUTV. They were interested in obtaining interviews with people after the match but, for me, as soon as the final was over I was straight back up the road. I didn't even really bother with watching them pick up the Cup and do their lap of honour. It was just a case of: 'get back in the car, get back up the road and get packed and ready to go to Barcelona'. Even before the Cup Final everybody had been thinking about getting to Spain the following week and whether they would be able to get tickets for the European Cup final.

Manchester United 3 Millwall 0

Cardiff, 22 May 2004

Roy Williamson: The Millwall final was an excellent day out. Winning the Cup and Ronaldo's performance made the day special. Remember, when United opted out of the Cup it was to help the FA's bid for the World Cup. A lot of nonsense has been written since, though at the time United's directors should have told the FA where to get off; the FA Cup is sacrosanct, ask any match-going Red. I have to say that the Millwall and United fans were a credit on the day, we spent a few hours prior to the game, relaxing, having a drink amidst fans of both clubs. Winning the FA Cup will always be special – I had to wait 15 years before I was present to see them lift the Cup in '77. I would never take winning the Cup for granted.

Eric Halsall: OK, it's always good to win the FA Cup – at least it is to me, an old codger who still sees it as a special trophy. I still haven't forgiven my mum for not taking me with her to Wembley in 1948 because I was only eight. Naturally, it was good to rescue something from the season and to get a record 11th Cup but the final wasn't quite the climax that you always hope for: apart from Ronaldo's performance and Ruud's unselfish generosity in giving him the Man-of-the-Match trophy that he had so richly deserved in everyone's eyes other than the judges'.

Adam Bostock: Any Cup Final victory is good: the easier the win, the better on the nerves. With a really tight game such as the 1–0 over Liverpool, when Cantona scored the only goal late on, you can only enjoy it when it's all over. The 3–0 over Millwall and the 4–0 over Chelsea in 1994 were very enjoyable, from start to finish.

Simon Davies: It was a foregone conclusion, wasn't it? The real final was our semi-final win against Arsenal and I think you could tell that from the photos of the players celebrating in the dressing room afterwards.

Sir Alex Ferguson: When we didn't enter the FA Cup in 2000 we were dismissed as sidelining it but that wasn't the case: it was to do with helping England to try and get the World Cup and we were supporting the government and the FA in that. We've won the Cup more than any other club in the country and that tells you how much it's worth to Manchester United. It's a special tournament and I've never viewed it in any way other than that. In '99, against Arsenal, people forget I left out five players and we had to do that to take into account all the matches in which the players were involved, but it was not through any lack of respect for the FA Cup.

We didn't like getting knocked out by Barnsley in the year they eliminated us after we had rested several players but we had to do things like that. When you rest players in a League game, does that mean the Premier League is not important? People here at Manchester United believe that any cup is a priority. If we win a trophy year to year, we view that as success; we're not greedy. Hopefully, that trophy will be the European Cup; if not, then there is the League trophy and the FA Cup. There are eight great football clubs in this country: Newcastle United, Arsenal, Tottenham, the two Manchester clubs, Liverpool, Everton and Aston Villa; and you would now have to add Chelsea to those clubs, although you wouldn't have included them a few years ago. Every one of those clubs wants to win a trophy, so if you win one that's brilliant and that applies to the FA Cup.

Arsenal 0 Manchester United 0

(Arsenal won on penalties 5–4) Cardiff, 21 May 2005

Tony Whelan: Losing the FA Cup Final to Arsenal was so disappointing and you could see that disappointment on the faces of everyone who went down to Cardiff with the United party. We were so unlucky in that game, played so well and had so many chances but could not get the breakthrough. Arsenal did well in the penalty shootout – several of their penalty kicks were excellent and that is part of the game – but I see no reason why there should not be a replay after the first match if the FA Cup Final is drawn. If the teams then play a second game and are still level at the end of that one, then penalties might be the best way to settle it, but I think it is maybe worth thinking about bringing back replays.

Simon Davies: I don't know why they scrapped replays, although, having said that, I wouldn't fancy sitting through another two hours of United dominating the other team and failing to score. To say it was frustrating is a huge understatement and I really can't see the benefit of playing five across midfield and one up front – particularly when Wayne Rooney is one of those five. Until someone comes up with a better idea for settling drawn matches, I guess we're stuck with penalties. Golden and Silver goals didn't really seem fair to me, but with both teams knowing that the match will go to penalties at the end of 120 minutes, it's fairer. And, to be honest, Cup-final replays always seemed a bit of an anti-climax for me when I was younger – you want a winner on the day, really. The fans who've gone all the way to Cardiff do, anyway.

We were unlucky but you make your own luck to an extent and not converting one of our many chances meant that it wasn't to be. It was the story of the season: playing well, dominating teams but failing to find the net enough. United fans are used to exciting, mesmerising, flowing football, with lightning-fast counter-attacks. It hasn't been like that for a while now and I, for one, miss it.

It was hard watching Arsenal's post-match celebrations but to be honest it would have been hard watching whoever had beaten us – I'm not sure it was any worse because it was Arsenal. Because there was none of the needle that everyone had been expecting, there wasn't much to get upset about. They won it fair and square on penalties and United only have themselves to blame for not scoring. I was more upset about that than Arsenal winning it, I think.

It was just a frustrating game, overall. To know we could and should have beaten them easily over the 90 minutes is disappointing but when Ruud's header was cleared off the line you just knew it was going to be one of those days.

12

Nights to Remember

Manchester United took on the role of pioneers in the 1950s when they defied convention and the wishes of the Football League to embrace European competition. Matt Busby saw European football as the future for his club and his vision led to numerous marvellous, unscripted dramas over the following five decades. Extra drama is added to European occasions through them being played midweek: the green rectangle of turf becomes even more sharply focussed by floodlights and looks even more than ever like a stage set for high drama.

It is the European Cup that has held special enchantment for Manchester United. The club has enjoyed participating in the other European tournaments – the Fairs Cup, the UEFA Cup and the Cup-Winners' Cup – but these have always been seen as primers for the main attraction, the tournament whose testing struggles against Europe's elite have done so much to forge the identity of the modern United.

The club's character was also tested severely by the 1968 World Club Championship matches between the champions of Europe and South America. United had come across underhand tactics in European football but none so vicious as those perpetrated by the Argentinian side Estudiantes. By 1999, when United faced Palmeiras of Brazil, that trophy was played for in a one-off game in Tokyo rather than over two legs. United's 1–0 victory saw them become the first British club to take the World Club Cup.

United have also suffered lengthy absences from Europe. They were out for five years after the Munich disaster. A lack of League and Cup success saw them miss out on European competition between 1969 and 1976. Then the ban on English clubs participating in European competition left United to concentrate on domestic issues between 1985 and 1990.

Every European tie is filled with intrigue. Especially in the early days of competition, little would be known about the opposition so the match in prospect could produce any amount of surprises. Certain games, however, stand out as being crucial to United's progress in European competition, from the clashes with Real Madrid, Red Star Belgrade and AC Milan before and after the Munich disaster up to the outstanding performances of the past decade in the Champions League.

Anderlecht 0 Manchester United 2
European Cup first round, Parc Astrid, 12 September 1956

Manchester United 10 Anderlecht 0
European Cup first round, Maine Road, 26 September 1956

Bill Foulkes: At the time of our very first game in Europe, against Anderlecht, we had a good team. We were quite confident. We weren't feeling as if we were going into Europe and we were second-best. We knew we had a good team, a young one. We were full of confidence and it showed, because Anderlecht were a good team; they were supposed to be one of the best in Europe, and we went out and we attacked them when it was right. We attacked them and we scored two goals and we won the game. It was 2–0 and there wasn't a lot of trouble at the back for us. I remember Mermans, the centre-forward, was one of the best in Europe and he hardly got a kick at the ball. Mark Jones obliterated him. So that gave us a lot of confidence.

The second game was unbelievable because we beat them 10–0. We played at City because there were no floodlights at Old Trafford in those days. We destroyed one of the best teams in Europe. We thought, 'It can't be that easy.' Matt wouldn't allow us to get over-confident after that game and he was right to do that, because we later came up against some really good teams. Matt was a psychologist long before you had ever heard of it! He was a manager, a coach and a psychologist all in one. I don't think anybody realized it, maybe not even himself, but that's the way he was. He'd speak in that quiet voice; he'd very rarely raise his voice. He had a nice quiet voice with its Scots twang, and you listened. You had to, just because of his presence and the way he did things. He made sure we were convinced after that game that European football couldn't be that easy.

Sir Bobby Charlton: Unfortunately I had to do my National Service like everybody else. For two years I was away. There was all this paradise here and I was down in Shropshire in a little camp doing something that I thought was an absolute waste of time, but there you go. Even then, Duncan Edwards and I were in the same camp and we used to come back on the half-past-five train from Shrewsbury to Manchester every Friday night. Then we'd get the midnight train back and change at Crewe and get in at half-past-four on the Monday morning. It kept me going.

When the European games started, in the first year we played Anderlecht, and Chalky White, who was the Regimental Sergeant-Major of the company, was a United supporter from Edinburgh. He said to me, 'I know somebody who's got a car.' Nobody had a car in those days. He said, 'If you can get the tickets I'll get us off.' So I got on the phone and got the tickets arranged. So we drove up and we saw United beat Anderlecht 10–0. And then you go back to the camp and all the ones from the South are saying, 'Bloody lucky! You were playing a load of nonsense.'

Atletico Bilbao 5 Manchester United 3
European Cup quarter-final, Estadio San Mames, 16 January 1957

Manchester United 3 Atletico Bilbao 0
European Cup quarter-final, Maine Road, 6 February 1957

Wilf McGuinness: Away to Bilbao we had been 5–2 down when Liam Whelan scored after a wonderful dribble, in snow. It rains in Spain, it snowed in Spain, on the plane. In the return we needed three goals to win, at Maine Road, because at Maine Road they had floodlights and we didn't. That stood out as the game with the greatest atmosphere from start to finish that I have ever seen. We beat them 3–0.

Ken Merrett: I can remember coming to Old Trafford to get the tickets because they were on sale here, although the match was at Maine Road, and the queue went down over the Salford Bridge and there used to be a railway ran along Trafford Road – the railway lines were there for quite some time – and we queued right down there and it was a very slow, long process. It must have been a Sunday sale. I remember getting the tickets and being very excited at the prospect of going to the game. The noise was non-stop as they pulled the goals back. I wanted United to win, even though I was a City supporter. That was the difference, then.

Jimmy Billington: The most exciting one ever was when they played Bilbao at Maine Road. From the kick-off the roar carried on right through the match, no matter what movement United made. When they got that third goal, Austin's the cap-makers must have been cheering too because so many lost their hats by throwing them up in the air. You couldn't see the sky because of all the caps and hats being thrown up in celebration – but nobody cared about losing their hat that night. A book called The Red Devils came out and in that book Bill Foulkes said the crowd at the Bilbao game was worth a goal.

Sir Bobby Charlton: We went to see them play Bilbao at Maine Road. We had lost 5–3 in the first match in Bilbao and they won the return 3–0. It was maybe the most exciting game I've ever seen: just magical. It was real Man United stuff, just like today, the way they go for it.

Real Madrid 3 Manchester United 1

European Cup semi-final, Bernabeu Stadium, 11 April 1957

Manchester United 2 Real Madrid 2

European Cup semi-final, Old Trafford, 25 April 1957

Sir Alex Ferguson: I always remember well when they got to the semi-final with Real Madrid in '57. Everybody was entranced by this great young Manchester United team going to play Real Madrid. At that time Real Madrid had an open stadium and I always remember seeing photographs of the crowd stretching up to the top of this massive stadium; it was some sight. These pictures are vivid in my mind. Real Madrid were just starting to get that romantic footballing team together, the one with Di Stefano and Puskas and Gento. They were unbelievable players – I was at the '60 European Cup final at Hampden when they beat Eintracht Frankfurt 7–3. Eintracht had put 12 goals past Rangers in the semi-finals so we thought they were gods and then they got slaughtered at Hampden. So we were thinking, 'What kind of team is this Real Madrid?' They were way ahead of their time, Real Madrid, when you think about it. Puskas was Hungarian, Kopa was French, Di Stefano was Argentinian. Only now, 50 years later, are we getting foreign players into the country. It's quite remarkable.

Bill Foulkes: When we first went into Europe I was doing my National Service. I was based at Aldershot and was captain of the Army team. I trained every day and trained various teams. So when we played at Real Madrid, because I was in the Army, I only got £7 from the club as an allowance – for playing against Real Madrid. The normal rate wasn't too clever – about £12 to £15 – but because I was doing my National Service the club were only allowed to pay me £7. There were about 130,000 people in the stadium and we lost 3–1 to one of the greatest teams ever. We learned so much from that.

Jackie Blanchflower was a good player – he could play anywhere. In this particular match he played at centre-half. He was a good centre-half, very good in the air. He looked a bit fat and a bit plump but he timed the ball well. He tried to nutmeg Di Stefano – to do that to him! – but he did it. Jackie was cheeky like that, he was clever with the ball. So he nutmegged Di Stefano and as he was going past, Di Stefano just clobbered him – he took him right through, all in one movement, you know. Jack went down and I was walking past him and he said, 'Hey, Foulkesy, have a word with him.' That's just what he said. And Di Stefano was a little bit worried about it. So I just went over to him and before I could say anything, he put his hands out and said, 'Foulk-ez – excuse.' He was saying, 'I'm sorry.' So I didn't have to say anything to him. He said it himself. He was a great player.

Sir Bobby Charlton: Matt took me to Madrid for the semi-final. In those days there were no substitutions and I was a reserve and so I didn't stay on the touchline. I remember being up in the stand right at the top, looking down, and we lost 3–1 and it was really Di Stefano's doing. He was just magic. It was like watching a Subbuteo game and I thought, 'Who's he? He's always got the ball. He takes it from the goalkeeper, he takes it from the full-back...' I'd never seen anything like it because we'd never seen them on television. This was a brand-new experience, playing against this quality of player.

I got picked for the second match here. We were a bit naïve. We didn't know how to go on tactically in Europe. It wasn't in our make-up to play defensive football. We played here in the second leg and we thought, 'We pulled three back against Bilbao. Why can't we pull three back here?' And the crowd thought we could do it, you know. And we were two down before we realized it; they just hit us on the break. It was a type of football we had not seen but your pride gets hurt a little bit and we piled on, and suddenly we got to grips with it all and we started playing. We got two back with about five minutes to go. If there had been another ten minutes we might actually have tied it up but it was so exciting. It was what everybody talks about – great European nights. Now it's not so sudden death, with the league system, so people say 'if you don't win this one, you'll win the next one', but, in those days, if you lost that was the end of it. They were brilliant days and it's the same now. We had a period when we were never in it and we missed it.

Sir Alex Ferguson: I think for United to have such a young team and go there and do so well in a semi-final is amazing. I remember they lost 3–1 over there and drew 2–2 in Manchester. It just tells you what the potential of the team was. That penetrated up to Scotland and I don't think it had anything to do with Sir Matt, really. Yes, everyone was hoping that Matt would win but I think it was more that they were playing Real Madrid in a semi-final with a young team like that. They were all kids, weren't they? It was fantastic.

I've spoken to Bobby quite a lot about that era and certainly Taylor, Edwards, Colman and Pegg were obviously fantastic players and they weren't even near their peak. Taylor was 26, Edwards was 22, Colman was 21 and Pegg was 22. That's startling. We've signed the boy Forlan, who's 22, from Argentina and we're saying he'll be all right in a few years' time. It puts it into perspective – and that was in an era when players would spend five years in the reserves before getting into the first team. At the time when I was a boy, Rangers had an outside-left called McCulloch who was understudy to Waddell for about seven years! Time and time again you would have spent five years in the reserves in those days. So for United to produce a team that could get to the semi-final of the European Cup and play Real Madrid, and for the scoreline to have been so close, it's hard to reason any other way than that they would have been the best team ever. There are too many bits of evidence there that tell you this was an exceptional team.

Manchester United 2 Red Star Belgrade 1

European Cup quarter-final, Old Trafford, 14 January 1958

Red Star Belgrade 3 Manchester United 3

European Cup quarter-final, Stadion JNA, 5 February 1958

Bill Foulkes: The game we played at home, I remember they had a big, blond centre-forward and a brilliant midfielder – only a little guy – who caused us a lot of trouble here at Old Trafford. They were a good all-round side and they caused us lots of trouble but we controlled the game and got one goal ahead of them. We knew it was going to be a tough game over there but in Belgrade, as a team, we played football on the day that was absolutely out of this world. We were three up before they had even seen what we were doing and they were flabbergasted.

I had some terrible experiences in Europe with referees – blatant fraud – and this was one, Red Star. He gave two penalties, one against me when I beat the guy to the ball on the edge of the box and he got hold of me and dragged me down. It was that centre-forward; he dragged me down and the referee gave a penalty-kick. It was unbelievable. Then one of their players was on the ball, hit it against somebody and the referee gave a penalty for handball; penalty-kick and they scored again. So it was 3–3 and there was about half an hour to go, but fortunately we held on. We were on the rack after having dominated and having played terrific football. Fortunately, Greggy had a really good match. Dennis Viollet and Bobby Charlton scored our goals and they were brilliant goals, well-worked, beautiful goals. The referee couldn't disallow them!

Their players were ready for fighting – they had great fighting spirit because they hated to lose. They would do anything to win and they were doing it, including cheating. There were over 100,000 people in the stadium – it was an unbelievable atmosphere – but we got through. We won the tie through the goals we got in Manchester.

Manchester United 2 AC Milan 1

European Cup semi-final, Old Trafford, 8 May 1958

AC Milan 4 Manchester United 0

European Cup semi-final, San Siro, 14 May 1958

Bill Foulkes: After the crash we came back by boat and Jimmy Murphy got a team together. I went with him once to sign Stan Crowther and also little Ernie Taylor from Blackpool, whose son had just been killed in a car crash. So his wife was delighted he would have something to take his mind off what had happened. So he came over to Manchester and played with us and he was brilliant. He would get the ball and distribute, get the ball and distribute. Whenever we were in trouble we would give him the ball and he was brilliant. We got a team together and we played in the semi-final of the European Cup with that team. We played AC Milan here at Old Trafford with that team. Ernie Taylor couldn't run, I was mixed up, and Harry Gregg, brave as a lion, was playing. Along with a lot of youngsters, youth team players, we beat AC Milan 2–1 at Old Trafford, which was unbelievable. There were 60,000 inside and there must have been 30,000-odd outside. I tell you, we might have done it over there but we were robbed. They got two penalty-kicks for nothing. They scored one goal where the fellow dragged it down with his hand and slotted it. The referee allowed it – it was unbelievable. In fact, I very nearly walked off. It was so blatant, but I was the captain. I felt like walking off because it was disgraceful. I played a few times in Spain and never felt that corruption but as soon as I stepped out on the pitch in Italy I could feel it.

Sporting Lisbon 5 Manchester United 0

European Cup-Winners' Cup quarter-final, Estadio Jose Alvalade, 18 March 1964

Bill Foulkes: We had a meeting in Lisbon before the Sporting game with the boss and Mr Edwards, who was very generous, to ask for a bonus and we were promised one – a good bonus as well. Then we went out and played like a bunch of idiots and went down 5–0. Like any good manager would do, Matt reacted angrily and that was the start of a whole new set of players coming in. Nobby came into the team after that and I'd have to say that the following five years – '64 to '69 – were the most enjoyable of my entire football career. I thought, when I saw him come in, and looked at the height of him, 'Oh, here we go, I'd better make sure I win everything in the air now.' But it was great to play alongside him – he was a great reader of the game.

Manchester United 3 Ferencvaros 2
Fairs Cup final, Old Trafford, 31 May 1965

Ferencvaros 1 Manchester United 0
Fairs Cup final, Nep Stadion, 6 June 1965

Ferencvaros 2 Manchester United 1
Fairs Cup final, Nep Stadion, 16 June 1965

Sir Bobby Charlton: That was the Fairs Cup. Well, we had a bit of a problem with that. The Danube was flooded and you couldn't go directly into Hungary. You had to fly to Vienna and then you had to go by bus because there were no air services at that time. We drew over two legs and in those days you had to play another game and you tossed for where it was. We had gone all that way and we lost the toss so we had to go to play one match and then go back to play another match the following week and the Danube was flooded and it took us about seven hours by bus, trying to find our way through to Budapest. We got there and they beat us. It was all right but it wasn't the top competition. I think we felt that at the time, the only thing was the European Cup. That was where the big lads were, you know, no question about that. If the Fairs Cup is there for you to go and win, you go and try to win it. The fans love it but, at the end of the day, you beat the best in the European Cup. When you are in the Fairs Cup or the UEFA Cup you don't actually beat the best, do you? It's still a good tournament and it's good for the game and it gives people the chance to see more exciting matches.

Benfica 1 Manchester United 5
European Cup quarter-final, Stadium of Light, 9 March 1966

Roy Williamson: I thought they should have won it in '66 when we beat Benfica 5–1 and Best scored three. My brother was listening to it downstairs on the radio and when he shouted up that we were 3–0 up after 20 minutes I thought he was pulling my leg.

Bill Foulkes: We had a meeting before the Benfica game and it was agreed that Denis should come back into midfield to help out. Denis would normally float about looking for chances. You should have seen his face when it was suggested but he did it – he was up and down the pitch all night – and it worked. We had loads of space to play in that night. Maybe we should have done more of that – players tend to rely on the manager a lot and should take responsibility on themselves.

Partizan Belgrade 2 Manchester United 0
European Cup semi-final, Stadion JNA, 13 April 1966

Manchester United 1 Partizan Belgrade 0
European Cup semi-final, Old Trafford, 20 April 1966

Roy Williamson: They were fantastic that year – they should have won it but Partizan knocked them out in the semis. I thought we underperformed in the two games against them, particularly away. That's one of the best sides I've seen. I thought we were at our peak then – George, Denis, Bobby and Pat Crerand – everybody was playing really well, whereas two years later I think some of the players had kind of gone off a bit.

Bill Foulkes: We were twice the team they were. We had murdered teams like that, you know, teams like Partizan and Sarajevo.

Cliff Butler: Nobby Stiles scored off Soskic, the goalkeeper, late on. That was our fourth semi-final and you started to think we would always be semi-finalists.

Real Madrid 3 Manchester United 3
European Cup semi-final, Bernabeu Stadium, 15 May 1968

Bill Foulkes: In '67 I got a really bad injury – a cruciate ligament injury. I didn't get it through playing football; I was fooling around in the gym, wrestling with Brian Kidd, and I did my cruciate ligaments and I thought, 'That's it.' I was 36 years old and I really thought that was the end of my career. I kept training; I wouldn't have an operation. They asked me to have an operation and I said, 'No, just leave it.' So I trained and I got very fit, training every day, morning, afternoon and night, weights, running, and the boss came up to The Cliff one day. One afternoon he came up and watched me training. He said, 'I think you're ready for a game, Bill, because you're looking really fit.' I said, 'Yes, I am fit, but I can't stop and turn.' He said, 'We'll give you a game and see how it goes.'

Well, I played but I didn't move. I had Nobby Stiles in front of me and Tony Dunne at the back of me. High balls I could go for and get but I wasn't too happy. Anyway, City won the League; we came second. The following week, he said, 'Do a bit more training and I think you'll be ready to play at Real Madrid.' This was the semi-final of the European Cup and there was no way I could play. So I told him so. He said, 'Just see how it goes.' Now I had done this before with him. I had played when I was injured. I had played when I had had a damaged shoulder; I'd played with two broken ribs. I had played. So I thought, 'Here we go again.' This time, though, it was really bad. I did play in the game, though, and we came in at half-time and we had been murdered.

The defence had played well; Alex Stepney had had a brilliant game but we had seen nothing of our attack. The goal that we had got in the first-half was an own goal from their centre-half, Zoco. We were just stopping them about 30 yards from goal but they got in and they got three goals before half-time and we were 3–1 down. That was when Real Madrid made a big mistake – they decided that that was it. They didn't make many mistakes but they made a big mistake that day. They decided that we were beaten – you could see it – and they gave us a bit of space to play in. Bobby Charlton came into the game and George Best started to come into the game. They had been kicking hell out of him all night. Brian Kidd started to get confidence. Things started to move a bit and we started to play. We got a corner-kick and I went on the near post and got a touch, David Sadler went up to head it but he misjudged it, it hit him on the shoulder and went in the net; 3–2 on the night and 3–3 on aggregate.

I don't know why Real Madrid allowed us the space to play because we had some good players in our team. With about 20 minutes to go I felt as if they weren't playing and we weren't doing anything and I could see Paddy Crerand on the halfway line with the ball. I could see two players still on George because two marked him all night; he didn't get a kick.

I thought, 'If I make a run and pull somebody away from George, something might happen.' I had scored a few goals – not many, but I had scored a few. In fact, I had scored one against Fulham from a cross from George when we had beaten Fulham 2–1 here at Old Trafford the previous season. With my dodgy left knee I went on a slow run. I said to Nobby, 'Stay here. Don't move from here.' He said, 'Where are you going?' I said, 'Just don't move from here.'

So I jogged forward, Paddy threw the ball to George, the cover came off, and George was away, beating one, two, three. He came to cross the ball and looked up and saw me; I was the only United player in the box. He couldn't believe it; I could see it. You could see it in his face. I thought he wasn't going to cross it or pass it. I thought he was going to shoot because it was me in the box. So I thought I would get in closer to get the rebound, but he crossed the ball. It was the most gorgeous pass. He knew what he was doing. As he feinted, I could see what he was doing and I just withdrew quickly. The ball came to me and the only thing was it was on my left foot. So I turned my body, got across the ball and hit it with the outside of my right foot, which was even better really, when you think about it, because it just sliced inside the post and went in. Silence – you could hear nothing. The entire ground went absolutely quiet until all of a sudden everybody was on top of me and then I was scared in case somebody hurt my knee. And who was there but Nobby Stiles? I said to him, 'Didn't I tell you to stay up there?'

People have asked me, 'What were you doing up there?' I'll tell you now, I've got no idea. It was just something that happened and I can't explain it. I shouldn't have been playing in the first place because I was injured and I played nearly 700 games and only scored nine goals although I had, as a junior, played at centre-forward and scored a lot of goals. Matt had tried me out as a centre-forward because he had seen something and I had scored 16 goals in the reserve team at centre-forward. I scored four in one game against Newcastle and that's when he decided to give me a chance in the first-team at centre-forward. Fortunately, I was injured, because I don't think I'd have liked being a centre-forward. It was Jimmy Murphy who convinced him I was a defender, not a centre-forward.

Estudiantes 1 Manchester United 0
World Club Championship, Bombonera Stadium, 25 September 1968

Manchester United 1 Estudiantes 1
World Club Championship, Old Trafford, 16 October 1968

Bill Foulkes: We played Estudiantes in that World Championship and it was a farce. We went over there and, I'll tell you, we weren't allowed to tackle anyone. Matt told us. He said, 'Look, don't tackle. Stay off, just run off them. If you are anywhere near the box, don't go in and tackle because they'll get a penalty-kick.' We beat them on the offside trap, which they were using a lot. We worked it out and they didn't expect Nobby to break but he did it perfectly and he was clean through, one on one with the goalie, and the referee blew for offside. Nobby just put his arms out by his sides as a gesture and was sent off. So we had ten men and they cheated us. We scored a goal. David Sadler scored a goal from a corner-kick and they disallowed it. He gave a goal that was absolutely unbelievable. The player brought it down with his hand. We had the same thing most of the times we played in Italy. I think I'd have retired if it had been like that here – fortunately it wasn't.

Cliff Butler: We knew what was going to happen. Celtic had had it the year before with Racing Club in three matches. I didn't go to Argentina but I saw these silvery pictures on the television, and some of the things that happened were terrible.

You knew it was going to be a battle here. It was a total disappointment that night. From high up in the stands you couldn't see specifically what was happening but there was always something going on because players were stopping nearly all the time after a tackle to sort of turn on the player... stopping in their tracks and turning back to say something. It was happening all the time; they were kicking their ankles, pinching, spitting, all sorts. A lot of people were saying they shouldn't bother after what had happened to Celtic. As he did with Europe, Matt Busby said that you had to look to these new horizons and embrace them. I think it was good that we went and played in it but I think it would have been a lot nicer if we had won it.

I remember a picture in the *Evening News* on the day after, when they were flying back. They were in the departure lounge and the trophy was at the end of some chairs, and I thought, 'That shouldn't be there. That's ours, that.' I wanted United to be the first British world champions. It wasn't to be. Strangely, 30 years on we became the first British club to win it, didn't we?

AC Milan 2 Manchester United 0
European Cup semi-final, San Siro, 23 April 1969

Manchester United 1 AC Milan 0
European Cup semi-final, Old Trafford, 15 May 1969

Roy Williamson: The AC Milan one was a new experience for people – they showed the away match live on two big screens that were situated on the pitch at Old Trafford. People forget that you wouldn't have seen it on telly because they didn't have the same amount of live football then as they do now. So you either came down to Old Trafford and paid a couple of bob or you didn't see it at all. It was good coming to those sorts of things – the club would even do a programme for those games.

Cliff Butler: I've never witnessed anything like the Milan game in 1969 in my life. There was an incredible atmosphere – it was the nearest I've ever seen in my life to mass hysteria. It wasn't just a semi-final. We were the champions then and that was slipping away from us. About 20 minutes from the end of the game we scored a goal – and there was no question we had scored a goal. I was in line with it, I was in the little strip of terracing that ran along the front of the stand. I still wanted to be in the Stretford End, so I got as near as I could to it, which meant I was right in line with the goal-line at the Milan match in '69 and the ball went well over the line. I'll never forget that.

The noise was incredible and the back of my neck went tense. I couldn't move my head with shouting, and everybody was the same. I turned round and looked into the stands and normally tranquil people were on their seats, little old ladies were on their seats, shouting, and it was absolutely astonishing. Half the time during that game you felt that you weren't in control of yourself. The passion in those days was incredible because Old Trafford was packed, on the whole, with Mancunians who lived the part, day in and day out.

I think the United players themselves felt that they had been pretty badly done to in Milan – John Fitzpatrick was sent off in that game and in those days we tended to look on the Latins as the real enemy, didn't we? We thought the Italians and the Spanish were up to all sorts of tricks in matches so the hackles were up for that game anyway. I think Bobby Charlton scored about 20 minutes from the end and when Denis's 'goal' went in I remember looking in the Stretford End and it was an incredible sight because of the way everybody used to tumble down in there. There was just a mass of humanity in there, throwing themselves about, and the noise – I was shaking until I went to bed that night with the emotion of the occasion. Everybody solidly believed that that was a goal and that United had equalized.

There was a theory that the referee was a bit worried about going too near the Stretford End because at half-time, when the Milan goalkeeper Fabio Cudicini had taken up his station for the second half, missiles had rained down on him from the Stretford End. Whether anything was heavy enough to have caused him any harm we'll never know, but I think they claimed at the time that he'd been hit with a snooker ball or a billiard ball. Others claimed it was an orange or an apple. Anyway, he went down as if he'd been attacked from behind. So some people have suggested that perhaps the referee was a bit worried about going too near to there, and that if he'd followed the play and been up with it he'd have seen that it was a perfectly good goal. Whether we would have gone on to win it I don't know. My feelings are that we probably would, in those last ten minutes, because there was unrelenting wave after wave of attacks on the Milan goal. That was the greatest moment I can remember in watching Manchester United – the night we lost the European Cup!

Bill Foulkes: When we lost to AC Milan in '69, it was robbery at Old Trafford.

Roy Williamson: Against AC Milan, Denis Law 'scored' at the Stretford End – it actually went over the line; it looked over the line to me, anyway. I was in the Stretford End behind the goal and it looked like we had scored then. Everybody went bananas, thinking we had scored, but to be honest I've got to say that by that point, in '69, United didn't look the team that they had done.

Ajax Amsterdam 1 Manchester United 0
UEFA Cup first round, Olympic Stadium, 15 September 1976

Roy Williamson: At Ajax we got our tickets from a bar owner in Amsterdam who had been over to England a few months before and befriended a local publican and customers here. So my mate had the address of this guy's bar. The night before the game was madness in the bar. After about 11 no one could buy a drink unless you bought the whole bar one (about 20 people) and you had to ring the bell behind the bar to let everyone know it was time for another. Also, being my first trip to Holland, I underestimated the beer strength and ended up leathered.

The match was played at the Olympic Stadium and we were on the side. There was quite a big crowd there and we were sat amongst the Ajax supporters but it was more the kind of moderate, sort of 'old men with the flat caps' type of stuff and the United supporters were behind one of the goals. It felt a bit odd really on the night, because losing 1–0 felt all right. You didn't feel as though you had lost really – we were fairly confident we would beat them over here, which we did. So although it was at a time when there was a lot of trouble in Europe, the atmosphere between the fans was quite good, as far as I remember. They were happy they had won on the night and we were confident we'd win the tie overall.

Manchester United 1 Juventus 0
UEFA Cup second round, Old Trafford, 20 October 1976

Juventus 3 Manchester United 0
UEFA Cup second round, Stadio Comunale, 3 November 1976

Lou Macari: European nights at Old Trafford were always special occasions, but at that time we were nowhere near good enough to conquer Europe. Even now, United still find it a little bit more difficult to adjust to the demands of Europe as opposed to those of the Premiership. So many things can go wrong for you in Europe. For example, when we went to Juventus with a 1–0 lead I didn't think that was a particularly big advantage. In those days referees were maybe more intimidated by the home crowd and that meant that vital decisions could go against you. I'm not saying the referee on the night in the Juventus match did not do his best, but things were made very difficult for referees at that time.

St Etienne 1 Manchester United 1
European Cup-Winners' Cup first round, Stade Geoffroy Guichard, 14 September 1977

Manchester United 2 St Etienne 0
European Cup-Winners' Cup first round, Home Park, 5 October 1977

Roy Williamson: The strange one was the St Etienne one the year after. My mate went – I couldn't afford to go – and there was supposedly a lot of trouble through people throwing bottles and things like that but he said it started out with people throwing bread rolls at each other, and although it all got a bit out of hand he said it wasn't anything like as bad as the press made out.

But we got blamed for it and banned from Old Trafford for the second leg. I was working so I couldn't go to Plymouth. Instead, I went to the televised version up here at Old Trafford.

In '69 we had done that against AC Milan when we lost in the semi and they televised it here and I remember it being all right, yet when you think back to what the technology was like you wonder how good it could have been. Still, I can't remember it being anything other than good. They had two big screens – I think there was one at either end, at the goals. It was like watching it on a big telly and I remember it seemed clear enough. So it was good on closed-circuit telly, it wasn't a problem.

Manchester United 5 Porto 2

European Cup-Winners' Cup second round, Old Trafford, 2 November 1977

Chris Yeamans: Porto in 1977 at Old Trafford in the Cup-Winners' Cup was the first European match that I'd actually been to and the atmosphere was like nothing I'd witnessed before. We were 4–0 down from the first match and it looked a pretty hopeless case but the boys gave it a go and scored five, though we lost two. Even though we went out, they were applauded off the pitch. The crowd had sung their hearts out right through the game.

Barcelona 2 Manchester United 0

European Cup-Winners' Cup quarter-final, Nou Camp, 7 March 1984

Manchester United 3 Barcelona 0

European Cup-Winners' Cup quarter-final, Old Trafford, 21 March 1984

Martin Edwards: I remember going to Barcelona and being very depressed because we gave away an own goal by Graeme Hogg, I think it was, very late on. We'd actually done OK and we were losing 1–0 and we thought, '1–0 is not the end of the world'. Blow me – right near the end of the game Graeme Hogg scored an own goal. So 2–0 was a bit of a mammoth task, but I remember the atmosphere here that night when we played Barcelona and, of course, they had Maradona and Schuster in their side and to win by three clear goals was clearly going to be an uphill task, but I can remember there was a fantastic atmosphere that night. Robson was superb, absolutely magnificent and, of course, he scored twice and Stapleton scored. I think we scored the first three goals quite early in the first half and I can remember it being a fairly tense second half because if they'd scored one goal on the away goal rule they'd have gone through. There were great scenes at the end with the crowd coming on and chairing Robson off the field. I remember I thought they should have had a penalty. Mark Hughes tripped Maradona – he was tracking back and he caught Maradona's foot in the penalty area. Maradona went flying and the referee didn't give it.

Manchester United 1 Juventus 1
European Cup-Winners' Cup semi-final, Old Trafford, 11 April 1984

Juventus 2 Manchester United 1
European Cup-Winners' Cup semi-final, Stadio Comunale, 25 April 1984

Lou Macari: We were playing Juventus and the day before we played them the British press were playing a match against the Italian journalists at The Cliff. David Meek was in charge of organizing it all. When they all went out to play the match I went into the Italians' dressing room and cut all the toes off the Italians' socks and put them in the teapot. I then put the socks back in their shoes so that they couldn't see the toes were missing. When they came in from the game, Gordon McQueen and I were looking through the keyhole to see their reaction. Then you heard somebody screaming in Italian because they had started to put on their socks and the sock had gone straight up to their knees. They were complaining to David Meek – then they saw the funny side of it. So they started to drink their tea, and after six or seven of them had poured cups they couldn't get any more tea out of the pot because the spout was blocked. They looked in the pot and the guys who had started drinking their tea soon realized just why their tea was tasting a bit strange.

Martin Edwards: We then went into the semi-final with Juventus and we had a string of injuries. We had a lot of reserves playing that night and we drew 1–1 here. It was a good draw under the circumstances but we knew it was going to be tough after they got the away goal. We knew we would have to win away from home.

They scored early on over there, through Boniek, and we made a substitution with 20 minutes to go. We brought Norman Whiteside on and Norman scored and it really set the cat amongst the pigeons. They were looking tired but, blow me, Rossi scored in the very last minute and I think – and Ron felt very strongly – that if it had gone to extra-time we would have won that night.

Manchester United 1 Montpellier 1
European Cup-Winners' Cup quarter-final, Old Trafford, 6 March 1991

Montpellier 0 Manchester United 2
European Cup-Winners' Cup quarter-final, Stade de la Masson, 19 March 1991

Legia Warsaw 1 Manchester United 3
European Cup-Winners' Cup semi-final, Wojska Polskiego, 10 April 1991

Manchester United 1 Legia Warsaw 1
European Cup-Winners' Cup semi-final, Old Trafford, 24 April 1991

Cliff Butler: I had always been of the view that the Cup-Winners' Cup was the third-best of the European trophies anyway. The teams we played that year were rubbish. If we had played Legia Warsaw in the first round we would have been happy – we played them in the semi! We played Pesci Munkas – it sounds like some sort of nasal problem. We played Wrexham - no disrespect to Wrexham. Montpellier were the best team we played. They gave us a struggle here and we beat them away. Then Legia Warsaw, who were all right for about ten minutes in Warsaw and then that was it. We even drew the second leg here because it didn't matter.

We played a half-decent Montpellier and then a half-decent Barcelona in all the games. It was a poor competition, that. The best match – apart from the final – was Montpellier here, because there was a good atmosphere.

Brian McClair scored early on and then they equalized. It was a good match because it was a struggle – Laurent Blanc was in that Montpellier team and Valderrama, the Colombian with the mop of ginger hair. So they weren't a bad team. They weren't the most famous of the French clubs but I didn't think we would do it against them in France. It was a really good performance to turn it round. We went in 2–0 ahead at half-time, so that was quite surprising and good to see.

Galatasaray 0 Manchester United 0

European Cup second round, Ali Sami Yen Stadium, 3 November 1993

Barry Moorhouse: Part of my role is not just membership. I have other roles as well and I organize all the travel and ticket distribution for all the European away games. On the first trip to Galatasaray we had good co-operation from the club itself. We organized the official trip and in those days, in the interests of safety, all the match tickets were sold as part of travel packages. I organized the official trip and we had no problems whatsoever. Everybody was fine and had a great time but unfortunately the police authorities, in their wisdom, went round all the boarding houses, guest houses and accommodation and rounded up everybody – this seems to be the picture now – who was not part of that official trip and treated them as English hooligans, which they weren't.

It's just that they weren't part of that official trip; they got tickets elsewhere other than through the official allocation and quite a lot of them, including elderly gentlemen and some elderly ladies as well, were pulled out of their beds and locked up the night before the game and remained locked up until the game was finished. They were then chipped off home, which I thought was scandalous, to say the least. One of those gentlemen was 78 years old!

It took a long, long time to try and calm our fans down afterwards because there were so many complaints about that. Some of them went through trauma; to be locked up when they'd never been in an ounce of trouble in their lives before was very, very difficult for them. It put a lot of people off travelling abroad again.

Barcelona 4 Manchester United 0

Champions League group stage, Nou Camp, 2 November 1994

Gary Neville: I was a sub that night, along with David Beckham and Paul Scholes. Nicky Butt played in the game and Scholesy came on for about ten minutes. That was an eye-opener. As young players, watching it there on the bench, we couldn't believe what we were seeing. They were just head and shoulders above the level that we were at. We felt we were at the top level in England, but in terms of European standards it just showed that night how far we were behind. Watching from the bench, I remember thinking, 'I don't want to go on here.' That's the only time I've ever thought that. I was only 19 at the time and I thought to myself, 'I don't want to be exposed to this.' It was 4–0; there were 110,000 people there and Barcelona had fantastic players: Romario, Stoichkov, Koeman, all these players. It was just a really frightening thing to see as a 19-year-old player and to see what you feel is a great team get absolutely demolished did really put into perspective how far we were behind.

I think sometimes that when people compare the '99 team with the one that won the double in '94 there can be no comparison because we're just head and shoulders above them in terms of the development of European football, but it is also true that we've benefitted from those experiences that they had. I think, in terms of which team was better, we've got to the quarter-finals in the last six years on the trot. They never got out of the group phase, so it's a case of we are head and shoulders above them in terms of performances in Europe and the way that we've progressed as a club – but we needed those early defeats to actually get where we are now.

Juventus 1 Manchester United 0

Champions League group stage, Stadio Delle Alpi, 11 September 1996

Gary Neville: After our first real campaign, when we won the Championship in '95–96, we played Juventus the following year, in Turin, and we lost 1–0, but that's the biggest beating that I've ever been part of in Europe. We've been beaten 2–0 or 3–0 in other games but that was the biggest beating in terms of coming off the pitch and feeling 'We weren't even in that game.' It's the only time I've ever played for United and never had a chance in a game. They could have scored five or six. That was daunting – thinking you were such a long way behind. They were European champions at the time and you think to yourself, 'We've got a long way to go before we get where they are.' We needed three more years of those sorts of experiences but we were getting better all the time.

The front line of that team was Vieri, who now plays for Inter Milan, Boksic, del Piero and Zidane, which is just incredible. They also had Deschamps, who was the best midfield player in the world at the time, and played for the French national team, Conte, who was flying, and they had a great back four and 'keeper as well. It was amazing to feel that experience of playing against a team of that calibre. They're the best team that I've ever played against, the hardest team I've ever played against – physically strong, quick, they just had everything – and I think that those two experiences, playing against Juventus in '96 and Barcelona two years earlier, taught us a lot. Since then, teams who have played us may feel that we are one of the toughest teams they've played against. It's nice to feel that now when we go into European games we can stand next to teams like that on an equal level and think, 'We're going to give them a game tonight', whereas in those days it was more like damage limitation, really.

Porto 0 Manchester United 0

European Cup quarter-final, Estadio das Antas, 19 March 1997

Ole Pedersen: I have to mention 1997 and Porto, though, because of the horrendous surroundings you sometimes have to endure as a football fan. How that stadium was ever accepted as being up to UEFA standards, I will never know.

Cameron Erskine: At Porto in '97 we had tickets for the handicapped section but the Portuguese stewards directed us into this section behind the goal. When we got in we could hear the crowd outside banging the tin sheeting beside the entrance to try to break it down and break into the ground. These were United fans who were becoming very impatient because the turnstile attendants were letting them in too slowly and kick-off time was getting closer and closer.

I thought our time had come, that night. When we saw the fans rushing in we thought it could become another Hillsborough so we carried Nigel down to the front of the terracing and begged the stewards to let him out. More and more people were coming into the section we were in but the stewards wouldn't open up and let us out. They were arguing among themselves – I think they were waiting to get some sort of authorization. Then Gary Neville and Cantona came over to tell the stewards to get the wheelchairs out. They pleaded with the stewards – it was only when they came over that the stewards opened up the gates. If we had stayed in there for another 15 minutes it would have been a catastrophe, especially if we had stayed with the wheelchairs in the place where we had gone to start with – right at the top of the terracing. The wheelchairs could easily have been pushed over. These stewards had put the handicapped people into the crowd instead of at the side of the pitch, as they should have done and as they eventually did. It was just as well they moved us. Towards the end of the match, the Portuguese riot police started firing rubber bullets into the section where we had been, creating mayhem in there.

Barry Moorhouse: The riot police were just batoning people for fun – it was absolutely disgraceful. We had three great days on our official trip until the day of the game. I just can't understand the mentality of the police; why they would want to baton people who were walking on the road when you can't get on the pavement. They were manhandling and pushing people about before the game. It was very, very frightening. Their batons are not short, little things. They're great big batons and they were just wielding those at anybody; not anybody who was causing problems, just anybody, any supporter. One of our security guards had his arm broken by the police when he was only trying to help. It was just crazy.

One of our supporters was shot in the leg and the police denied any shooting had taken place. Then they said, 'OK, it was rubber bullets.' The guy came to see me and showed me his wounds, which were all down his leg, and he brought the pellets that were taken out of his leg and they were metal pellets. That particular guy would not say boo to a goose and they shot him in the leg to set an example. What's that all about? We were there to see a game of football.

Borussia Dortmund 1 Manchester United 0
European Cup semi-final, Westfalenstadion, 9 April 1997

Manchester United 0 Borussia Dortmund 1
European Cup semi-final, Old Trafford, 23 April 1997

Phil Neville: It was very disappointing, because if we had got to the final that year it would have been a great achievement because we still had a lot of inexperienced, young players. Although Dortmund went on to win the competition, in the two matches we played against them we were unlucky to lose 1–0 each time. Out in Dortmund we lost to a deflected goal and at home we could have won 7–1. We missed an awful lot of chances: the 'keeper was blocking shots and defenders were on the line. It was just the most unbelievable night of football I've ever played in really. They took an early lead but we missed chance after chance after chance. You couldn't describe what went on that night because we played so well and created so many chances against a German side that were renowned for not giving chances away. If we had converted all our chances we could have won 7 or 8–1 that night. You come off afterwards and you try to pick holes in your performance, but all that was missing were the finishing touches; the goals. You just think to yourself, 'Maybe that wasn't our night.' Good luck to Dortmund, who went on to win the trophy. It was all part of the experience of the European Cup, because that's what it's like. You've got to take your chances to win.

Manchester United 3 Juventus 2

Champions League group stage, Old Trafford, 1 October 1997

Phil Neville: I remember beating Juventus at Old Trafford, 3–2. We went a goal behind – they scored with probably about 30 seconds gone. We had quite a depleted side because Keanie had got injured on the Saturday against Leeds; he had done his cruciate. I ended up playing centre midfield in the second half, we had Scholesy up front with Teddy and we beat Juventus, which was a very important result because we'd never beaten one of the great European clubs. That night we went 3–1 up and they scored in the last minute. We'd played really well and Giggsy had had a great night. It was probably the start of our confidence in beating these big clubs. We'd played Juventus three or four times before and got beaten so questions were beginning to be asked. It was an important night for us, that, because it gave us the confidence to go on and play better.

Internazionale 1 Manchester United 1

European Cup quarter-final, San Siro, 17 March 1999

Paul Hardman: I remember Milan, when we played Inter, on 17 March 1999. We were in a cage and everything was coming over on to us, full bottles, coins, the lot. I got hit three times. A girl got hit by a plastic bottle full of water. She was concussed and I remember the ambulance people coming to help her. They were wearing these yellow and white builders' hats and were trying to persuade this woman to go out because she had a big cut on her head. She refused because she didn't want to miss the game. She wouldn't leave, so this guy gave her his hat and she was standing there with this hard hat on whilst watching the rest of the game. Scholesy scored that night – it was 1–1 – but for me it was probably more memorable for getting a rifle butt round the head from the Italian police. It's kind of a tradition between Kath, the girl I go to football with, and I that I keep hold of the tickets until the last minute as we are going into the ground. That night Kath, for some reason, had got absolutely paralytic and she took the tickets and wouldn't give me them back. I kept asking her for them, but the more I did so, the more rowdy she got and the more jumpy the police got. They thought I was trying to steal her tickets and one of them just swung round and lamped me with the butt of his rifle. I thought, 'You can't do that' but then I thought again and realized that if I made any kind of protest I'd probably get shot.

Juventus 2 Manchester United 3

European Cup semi-final, Stadio Delle Alpi, 21 April 1999

Gary Neville: That was the pinnacle, that night. We had drawn against them 1–1 at home and they'd given us a little bit of a doing first half, to be honest with you. In the second half we came out and really went at them and could have had a couple of goals ourselves. We'd played them five or six times, but that night at Juventus was the making of us in terms of becoming European champions. They were the benchmark for four or five years – they were the best team. They were 2–0 up and 3–1 up on aggregate and we needed to score two goals if we were to win the European Cup that year, and you just don't do that at Juventus. No team had done that in the previous five or six years; you don't do that against an Italian club. So for us to go and play the way that we did after going 2–0 down was really the making of us as European champions, because we'd beaten the best team in Europe. There comes a defining moment in the European Cup where you have to beat the best team; it might be in the final or the semi or the quarter-final. There comes a time when it's do or die, and that night in Juventus was the one for us. We had had a few defeats against them where you would come off the pitch and you hadn't even been in the game. To come off the pitch and have their fans clapping us in the way that they did was just an amazing feeling.

Manchester United 2 Real Madrid 3

European Cup quarter-final, Old Trafford, 19 April 2000

Simon Davies: I was sat in the East Stand for that one and Real Madrid scored just in front of us. I didn't have a clue what had happened at the goal until I went back home and watched the replay on telly. One minute Berg was in control of the situation and just tracking back and then, all of a sudden, they had scored. You were wondering, 'How did the ball get from there to there?' Their player had sort of backheeled it through Berg's legs. Berg wasn't sure what had happened and no one in the stand was sure what had happened. I think they still show it in the credits of the Champions League highlights.

Beckham then decided to go weaving past several Real Madrid players to score his goal, but we ended up losing 3–2. I was gutted about that, probably because you think that once you've got the European Cup you're going to hold on to it. You sort of feel you own it once you've won it once, especially when you've won it the way we did. You feel you're invincible and to be shown you're not at all doesn't make for a good feeling. Then again, once you sit down after the game and think about it you're not that gutted because it means that that game in Barcelona stays special. It's a sort of strange double-edged sword: part of you wants to win the European Cup again but then the other part of you thinks that that Barcelona win was so special that you don't want the European Cup to become like the Premiership. If you won it six or seven times you'd just think, 'Oh yeah, we've won the European Cup again.' That would be terrible. So you could console yourself with the thought that even though we were out of Europe, that night in Barcelona would remain special.

Dynamo Kiev 0 Manchester United 0
UEFA Champions League first group stage, Stadium Respublikanski, 19 September 2000

Voni von Arx: I've been to Kiev with 500 United fans and I think it motivates the players on the pitch when, miles away from Old Trafford, they hear United fans, 500 or whatever. Kiev is my favourite memory of following United in Europe. I like the eastern part of Europe anyway because it has something special. Paying £1 for a taxi for a two-hour drive, trying to talk to the people, going to the ground; the people there were so friendly, so cool and so impressed with the fact that so many United fans had made the trip. The fans had this special type of hooter and it made a great noise. To me, even including Barcelona, it was the best trip I ever made. I hope we get a Moscow club this year so we can make a similar type of trip.

I haven't missed a match in Europe since the end of '96. You go to the town, you go to the bars, you have a few beers and speak to the supporters from the opposing team. I like talking anyway and I like talking to those fans about how they feel about their clubs. It's one world to me, we have the same interest in football and I just like talking to them. Experience has shown me that it's a bit difficult to do that in Italy, actually, but elsewhere it's usually easy to go up to the other team's fans and have a chat.

Manchester United 5 Nantes Atlantique 1

Champions League second group stage, Old Trafford, 26 February 2002

Phil Neville: We didn't lose a game in the second group and, particularly at home to Nantes, we played some fantastic football. When we are on form, teams can't live with us. We pass the ball, we move, we've got pace and Nantes couldn't live with us that night. We've got players that score goals, players that can cross, players that can defend and tackle. When we're on song, I don't think there's a better team in Europe.

Manchester United 3 Deportivo La Coruna 2

European Cup quarter-final, Old Trafford, 10 April 2002

Eric Halsall: I don't think I've ever been more nervous before a European match – don't ask me why, except that they have such a good track record against us and other top sides and I didn't want the awesome display in the away leg – which I didn't get to – to go to waste. The quality of United's play – even without Keano driving them on – was as good as I've ever seen it. Pity about the injuries. The atmosphere was also really very good and it was a joy to be on the Stret in such a rousing, supportive and funny mood.

Manchester United 1 Porto 1

European Cup last 16, Old Trafford, 9 March 2004

Eric Halsall: An experience that will rankle with me for years was that of seeing United go out to the eventual winners, Porto, at Old Trafford, 3–2 on aggregate, in a game that United should have won – and morally did win – but that was most notable for the orchestrated diving and other disruptive tactics of Porto, the horrendous performance of the officials, including a disallowed Paul Scholes goal with not one but two Portuguese playing him onside, the kind of goalkeeping blunder that we're becoming used to again after being spoilt for so long by Schmikes, and, finally, Mourinho's hysterical gallop along the touchline at the final whistle. That was a night to define comprehensively the phrase 'sheer frustration'.

Manchester United 6 Fenerbahce 2
European Cup group stage, Old Trafford, 28 September 2004

Simon Davies: This match springs straight to mind, just because of Wayne Rooney's impact. Every time he got the ball, you thought he was going to score – and he did. You just thought, 'If he can do this every game, we're laughing.' Of course, that would be impossible but on that night, anything was possible. It was the most stunning debut you could ever wish to see. Otherwise, in Europe recently, it's defeats that stand out: the Ronaldo hat-trick for Real Madrid at Old Trafford that all the fans stood up to applaud; the heartbreak of Porto and Mourinho taking off down the touchline after they had knocked us out with a last-minute goal in 2004; and the class of Milan in the 2004–05 season. They were the last of the big clubs that we hadn't faced in recent years and I have to say they were the most impressive.

Eric Halsall: I'd have to include the Old Trafford game against Fenerbahce – just for Wayne Rooney's hat-trick debut. After that, even Arsène Wenger said, 'Would I like to work with Wayne Rooney? Who wouldn't want to work with him?' It was certainly a night to remember and I'm privileged to have been there. Till the end of time there isn't likely to be another Scouser who will have the Stretford End drooling over him as Rooney did on Tuesday, 28 September 2004.

Milan 1 Manchester United 0
European Cup last 16, Giuseppe Meazza Stadium, 8 March 2005

Roy Williamson: Since 1999 there has been a decline in the club's successes. Of course, United don't have any divine right to win everything all the time and a couple of league titles and cups is hardly a disaster. In Europe, though, rather than Barca '99 getting rid of the monkey on the back, there seems to have been even more of an obsession with winning the European Cup than before. In my view, especially in season 2004–05, too much emphasis has been put on a European style of play, one up front and so on. It isn't United's way. If we are going to go out in Europe, then let's do it with all guns blazing. Its no coincidence that playing 'our' way in '99 led to success; playing cautiously since has led to only a single knockout victory in Europe in six years. What does that tell you?

Sir Alex Ferguson: The last couple of years have been disappointing. In the Porto game we were subject to some curious refereeing decisions. This year we got Milan at the wrong time: I think their legs had gone by the end of the season – Maldini, Stam, Cafu, are all 34 and upwards. The statistics of the game were that we had eight clear chances when we were in on the goalkeeper and never hit the target once and if you don't hit the target...

Against Leverkusen, in 2002, if we'd had Keane on the pitch at 2–1 up, we'd have won. At the second goal the ball was bouncing about on the pitch and I think if Keane had been on the field he would have introduced some very necessary composure. Over there, we hit the woodwork three times. Against Dortmund in 1997 we had 15 chances and were hitting the post, so we've not, I would say, underachieved on the whole. There have been unlucky occasions and very occasionally we have underachieved – against Milan, not hitting the target, but that was indicative of the season we've just had – against West Brom in our final home game, for example, we should have won by six or seven but drew 1–1.

13

Wembley-Rotterdam-Barcelona

Benfica, Barcelona and Bayern Munich are rarely bit-part players on the European stage. Yet they found themselves relegated to a supporting role as United powered their way to their three European trophies on three drama-packed nights. The intoxicating thrill of victory in those three one-off matches made them outstanding occasions in United's history.

Benfica 1 Manchester United 4
European Cup final, Wembley, 29 May 1968

> **Roy Williamson:** As a 15-year-old in 1968 I had a blind faith that United would beat Real Madrid to get to the final. We should have won it two years before when we had slaughtered Benfica 5–1 in Lisbon, the game that led to George being dubbed 'El Beatle'. So I could not see us blowing it a second time. Being so confident, I applied for final tickets before the outcome of the semis. My correspondence from Wembley was numbered EC1; I assume because it was the first request for tickets they received. In short, I had my two seats on the halfway line guaranteed in writing before the second leg in Madrid. At 3–1 down, I have to confess I was thinking about how to dispose of those tickets – at 3–3 I could have named my own price!

Cliff Butler: I just couldn't believe we had got there. I was really, really annoyed when Celtic won it the year before, because I wanted us to be the first British team to win it. We became the first English team, but that's not the same thing.

Ken Ramsden: We had arranged with Wembley that we would go down the day after we played Real Madrid in the second leg of the semifinal. There were only three of us in the ticket office at that time: me, my wife and a colleague. So we all got into a little car I had and drove down to London to collect the tickets. We didn't have a strongroom although we did have a safe, but I was really, really worried, so I made an arrangement with the police at Stretford to lodge the tickets with them in the cells – nobody ever steals from a police cell, do they? We had them locked in big, wooden bullion boxes that we used to carry our cash in. Every morning I went to the police station, into the cells – it's the only time I've been in a police cell, I hasten to add – took out the boxes, put them in the car, brought them here to Old Trafford, worked on them all day, and every night went back to the nick and put them back in the cells. The police then locked the cell for me and I went home and could sleep safely. I was worried about leaving them inside Old Trafford during the night because you didn't have burglar alarms in the late '60s.

Roy Williamson: The story of how I got to the final becomes ridiculous. My brother, who had first introduced me to the Reds, had an A-level on the day of the match and could not go; a stupid decision, I know, and one regretted ever since. The second-in-line was my Dad but he had to have all of his teeth out on the day to have them replaced by falsies. So for the one and only time in my life I went to see the Reds with my mum. It was the only United game she ever saw live – the European Cup final in 1968.

Nesta Burgess: I remember Georgie's mother and father were sat in front of us and Lady Jean was sat in the Royal Box and, of course, we scored, and in her excitement she got up and waved to all of us. We stayed at the Russell Hotel – it was a wonderful few days.

Cliff Butler: Playing at Wembley gave us a terrific advantage. I think the crowd that night was officially 92,000 and of those only 4-5,000 were Benfica. They were just swamped. The atmosphere that night was something else. If a shout started at one end it just continued right round the place.

Bill Foulkes: I played one of my best games for United in the '68 European Cup final. I was up against Torres, who must have been about six feet four inches. I remember getting a taxi with Jock Stein two or three weeks before the final and he said, 'You've got to get hold of that fellow Torres or he'll really punish you.' I was very pleased with how I played that night. I had still been carrying my injury but in the weeks before the final I did a lot of training to build myself up and keep in peak fitness before the final. The other lads would be off playing golf and I would be training, even though I would rather have been playing golf.

I still had my injury and I thought he was going to leave me out. I wouldn't have questioned it if he had – I had such respect for him. I never thought we were in any danger of losing that game. David Sadler should have scored four goals!

Sir Bobby Charlton: It was a hot, humid night and they were fantastic, really; they're great people, the Portuguese. It was a tough game, a hard game, but it was as if it had to be. People here felt there was no way we could lose this.

At the first goal I went on a decoy run, to be honest. I went to the near post to pull somebody in, thinking that David Sadler was going to cross it. David Sadler came on his right foot and so I ran to the near post, which I was always taught to do, to create space behind me, and I expected the ball to go over the top for somebody else to be there but he didn't do that. The ball came in towards me and I thought I would just help it on. That's what I was doing. It flew right in the bottom corner. The goalkeeper had no chance, and that was the first goal. So we'd broken the ice.

We scored one and then they equalised. Torres knocked the ball down and Graca scored, and I thought, 'This isn't in the plan.' It certainly wasn't in the plan for them to get another one and I have visions now of Eusebio running through. I thought, 'How has he got there?' And you would never expect him not to score. Anyway, he hit it and Alex Stepney held it. He didn't parry it or block it – he held it, and I think that was the turning-point, I really do. Suddenly, the referee had blown for full-time and there was an extra half an hour and we thought that there was no way we were going to lose now.

We were always trained to play for an extra half-hour but we never thought that foreigners, especially Latins, were. They didn't like it and they didn't like playing too many matches close together, whereas we used to do it all the time, with three matches at Christmas or Easter. We were doing it all the time. It proved to be right. They absolutely collapsed. Alex hit a long ball and the centre-half made a mistake – in trying to trap it he went too far forward and it went through him. George was round the goalkeeper, as you would expect him to do, and slotted it in. There was no danger then – as soon as the second goal went in we were going to win. It was to be.

When I scored the last goal, the game was done. Brian Kidd got it, and by that time Benfica were desperate, so the full-back dived into a tackle he should never have gone for. Brian Kidd skipped over him, got to the dead-ball line and just rolled one in, expecting somebody to be there and again I had gone to the near post. Again, I couldn't see the goals. I couldn't see the goals for the first goal I scored and I couldn't see them for the second goal, but again I literally thought, 'I'll just help it on its way.' It wasn't a shot, and it just looped over the goalkeeper to make it four, but the game was finished long before that.

The whistle went and everybody was charging over to Matt. I was so tired. I couldn't believe how tired you could be. I've never been so tired in my life. They didn't give you any water in those days; they didn't put any water on. I think people even thought water wasn't good for you. They used to give you tea at half-time. I was so tired and drained and we were probably all dehydrated because it was humid.

I couldn't see the fans because it was at night and Wembley was floodlit but I knew they were there. You could hear them. It was just great and I was pleased that everybody who should have been playing was playing: Bill Foulkes, Nobby Stiles and Shay Brennan at right-back, all the ones who had been part of it all. It was right. I was really pleased about it, the whole thing. It's all part of the history, and we had to wait a long time before we did it again.

We had won it, and all the emotion about what had happened before and during the Munich air crash seemed to be all put in its place. The players had done justice to them and it was a very big, emotional day. In fact, there was a dinner at night for all the old players, some of the ones that had survived the accident, and I couldn't go. Every time I got off the bed I started to faint. I think it was because of the dehydration and the nerves. My wife had to go down on her own. I missed the celebrations that night and the following day because Nobby and I had to go off to play with England. I wasn't bothered about that. We had won and that was the important thing. It was all part of the ongoing history of this place.

Ken Ramsden: There was a '60s Manchester pop group called Freddie and the Dreamers and the singer, Freddie Garrity, several members of the group and their manager had season tickets for Old Trafford. They were red-hot fans and it so happened that Freddie and his manager were sat behind my wife and I at the final and Freddie had one of those goatskin containers for drink that you hold up to your lips and he was sharing that round – that was in the days before it was illegal to drink at football matches. I can't remember what was in it but it tasted good! The game was exciting – I particularly remember Stepney's save near the end of the 90 minutes when we could have lost and, indeed, Benfica ought to have scored. Then all the staff went back to the Russell Hotel for a banquet and Joe Loss's band played. When Matt walked in they struck up 'For He's A Jolly Good Fellow'. You never ever forget things like that. We took the train back to Manchester the next day and the streets were packed with people to see Matt Busby and the players with the Cup.

Wilf McGuinness: In '68 we won it for Manchester United and Matt Busby and the players who had died, especially the players who had died; my friends. I felt that and we all felt it, and that showed in the way everybody ran at Matt Busby and applauded him and kissed him and loved him, because we knew what it meant to him and the families of the ones who had died. It meant that much; yes it did.

David Meek: The European Cup final of '68 is an outstanding memory, again because of the emotional background. Ten years after Munich, here was a team becoming champions of Europe, and the enormity of that achievement has never really been given full credit. The fact that Busby picked himself up from the deathbed and built another team within ten years is, I think, an incredible achievement. It was a lovely team and they played well right through. In football generally, people seem to have taken it for granted that United won the European Cup. Few people focus on the fact that it was done within ten years of having a club virtually wiped out. The drama of extra time and George Best surging through sticks in my mind most vividly and then the sight of Bill Foulkes and Bobby Charlton, the two survivors, embracing Matt Busby at the end.

Martin Edwards: I remember just being relieved that we'd done it and that we'd done it before Matt retired. That was the big thing.

Sir Alex Ferguson: I watched it in the house. The disappointing thing for me was that Denis Law wasn't playing. I was a Denis Law fan; he was my hero and I was devastated that he didn't play in the final. It was a great moment nonetheless. We were so glad in Scotland that Celtic had won it the year before because we didn't want an English team to be the first to do it. So that allowed you to relax and support United! I think when history plays its part, the real story about the '68 final is Matt Busby. It was Matt Busby's game, because to lose a team and then within ten years rebuild and win the European Cup is fantastic, amazing, the way he pieced it together. Obviously Bill Foulkes and Bobby were still there after the crash but all the rest were new players: John Aston, Brian Kidd, David Sadler, Nobby Stiles, Shay Brennan, Tony Dunne, George Best – all of them produced by the club – and with Bill Foulkes and Bobby already there the only two bought players were Crerand and Alex Stepney. So, similarly to Celtic, they produced a team from home-grown players, which was fantastic. That's the real story there, to my mind, in the history of the club.

Sir Bobby Charlton: It was very emotional for the fans and from a club point of view, because of what happened with the accident, and it seemed right. Once we got to the semi-final and beat Madrid I thought there was no way we would lose at Wembley, and we were playing a Portuguese team with whom we were very familiar. There was nothing strange about the opposition. We knew most of them inside out: we had played against most of them in the World Cup and we had played them before in the quarter-finals two years previously. It was quite emotional, because the accident happened when we were at the start of the European adventure really, and potentially going on to be a great team, and that was taken away by the accident. So there was a lot of emotion about winning the European Cup.

Roy Williamson: Nobody who was there will ever forget that night. My over-riding memory is of the final whistle blowing and the tears being shed by most of the adults around me. Having been too young to understand the magnitude of the Munich crash when it happened in 1958, I knew at that moment what it meant to those who had experienced it as United fans. The tears were mixed; tears of joy for Matt and the magnificent eleven on the pitch, and tears of sadness for 'absent friends' lost in the air disaster.

I will never forget those magical moments and the reaction of the 'United family' around me on that night. When that final whistle went the atmosphere was all about the connection between that night and Munich. I just looked at people and the emotion – I think people were actually seeing the Munich side playing and running round with the cup. I actually think they could visualise it – it was so emotional. I'm so glad I was there – it was such a good occasion.

Barcelona 1 Manchester United 2

European Cup-Winners' Cup final, De Kuip, Rotterdam, 15 May 1991

Cameron Erskine: For Rotterdam in '91 we went by coach. It was out of this world. When they were doing a lap of honour Les Sealey threw the towel over the fencing. A guy was about to get a hold of it and I just grabbed it and gave it to Nigel. We were there for only five or six hours because the coach was leaving for Calais immediately after the game. The fans were so elated that night – to see the team win a trophy in Europe was just fantastic.

Cliff Butler: I was club photographer then, so it was a different sort of occasion for me. I was working rather than supporting. I did enjoy it, though, I enjoyed being part of it, being on the inside. I don't think it was anything like winning the European Cup. It was a good occasion because there were loads of United supporters there – a lot more than Barcelona had. Then again, Barcelona would get to a final just about every year, so it was like an away match to them. We had waited all those years to get to a final. It was a horrible day in terms of the weather but it was great to see so many United supporters in a foreign country.

Ole Pedersen: We drove down from Oslo. I got a ticket through the Norwegian FA, so I was in the main stand, five yards away from Bobby Charlton! We came up the stairs at the back of the stadium and saw the masses of red in the torrential rain... I think that was probably my second-best moment at a United game – it was only overtaken by Ole's goal at the '99 European Cup final. During half-time, you could feel United were going to win, because we owned the stadium. Watching the emotions on Sir Bobby's face when the game was over was also special.

Ken Ramsden: I was worried because the stand was bouncing where the bulk of our fans and my son were – there were so many people jumping up and down with excitement. It was a lousy night but a great day. Mark Hughes' goal – the second one – was a fantastic goal, and I remember Clayton Blackmore clearing one off the line for us late on. We had a new hotel to ourselves and the staff were fantastic with the players when they returned – they formed a guard of honour for them at the door. It was fantastic for the manager because he had done it with Aberdeen and to win another European honour, this time with United, was fantastic for him. It's only when you look back on it that you think it probably was the start of the club's domination, but at the time we just really enjoyed winning that trophy for its own sake. Matt Busby was there – he was in good form – and it was great for him because I know that Sir Matt was happy for Alex, because he wanted the club to succeed. Sir Matt had won a trophy in Europe but he was not envious or grudging at seeing someone else do the same thing. There is no doubt about that – he was so pleased and so happy to see the club doing well again in Europe. He was the biggest fan of all.

Chris Yeamans: I didn't actually get beyond Newcastle for this one, so I had loads of mates round. Unfortunately, I was the only Red there, but my mates, to their credit, were Reds for the night. I think my feelings when we won were of total disbelief that after all those years out of Europe we could win that cup and beat the mighty Barcelona in the process. Typical United, though, after going 2–0 up we let them back into the game and had to endure a nightmare last few minutes. After that, it was a wild house party.

Ron Snellen: I was, of course at the European Cup-Winners' Cup final in Rotterdam. And although winning this trophy was good, we just wanted one thing at that time: winning the title in England. But it was great seeing so many Reds in your country and their celebrations afterwards. When you look at it now, it was the beginning of a new era.

Bayern Munich 1, Manchester United 2

European Cup final, Nou Camp, Barcelona, 26 May 1999

Jonathan Deakin: I was teacher-training during the treble season and on practice at the time of the Barcelona match. I got Wednesdays off to go to Uni so on the day of the final I skipped Uni and left home at 5.00am. I did the one-day trip, returning to Manchester at 7.00am on the Thursday. I was in school that morning and no one believed I had been to Spain, apart from the fact that I was knackered and grinning like a Cheshire cat all day. In the run-up to the day I was too excited about the trip to consider the game and on the day I was too concerned about getting in, keeping the tickets safe and looking after my sister to really think about our chances. Obviously, seeing Reds everywhere in Barcelona and singing, 'taking over, taking over, taking over Barcelona' had been brilliant. I will also never forget coming off a tube train and singing the then-new Yip Jaap Stam song and it echoing around so loudly. Being in the Nou Camp, seeing all the flags and hearing the Champions League music are all great memories.

Gary Neville: We never thought we were beaten. I just thought, 'We can't break these down.' They just killed the game off, but then the game changed with 15 minutes to go. They started seeming to want to come and get a second, which they hadn't done previously. When Becks came over to the right I just started to seem to get a little bit more time to go forward and Becks got a couple of crosses in. With 15 minutes to go they hit the bar, and a few minutes later they hit the post.

I think Yorkie got a chance from a cross from me. For 75 minutes, 80 minutes we hadn't created a chance. We started to get a couple of sniffs at the goal and you thought, 'There's something still in this game.'

Ole got a header and then we got a throw-in in the corner and I sprinted over, took the throw-in and we then got a corner. From the corner it was just luck: a bad clearance from their lad, a bad shot from Giggsy, bad contact from Teddy and it ends up in the back of the net! You just thought at that time, 'Extra-time – I'm knackered!'

We got the goal and you just felt as if something was happening. We couldn't just let all the work we'd put in that year go out of the window with a 1-0 defeat to Bayern. So we scored, and the most incredible thing was for us to score again. When we got the second goal we knew we'd won the game. It makes you shiver now just thinking about that night.

When the second goal went in, I just lay on the ground and thought, 'I can't believe this has happened.' I was so tired. We had played so many games and I remember I was struggling at the time personally with my groin, and with half an hour to go in that game I just felt as though my legs had gone. I remember looking up and seeing bedlam in the crowd and thinking it was the happiest night of my life. I was thinking, 'If it gets better than this, I hope it happens soon.'

I don't think there are any words that can describe what happened, to be honest with you. It was just the most incredible feeling that I've ever had in my life. Nothing that has ever happened to me in my life has surpassed it. I hope winning the European Cup again would do it, but even in winning the European Cup again I don't see how it could be as special as that night in terms of the way it happened. To score two goals in the last minute to win the European Cup is just the most incredible feeling. I'd love to experience winning that trophy again. That's what we're all here for; to win that trophy again.

Anna Deakin: From the minute my brother and I received the letter saying we had got tickets to the game, we knew it was going to be a day to remember. The fun started in the airport lounge, which was filled with Reds. A middle-aged couple were keeping everyone amused with tales of how well they knew all the players, how their son had his hair cut by Nicky Butt's fourth cousin's next-door neighbour – that kind of thing. Arriving in Barcelona, the United steward in charge tried to pull my leg that there wasn't a ticket for me – but I soon had it in my hand, where it stayed until I was safely in the ground! The ground is incredible and seeing so many Reds there, all totally up for it, was brilliant. Obviously, conceding was a nightmare, but you had to be positive and still enjoy the atmosphere, appreciating how lucky we were to be there. When Sheringham equalised so late on, the ground went mad – everyone was throwing themselves all over the place, hugging everyone around them. I personally thought that that celebration could not be beaten, but when Ole scored two minutes later everything went mental. It was bizarre, because for practically the whole game we had resigned ourselves to losing – but now we had to squash all the feelings of equalising and then winning into two minutes – that euphoric feeling will never be beaten. I had tears of happiness rolling down my face, as the reality of our victory sank in. Looking back, as my brother and I do frequently, we realise just how lucky we were to witness that game. I'll always be grateful to all those players and to Alex Ferguson for giving me that day.

Voni von Arx: Barcelona – the result made that the best day of my life, although I should really say my wedding day. It was fantastic. Every day I think about those two goals. When I watch the video I still get shivers up and down my spine. I didn't have a clue about how much time had gone in the match until I saw Schmeichel coming up for the corner. Then I realised we were into injury time. It was 1-0 to Bayern and I thought it had at least been nice to be at the final – my hopes of United winning that final had disappeared. Then they equalised, and I was just jumping up and down and ended up about four or five rows from where we had been seated. We had just about calmed down when the second goal came and after about a minute I realised that I had no T-shirt and had been kissed on the mouth by a stranger – there was just chaos on the terraces; we were just partying like mad. It was really animal-style in a way – we were so happy. I think the greatest feelings were released after the second goal – it is something that I will never forget, ever. For the next two days we just walked around Barcelona cheering with the other thousands of Reds who were there.

Sir Bobby Charlton: That was one of the best days of my life, that. It was pure theatre. It was just Man United all over. Don't do it easy, don't do it playing defensively. We gave a goal away through a stupid free-kick but all the time I thought, 'If we can just get in the box....' Whenever it got wide, Bayern Munich thought, 'Well, we've got big lads. We can handle anything that comes in wide from wide situations.' They always had plenty of people in the box, but I thought if we could just get in there, down on the floor, even when there were only a couple of minutes left, I thought, 'There's a goal there if only we can get in.' But we couldn't get in the whole game. They were just solid at the back all the time.

Then Schmeichel came up for the corner and the Germans absolutely didn't know what to do. For the first time in the whole match there were spaces in the box and it fell to Dwight Yorke. Dwight Yorke knocked it back. It fell to Ryan Giggs. He knocked it back to Teddy Sheringham who was in the space; he helped it on and it's in the bottom corner. First of all, I thought, 'Offside.' Then I thought, 'It can't be offside. There's a full-back on the line. It's a goal.' Well, it erupted. I've never known anything like it. I thought, 'Well, at least we've got half an hour.' And I don't remember what I did when that ball went in. I know I jumped over about three or four rows because David Will, who is a member of FIFA, was there, and I had to apologise to him and he said, 'No, I understand, Bobby.'

I was jumping around with my wife. I gave her a cuddle and I had been waving trying to see my other daughter and my son-in-law, and I couldn't see them.

Then, just as it has settled down, we break on the left and there's another corner and then it came across and Teddy Sheringham got up and it went to Solskjaer. It was as though time froze. He was shooting. It went silent. And it was a goal. I honestly don't remember what I did then. I honestly don't. I don't know whether I ran down the tunnel or wherever. I just don't remember. It's the most dramatic finish to any European match.

Jonathan Deakin: The thing is, the game was in many ways horrible. We conceded so early and the German efficiency was so good that it nearly killed the atmosphere. There were sporadic chants but it was not the celebration it could have been. I remember people around us arguing, swearing at each other for not singing/slagging off the team etc. It really was that bad. Personally, I was trying to reconcile the day in my head. It had been a great day out. We'd met up with friends and had a top laugh. We'd seen a match in the Nou Camp. It was better to be there and lose than not be there. I was considering all the things I was going to say to those who would mock me in the aftermath of defeat, yet even I was not convinced by my own arguments as to why it had been worthwhile. And then we scored. It was mental. We had an awesome view, just to the side of the goal. I can remember the relief at simply seeing a goal. I turned to my sister and told her to look around at the Nou Camp. 'At least we've seen a goal!' I said as we watched the mass of United fans go berserk. It was one of the finest sights I've ever seen. Later, watching the TV version, I saw Teddy do exactly the same thing.

Then we had another corner. I noticed Schmeichel stay in his goal. 'Well, why risk it when there is extra-time to come?' I thought. And then I had another great view of that goal. I was shaking, screaming, crying. Repeating 'We've done it!' and 'I don't believe it!' like a mantra, hugging everyone. I have never physically experienced anything like it. My whole body was shaking like mad. The thing is, I was not expecting victory. I had not even considered it all day. In some Cup Finals you sit at 1-0 up thinking what it would be like to hold on. Others have been wrapped up long before the end, but not this one. I had gone from thinking only about defeat to winning the game in 132 seconds. The ultimate footballing low to the ultimate high. An emotional rollercoaster I will probably never again experience in football. A truly unique feeling. I knew it was 'history'. I was there! It was incredible. Looking back now it's hard to recall details, but I remember the Nevilles singing in front of us with the Cup. I remember singing all the songs in the songbook and the sheer delight on everyone's faces. I have several photos to remind me, but they don't truly capture things, but then with such a special moment I guess that's the way it's meant to be.

Wilf McGuinness: Those last few moments at the Nou Camp were the greatest moments in Manchester United's history as far as I'm concerned. They deserved the treble – I always felt we were going to get the treble that season. The replayed FA Cup semi-final with Arsenal ripped people apart and then lifted them up. Going down to ten men, the only way to win it was by doing something special and Giggsy did it. Then those last few minutes in Barcelona, on Matt Busby's 90th birthday; to win it on such a day is quite exceptional, quite a remarkable thing. And the way we won it too – out of the blue, if you like.

Simon Davies: I was in the press box and it was terrible most of the game, from the sixth minute on, because I was sat next to two German radio reporters and because I had studied German at university I could understand every word they were saying. From the sixth minute on they were loving it and I was getting more and more fed-up. The Germans were just bossing the game, Bayern, weren't they? They hit the bar and hit the post and they were screaming into their microphones, 'Champions' and all this. They started taking pictures and I think they were pretending to take pictures of each other but I'm sure they were taking pictures of me looking really fed-up.

Then there were those last two or three minutes. I was supposed to be typing this match report but I couldn't do it. I just didn't know what to say. I couldn't believe what had happened. I had already rewritten the last paragraph about three times so I wasn't sure what to write at all. I simply stood there for about five minutes. The two Germans had shut up pretty quickly. We shook hands at the end of it and I told them in German, 'That's life.'

Sir Bobby Charlton: The Germans didn't even want to stand up. They were all literally floored. They were all lying on the floor. The referee had to go and get them to start the game again. They couldn't believe it, but I could believe it. If you're a Man United person you can believe it. It's the way it is. It's not a Man United thing – it's a British thing. It's very British that, you know. You go for it, and if things get a little bit tough you keep your head but you keep going. The least you can do is to keep going and that's something they don't understand in a lot of countries. That's why they love watching the English game, they love it. It was pure British, pure Man United and Lennart Johansson, the president of UEFA, he came past me and he apologised, 'Sorry, Bobby,' as he was going down to present the trophy, and I said, 'C'est la vie.' And apparently by the time he got to the bottom we had scored two and they told him he wasn't going to present it to Bayern. What was it he said? He said he couldn't understand why a team that was winning was miserable and a team that was losing was celebrating because he thought it was still 1-0. By the time he got down the stairs he had missed both goals. It was just magic and sets a standard again; and Alex wants to win some more. He wants it again. The players want it again; they like winning. They know they're good players but you can only judge yourself on winning the big ones.

Phil Neville: I don't remember anything of the game; nothing at all. I've seen the goals and I've seen the last two minutes but I've not watched the game on video. I was sat on the bench, and all I can remember are two things, really: running down the pitch when Teddy and Ole scored to celebrate behind the goal, and all the subs chasing down after the players and then the celebrations afterwards, walking round the pitch. We seemed to be on the pitch for about three hours after the game, just celebrating. They couldn't get us off the pitch. That's what I remember most; the celebrations afterwards when each player held the Cup up in front of the fans, walking round the pitch, and the Bayern Munich fans applauding us. That's my abiding memory of the competition; the celebrations after the game.

I think that time was just the best two weeks, ever because we'd beaten Tottenham to win the League, we'd gone on to beat Newcastle in the FA Cup and then there was the final in Barcelona. It was just two weeks of football that you couldn't describe. There was the pressure of beating Tottenham in the last League game, after having gone a goal down, and then the FA Cup Final, which was a big competition, was sandwiched in between two massive games really, and was probably our easiest game of the lot. Then we went to Barcelona and it was just unbelievable.

Martin Edwards: I felt that the treble was a fantastic achievement. I'm not sure that it will ever be done again and it required a little bit of luck. It was amazing that season that everything came down to the last three games. Even the League wasn't sewn up; we had to win the last League game to win the title. Then, of course, at the Cup Final Alex made a few changes because he had the European Cup final the following Wednesday, so he rested a few players for the Cup Final. So there was a risk in that we might not have won that, but the overall goal was to win the European Cup. Then, of course, the European Cup itself, when you think that Scholes and Keane, two vital players that season, were missing for the final, I'd say that we probably didn't start favourites for that game. So to actually win it with those two players missing, and to win it in the way that we did was just a fantastic achievement and it all came together within two minutes of injury time in Barcelona. Luck was on our side at the end – there is no question about that.

We saw the Bayern Munich people afterwards and they were obviously shattered, as we would have been in their position. They were very good about it. Beckenbauer said, 'That's football.' I went down to see Hoeness in the dressing room afterwards and he was absolutely drained – shattered.

Greg Dyke: It was Manchester United's finest two minutes, wasn't it? It wasn't Manchester United's finest day. I was there. I didn't go over with United; I had to be in London working. One of my sons was doing his finals at university and wanted to go, so I leased a plane and flew my family and some mates out there. I got to the hotel too late and couldn't get my ticket. All my kids had tickets and I didn't, and I bluffed my way through. I told everybody I was a director of Manchester United and they kept letting me through and I ended up getting in to the ground and on to the pitch without a ticket. As a day; well, it was so emotional; we didn't play well, and then to score two goals in the last minute... That's what the season had been like, really. You had these incredible surges – it was just very exciting stuff.

Roy Williamson: We had travelled by coach with the Manchester United Supporters' Club – Leeds and Bradford Branch. Twenty-eight hours it took to reach the hotel at the coast. Arriving back after the game, at about two in the morning, the hotel next door reopened its doors and hundreds of Reds celebrated into the night. Realising the significance of the events that had taken place in the Nou Camp, and knowing that the drama of it all would quickly pass into folklore, some of us wanted the day to last for ever. So when the bar shut a group of us moved on to the beach with what remained of the duty-free. As might have been expected considering what had happened, the situation moved from the sublime to the ridiculous. Without a ball, we re-enacted famous United goals from the past. One big bloke decided he wanted to be Cantona, with which we were all inclined to agree, and I took my place in the imaginary goal as the infamous David James. It was Wembley 1996 all over again as I 'flapped' at the ball in true James style as 'big' Eric arrowed the ball home. How we celebrated! As morning came, some of us lesser souls departed to bed. Others carried on for another 24 hours. The greatest night of my life!

Paul Hardman: Harry was a guy who sat behind us in K Stand for a while and the last time we saw him he was sitting on this wall in Barcelona. The last thing he said to us was, 'If I die today, I'll die happy'. He went back to Salou and a few hours later died of a heart attack.

Jonathan Deakin: I have around four sides of typed notes about that day, as I wanted to remember every detail I could. But I have a feeling that it will take me some time to put into words how it felt when we won. The thing is, I hadn't prepared myself for the win and that's why it was so amazing.

Paddy Harverson: The treble I was following as a journalist and as a fan, so I was lucky enough to go to quite a few of the European games, including the final. I was the *FT*'s only sportswriter and so therefore could do what I wanted, so I entirely self-indulgently decided to write about United as they went into Europe. So I wrote about the semi and the final in these rather embarrassing but, I think, very heartfelt and emotional pieces that for some reason found their way on to the pages of the *FT*.

I gatecrashed the United party at the hotel because I knew a lot of people at the club from my work as a journalist, which was fantastic. Everyone was knackered, including the fans, and it was in a big ballroom in the basement of the hotel and everyone was thrilled, but it was also exhaustion and relief and stunned amazement. I imagine everyone had the real celebrations when they got back; that would be when they really went to town. I remember standing in the queue for cold ham and potatoes next to David Beckham and his wife Victoria and being too shy to say anything, but thinking, 'I'm standing next to a guy who's probably participated in the greatest Cup Final ending ever and he's just deciding whether to have the salmon or the ham.' It was kind of surreal. I think for United the road to the treble was such a remarkable journey that in the end they had used up all their emotional energy getting there, so they didn't have any left to celebrate; not on the night, anyway.

Phil Neville: When you got home after the celebrations you just sat down and were shattered after the events that had taken place. They were two of the best weeks of my life – to be involved in winning the treble. The bus ride round Manchester after coming back from the European Cup final was probably the best bit of all that season. The scenes coming down Deansgate at the end of that fortnight just capped what had been a tremendous season. It proved what the club and that match meant to the fans and it's something that I'll never forget.

We came home on the Thursday, and on the Friday I had to meet up with England, which was not difficult because it is playing for my country, but in another way it was hard because you still wanted to be celebrating because of what you had just achieved. That was probably the best thing that could have happened, because it got it out of the system very quickly. At this place you can't rest on your laurels too long.

Appendix

The Cast List

Swallay Bandhoo is a PE teacher and part-time soccer school coach in Mauritius. He founded the first official Manchester United Supporters' Club in Mauritius in April 1991 and has been chairman since then. He has represented the Mauritius Supporters' Club at Old Trafford on several occasions and is regularly interviewed on local radio and TV for his thoughts on the latest news from Manchester United.

Jimmy Billington was born in 1923 but lost his mother at the age of two and consequently spent three years in an orphanage in Didsbury and nine years in an orphanage in Patricroft. He saw his first United match in 1934, a friendly against Third Lanark. He served in the Royal Navy during the war and in the Army in the post-war years. He became a general labourer for the remainder of his working life.

Adam Bostock is Editor of www.manutd.com, the official website of Manchester United. He previously worked for four years on the official Manchester United magazine as deputy editor. The author of *Access All Areas: Behind the Scenes at Manchester United*, he also contributed to *The Official Manchester United Illustrated History* and to *The Official Manchester United Illustrated Encyclopedia*.

Nesta Burgess started work for Manchester United in 1951 and fulfilled a variety of duties at Old Trafford. She still works at the ground on matchdays and, at 90, is the oldest person on the United staff. Known at Old Trafford as 'Mrs B', she was presented with an award by UEFA in Monte Carlo in 1999 for her long service to United. Lou Macari says: 'Nesta used to pour tea for me for years and years – she did everything for us.'

Sandy Busby is the son of Matt Busby, manager of Manchester United from 1945 until 1971. A former professional footballer, Sandy played for Blackburn Rovers in the 1950s. He attends every home game at Old Trafford as a guest of the club in recognition of the contribution made to Manchester United by the Busby family.

Cliff Butler grew up enthralled by the *United Review*, the club's match programme. He landed his dream job of Programme Editor in the late 1980s and has also served as Curator of the club museum, Club Statistician and Club Photographer. A veteran of the Stretford End, he has been on the club's staff since 1984 and was a co-author of 2001's *The Official History of Manchester United*.

Sir Bobby Charlton spent 20 years as a footballer with Manchester United. He scored 247 goals in a record 754 appearances, making him the highest scorer in the club's history. He played as an attacking midfielder, a winger or a centre-forward and won four League championship medals, one FA Cup and one European Cup medal. He has been a director of Manchester United since 1984.

Simon Davies is Picture-Desk Editor for Photography at Manchester United. A Manchester United supporter, he frequented the South Stand before studying for a degree at Kingston University.

Anna Deakin was born in 1979 and first saw Manchester United in a 0–0 draw with Everton at Old Trafford in February 1987. She started going more regularly in 1990, and is now a season ticket-holder in South Stand. She grew up in Sale, South Manchester, and after leaving school went to the

University of Salford – allowing her, in between lectures, to go and watch the lads train at The Cliff. She now works in communications at Manchester Airport.

Jonathan Deakin's devotion to United began when he moved to Sale at the age of ten. Within weeks he had seen his first game at Old Trafford – a 1–0 win over Luton Town in October 1986. Three weeks later Alex Ferguson became United manager. Now a teacher of English at Helsby High School, Cheshire, he is Anna Deakin's brother.

Angus Deayton was for many years the presenter of BBC TV's *Have I Got News For You* and also had a leading role in the series *One Foot In The Grave*. As a youngster he had trials for Crystal Palace, his local club. He has been a United supporter since 1963, when he watched them win the FA Cup against Leicester City.

Greg Dyke was a non-executive director of Manchester United from 1997 until 1999, when he became Director-General of the BBC. He has been a Manchester United supporter since the late 1950s despite originating from a Tottenham Hotspur-supporting family. As an amateur footballer he modelled his style on Nobby Stiles until he decided he was taking too much punishment.

Martin Edwards is President of Manchester United. He saw his first Manchester United match at the age of six in 1952, has been following the team avidly since 1958 and collects every book and video that is produced about the club. He joined Manchester United's board of directors in March 1970 at the age of 24 and succeeded his father Louis as chairman in March 1980 and remained in that role at the club for more than two decades, as his father had done before him.

Cameron Erskine has been a Manchester United fan since 1946. He originally followed the team's progress from his native Cardiff, without going to Old Trafford, watching the team only when they visited Ninian Park during Cardiff City's spell in the old First Division. He started going to

Old Trafford regularly in 1972 with his son Nigel, who suffers from Stills' Disease and is wheelchair-bound.

Sir Alex Ferguson has been Manager of Manchester United since 1986. In that time he has led the club to eight Premier League titles, one European Cup, one European Cup-Winners' Cup, one League Cup, five FA Cups, one Inter-Continental Cup and one UEFA Super Cup. He had planned to retire from management in the summer of 2002 but in February 2002 he reversed that decision and signed a new contract to extend his period as manager.

Bill Foulkes made 679 appearances for Manchester United between 1952 and 1969, the second-highest total of appearances by any player in the club's history. Playing at full-back in the 1950s and at centre-back in the 1960s, he won four League championship medals, an FA Cup-winner's medal and was a member of the 1968 European Cup-winning side. He considered becoming a professional golfer in 1969 after retiring as a player, but instead embarked on a coaching career which took him to the USA, Japan and Scandinavia.

Dennis Giggs is grandfather to Ryan Giggs. He has followed Ryan's career at Manchester United from the day he signed for the club from school and has seen almost every home United game since Ryan's debut for the club against Everton at Old Trafford in 1991. A policeman for 32 years, Dennis is now retired and lives in Cardiff.

John Gladwin, a Manchester United supporter, lives in Worksop and played professionally for Rotherham United. His father, George, was a half-back for Manchester United in the 1930s but was seriously wounded in Burma during the Second World War and was unable to resume his career in football in the post-war years.

Eric Halsall has been following Manchester United since he was a small boy during the Second World War. A former high school headmaster, his attendance at matches was interrupted for years by exile, parenthood and penury, then by a seven-day-a-week job. Now living in Worcestershire, he is enjoying a retirement which allows him to get to every United game for which he can get a ticket.

Paul Hardman, a business manager with a major high-street bank, has known Sir Alex Ferguson since shortly after Sir Alex's arrival at the club in 1986. Paul is treasurer of The Elizabeth Hardie Ferguson Charitable Trust Fund, the charity set up by the manager in memory of his mother.

Paddy Harverson was Director of Communications from 2000 until 2004. He was previously a journalist on the *Financial Times*, for which he often wrote about football and, in particular, Manchester United. He has been a Manchester United supporter since the late 1960s, when he was given a book on Bobby Charlton's soccer skills.

Keith Kent was the Manchester United groundsman from 1987 to 2003. He joined the club having previously been groundsman at Leicester City for 17 years. He has been a follower of both Leicester City and Manchester United since watching them contest the 1963 FA Cup Final.

Les Kershaw was recruited by Alex Ferguson in 1987 for the post of Manchester United's Chief Scout. Chief Scout at Manchester United was, says Les, the only position in football that he would have taken – at the time he was recruited he was working as a senior university lecturer. He is now the director of the club's football academy. Les is responsible for coordinating all aspects of the academy.

Martin C.Y. Lai was born in London in 1970 and named after Martin Peters by his West Ham United-supporting father. His mother tells Martin that he started supporting Manchester United when he was four years old. He moved to Hong Kong on his 20th birthday, is now married to Joyce and has two children, Sheryl and Trafford. He works as a digital artist for a presentation company, doing 3D, photo-montages, animation and video work.

Paul McGuinness is Assistant Academy Director at Manchester United. Formerly a youth and reserve team player on United's books, he had two spells at the club as a player. He holds a UEFA 'A' Coaching Licence and is based at the Trafford training centre at Carrington. He arranges coaching, training and playing programmes, tours and tournaments for nine- to 16-year-olds with the club.

Wilf McGuinness played for Manchester United in the 1950s until a serious leg break forced his retirement as a player. He was a member of the coaching staff in the 1960s and was then appointed Head Coach in 1969 and manager in 1970. He was also a member of the England coaching staff at the 1966 World Cup. He is a popular speaker on the after-dinner circuit, and is the father of Paul McGuinness.

Sammy McIlroy was discovered by Manchester United's Northern Irish scout Bob Bishop, who had recommended George Best to the club several years previously. Sammy proved to be Matt Busby's final signing for Manchester United when he joined in 1969, and after making his debut in 1971 the midfielder was a fixture in the first team for 11 years, scoring 70 goals in 390 games for the club.

Lou Macari joined Manchester United from Celtic in January 1973 for a United record transfer fee of £200,000. One of Tommy Docherty's first signings, in his 11 years at the club he made 373 appearances and scored 97 goals. Excellent as a striker or a midfielder, he was a member of the United side that won the Second Division in the 1974–75 season and the FA Cup in 1977.

James Marshall when a teenager, sold the *United Review* at the top of the Stretford End and had work experience, when a 17-year-old at Knutsford High School at Manchester United in 2002. He has been a United supporter since 1989, when he got his first video, a season review.

David Meek is the son of Wilf Meek, who covered York City for the *Yorkshire Evening Press* for 45 years. David started writing about

Manchester United for the *Manchester Evening News* in February 1958 and he has enjoyed a fascinating career writing about what he describes as 'the major football club of Great Britain'. He retired from the *Evening News* in 1995 and still contributes to MUTV, MU Radio and the MU website.

Ken Merrett is the Club Secretary of Manchester United. He joined the z staff in January 1966 as a bookkeeper and wages clerk. His first job at United involved processing money from the ticket sales for the three 1966 World Cup matches that took place at Old Trafford and managing the grants and loans given to the club by the Football Association for the use of Old Trafford as a venue.

Barry Moorhouse is Players' Liaison Officer at Manchester United. He has worked for the club since the late 1960s and has been a full-time member of United's staff since 1976. He began running the club's membership scheme at the request of Martin Edwards in 1987.

Gary Neville joined Manchester United as an apprentice in July 1991 and made his debut for the club at the age of 17 in September 1992 in a UEFA Cup tie with Torpedo Moscow. He is equally accomplished as a full-back or a centre-back. In 2001 Gary, in common with his younger brother Phil, signed a six-year contract with United.

Phil Neville made his Manchester United debut at the age of 18 in January 1995. The following year he was still a teenager as he won his first League championship medal and made his first appearance for England. He signed, in 2001, a six-year contract to stay at the club. Bury-born Phil has played in defence and midfield for United and also scored world-class goals.

Ole Pedersen has supported Manchester United for 25 years. He lives in Oslo and works as an internet editor for a weekly newspaper that covers politics and economics. He has been on the committee of the Scandinavian branch of the official Manchester United Supporters' Club since 1988 and worked full-time for the supporters' club in 1997 and 1998. He has now watched United play in 11 countries.

John Peters worked as a photographer on Granada TV's *Kick-Off* programme, presented by Elton Welsby, in the 1980s. He also worked as a photographer for Manchester City but has been the official Manchester United photographer since 1993. His son Matthew now works with him.

Ken Ramsden joined Manchester United as an office boy at the age of 15 in 1960 and was put in charge of the ticket office at the age of 18. He became assistant secretary in 1989 and was also press officer for a period of time in the 1990s. He is the longest-serving full-time member of staff at Old Trafford – although keen to stress that he is not the oldest. He deals with football administration and event management at Old Trafford, with responsibility for Champions League matches.

Leo Rocca was born just as Manchester United were settling into Old Trafford, the ground they acquired in 1910, and his father, Louis, was also Old Trafford's first groundsman. Louis had a lielong relationship with the club.

Ron Snellen was born in 1964 and has been Chairman of the Dutch Mancunians since that branch of the official United Supporters' Club was formed in 1995. When not in England or Europe following United he works as a loss adjuster in Amsterdam.

Rebecca Tow grew up in a Manchester United-supporting household and began her career at Manchester United as a tour guide, a job she did for 18 months. She is now Editorial Co-ordinator on *United*, the official magazine of Manchester United. She writes news stories and interviews players for the magazine and, as the link person between the magazine and players and coaches, she organizes photoshoots and interviews.

Christoph 'Voni' von Arx is a 25-year-old member of Manchester United's official Swiss Supporters' Club, the Swiss Devils. He is a specialist in telecommunications in Zurich and has been a frequent visitor to Old Trafford since attending a match with Leeds United in 1992. He hasn't missed an away match in Europe since 1996.

Tony Whelan is Manchester United's Deputy Assistant Academy Director. A former professional with the club, he joined United as an apprentice in 1968. On being released by Tommy Docherty he joined Manchester City and later played alongside George Best and Brian Kidd for the Fort Lauderdale Strikers. He now assists with academy coaching and administration. He holds the UEFA 'A' Coaching Licence.

Roy Williamson has been attending matches at Old Trafford for 40 years. He believes he is due a testimonial for his long service to United. He was Vice-Chair of the Independent Manchester United Supporters' Association and sits on the committee of the Football Supporters' Association. He watches matches from the Stretford End and his son and daughters have followed him in supporting United.

Mark Wylie has been the Curator of the Manchester United museum since 1991. Having completed a postgraduate certificate in Museum Studies at Leicester University, he replied to an advertisement by United for a curator and became the club's first trained museum curator. A St Johnstone supporter, he feels that this helps him retain his objectivity about things United and prevents him getting too 'Red-eyed' a view.

Chris Yeamans was born in Warrington in 1962 and lived in Lymm in his teens. At 18 he moved to Newcastle-upon-Tyne to go to college and is now settled there. A professional musician, he writes music from home – early in 2002 he created the music for a David Bellamy eco-holiday video but he is now concentrating on writing original pop tunes for his agent to try to sell to what he describes as 'today's bland popstars'.

The publishers would like to thank the following sources for their kind permission to reproduce the pictures in this book. The page numbers for each of the photographs are listed below, giving the page on which they appear in the book.
Any location indicator: (c-centre, t-top, b-bottom, r-right, l-left).

Empics: /Jon Buckley: 4bl, **Laurence Griffiths**: 2b, 3t, /**Phil O'Brien**: 1, /**Neal Simpson**: 2t, /**Michael Steele**: 5b; **Getty Images**: /**Michael Steele**: 4t; **Manchester United PLC/John/Matthew Peters**: 3b, 4br, 5t, 6, 7t, 7b, 8.